SECOND EDITION

TAXATION FOR SUSTAINED PROSPERITY

Collaborative Tax Policy Setting & Administration

Dr. Samuel Taddesse

ISBN: 978-1-647046-55-2 (paperback)
ISBN: 978-1-647046-54-5 (ebook)

Because of the dynamic nature of the internet, any web addresses or links contained in this book may have changed since publication and may no longer be valid.

The views expressed in this work are solely those of the author. They do not necessarily reflect the views and opinions of the publisher.

ACKNOWLEDGMENT

The writing of this book is inspired by my desire to understand the theory and practice of taxation. It is also to convey to fellow citizens why we must pay taxes, how tax administration functions, and how import duties and taxes are assessed. In 1967, as a young university student, I took a test one Saturday morning along with 2,000 other candidates. I was in my senior year, getting ready for my national service. My friend and I took the test for fun to see how well we compared with those engineering and building college students. We were science students aspiring to become medical doctors. However, that dream was shattered when four police officers showed up at our science laboratory three weeks later and told us the government was looking for us. It was a shock. When we got outside the laboratory, the police officers said that we had passed the examination and that the government was serious about hiring us. I was assigned to work with the Ministry of Finance (MOF) and my friend for the Electric Power Authority. They said only 15 out of the 2,000 people who took the test had passed.

Two police officers escorted me to the deputy minister's office in the Ministry of Finance. After welcoming me, the deputy minister asked me when I could start my training to manage the Revenue Directorate. At that time, tax administration was under the Ministry of Finance. I told him I was not interested in a job with the ministry and preferred to pursue a career in the medical field. The deputy minister quickly indicated to me that that was not an option. If I refused the position, I would go to jail, and my future would be ruined.

After my national service and following my graduation from Haile Selassie 1st University in Addis Ababa, I went abroad to study finance and economics. After finishing my doctoral thesis at the Wharton School of Finance and Economics at the University of Pennsylvania in the United States, I received a telegram that instructed me to prepare to return to Ethiopia. At that time, I was an assistant professor of finance at Bernard Baruch College in New York City, teaching portfolio analysis and undergraduate microeconomics. Most of my graduate school students were from Wall Street, America's financial center in New York City. Thus, our discussions centered around stocks and bonds markets and derivatives and not on taxation or fiscal policy.

On September 11, 1974, which happens to be the Ethiopian New Year, Emperor Haile Selassie, King of Kings and Lion of Juda, was deposed by the military junta. He was taken out of his palace and imprisoned. The military junta, the Derge, took over the government. I was advised by family and friends not to return to Ethiopia. So my opportunity to manage the Revenue Directorate at the MOF evaporated. I continued living and working in the United States.

In 1979, while working at the Federal Reserve Bank of New York in New York City, I had the chance to work in the tax policy division at the U.S. Internal Revenue Service. I went for a job interview in Washington, DC, where I was given a tour of the building and was shown the office where I would be working from. It was a shocker. While the building looked majestic from the outside, the offices were tiny, and the furnishings were from the eighteenth century. I declined the job offer and decided to stay with the Federal Reserve Bank of New York, developing commercial banking policies.

In 1980, I accepted a position with American Telephone and Telegraph (AT&T) to lead their restructuring team. When I joined the company, AT&T had 1.2 million employees. When I left in 1989, it had less than 350,000 employees and 11 independent telephone companies. AT&T was no longer a monopoly. Soon after leaving AT&T, I became an independent consultant and worked on different consultancy task orders.

For the past seven years, I have been working in Ethiopia with teams that provided technical assistance to the Ministry of Finance and Economic Cooperation (MOFEC), the Ministry of Revenue (MOR), and the Ethiopian Customs Commission (ECC). From 2015 to 2017, I worked on the Department for International Development (DFID)-funded Tax, Audit, and Transparency (TAUT) Programme implemented by Development Alternatives Incorporated (DAI). And between 2019 and March 2021, I worked on the Tax Systems Transformation Programme (TSTP), implemented by Cowater International, a Canadian company. Both projects focused on strengthening the Ethiopian tax administration and customs and promoting and fostering voluntary tax compliance.

Working with TAUT and TSTP was an excellent opportunity to learn about and understand the Ethiopian tax system. The knowledge and understanding acquired from these two projects inform the writing of this book. The book also benefited from the intellectual exchanges I had with the tax experts on both projects and the literature review on tax and taxation.

I thank all my colleagues in the TAUT and TSTP programs, where I served as deputy team leader. I also want to thank our counterparts in the MOR, the ECC, the MOFEC, the Ministry of Civil Service Capacity Building, the Anti-Corruption Commission, the Federal Auditor General's Office, and Her Majesty's Revenue & Customs (HMRC) for meaningful engagements and dialogues on tax and other governance matters.

I also would like to thank my wife, Menbere Tsheay, for reading parts of the book and giving me feedback as a taxpayer. Her comments as a taxpayer were important for simplifying the language of the text. It is now less technical and easier to understand. I also thank her for her patience and support. I also thank my son David for supporting me with the artwork and graphics.

While I have gained knowledge to enrich my understanding of taxation from numerous sources, I take full responsibility for omissions and errors. I also invite readers to email comments and corrections for the next edition at samtad@yahoo.com.

CONTENTS

BOXES

FIGURES

TABLES

ACRONYMS

AABE	Accounting and Auditing Board of Ethiopia
AICPA	American Institute of Certified Public Accountants
ATA	Agriculture Transformation Agency
BL	Business License
BLI	Better Life Index
BPR	Business Process Reengineering
BSC	Balanced Scorecard
CEW	Community Extension Worker
CIF	Cost, Insurance, and Freight
CIT	Corporate Income Tax
CLTSH	Community-Led Total Sanitation & Hygiene
COA	Chart of Accounts
COM	Council of Ministers
COMESA	Common Market for Eastern and Southern Africa
CRM	Cash Register Machine
CSA	Central Statistical Agency
DAI	Development Alternatives Incorporated
DFID	Department for International Development
EABC	Ethiopian Agricultural Business Corporation
ECC	Ethiopian Customs Commission
EFDA	Ethiopian Food and Drug Administration
EFFORT	Endowment Fund for the Rehabilitation of Tigray
EIC	Ethiopian Investment Commission
EPCP	Ethiopian Prosperity Corps Program
EPRDF	Ethiopian People's Revolutionary Democratic Party

EPSA	Ethiopian Pharmaceutical Supply Agency
ERCA	Ethiopian Revenue and Customs Authority
ETB	Ethiopian Birr (currency)
ETC	Ethiopian Telecommunication Corporation
EthioSIS	Ethiopian Soil Information System
FCDO	Foreign, Commonwealth & Development Office
FDI	Foreign Direct Investment
FDRE	Federal Democratic Republic of Ethiopia
FIA	Freedom of Information Act
FMA	Food & Medicine Administration
FOB	Free on Board
FPD	Fiscal Policy Directorate
FY	Fiscal Year
GAAP	Generally Accepted Accounting Principles
GDP	Gross Domestic Product
GNH	Gross National Happiness
GNI	Gross National Income
GNP	Gross National Product
GNW	Gross National Well-Being
GOE	Government of Ethiopia
GTP	Growth and Transformation Plan
HDI	Human Development Index
HEW	Health Extension Worker
HIV/AIDS	Human Immunodeficiency Virus/Acquired Immuno Deficiency Syndrome
HMRC	Her Majesty's Revenue & Customs
HOF	House of Federation
HS	Harmonized Commodity Description and Coding System
ICC	International Chamber of Commerce
ICT	Information and Communication Technology
ID	Identification Card
IFRS	International Financial Reporting Standards
IIM	International Institute of Management
ILO	International Labor Organization
IMF	International Monetary Fund

IT	Information Technology
IVR/SMS	Integrated Voice Response/Short Message Service
JAP	Joint Action Plan
KPI	Key Performance Indicator
MIC	Middle-Income Countries
MOF	Ministry of Finance
MOFEC	Ministry of Finance and Economic Cooperation
MOH	Ministry of Health
MOR	Ministry of Revenue
MPMD	Macroeconomic Policy Management Directorate
MTI	Ministry of Trade and Industry
NEDMS	Networked Enterprise Data Management System
NTPC	National Tax Policy Convention
OFAG	Office of the Federal Auditor General
PCP	Public-Community Partnership
PLC	Private Limited Company
PM	Prime Minister
PMAC	Provisional Military Administrative Council
PMO	Prime Minister's Office
PPP	Public-Private Partnerships
PSA	Pharmaceutical Supply Agency
PSNP	Productive Safety Net Program
QOL	Quality of Life
R&I	Research & Innovation
RRB	Regional Revenue Bureau
RSFEDB	Regional States Finance & Economic Development Bureaus
RSRB	Regional State Revenue Bureaus
SA	Social Accountability
SAC	Social Accountability Committee
SDG	Sustainable Development Goals
SDSN	Sustainable Development Solution Network
SIGTAS	Standard Integrated Government Tax Administration System
SNNP	Southern Nations Nationalities People

SNNPR	Southern Nations Nationalities Peoples Region
SOE	State-Owned Enterprise
SOL	Standard of Living
SSA	Sub-Saharan Africa
TAUT	Tax, Audit, and Transparency Programme
TB	Tuberculosis
TDD	Taxpayers Data Directorate
TFCP	Tax Fairness Cooperation Project
TIN	Taxpayer Identification Number
TPD	Tax Policy Directorate
TPLF	Tigrayan Peoples Liberation Front
TPU	Tax Policy Unit
TSTP	Tax System Transformation Programme
TTO	Tax Transformation Office
TVET	Technical and Vocational Education and Training
UN	United Nations
USAID	United States Agency for International Development
VAT	Value-Added Tax
WASH	Water, Sanitation, and Hygiene
WEDGE	Women's Entrepreneurship Development & Gender Equity
WTO	World Trade Organization

GLOSSARY OF TERMS

Base erosion

Base erosion relates to the tax planning strategy used by foreign corporations to "shift" profits out of higher-tax countries to lower-tax countries through affiliated companies, thus "eroding" the tax base of the higher-tax country. OECD defines base erosion as "exploiting gaps and mismatches in tax rules."

Debt adjustment

Debt adjustment is a form of debt relief that allows a country to repay the debt it incurred over a more extended period and with smaller payment amounts than the original agreed-on terms of the borrowing. It is done to avoid the insolvency of the borrowing country.

Economic growth

Economic Growth is the increase in the inflation-adjusted market value of the goods and services produced by an economy over time, represented by a country's real gross domestic product (GDP). It is measured as the year-over-year percent increase in the real GDP.

Ethnopolitical tension

Ethnopolitical tension relates to the politics of ethnicity and the conflict over the control and distribution of economic resources, income-generating opportunities, and political positions.

Fiscal policy

Fiscal policy refers to government spending and tax policies to influence economic conditions, especially macroeconomic conditions, including aggregate demand for goods and services and employment.

Income inequality

Income inequality relates to the degree to which the total income of a country is distributed unevenly throughout the population. In many cases of income inequality, wealth flows disproportionately towards a small number of already financially well-off individuals. Such income disparities undermine a country's tax and governance system.

Informal sector

The informal sector, also known as the underground economy, black economy, shadow economy, or gray economy, is part of a country's economic system hidden from the government's eyes. The traders and merchants in the sector do not declare their income or pay taxes.

Poverty

Poverty refers to a condition where individuals and families do not have enough material possessions or income for necessities. Absolute poverty is when an individual or a household earns less than what is needed to pay for basic needs, such as food, clothing, and shelter.

Profit shifting

Profit shifting is a tax planning strategy employed by affiliated companies to lower their tax liabilities or avoid paying taxes by allocating income and expenses among themselves.

Prosperity	Legatum Institute defines prosperity as the condition where people have opportunities to thrive. People are better educated, have meaningful and well-paying jobs, and can afford to pay for food, clothing, and shelter. According to Legatum, prosperity is underpinned by an inclusive society with a robust social contract protecting every individual's fundamental liberties and security.
Tax administration	Tax administration is about the management, conduct, direction, and supervision of executing and applying a country's tax laws. It includes assessment, collection, and enforcement of tax laws.
Tax capacity	Tax capacity relates to the maximum amount of tax revenue a country can collect, considering a country's specific macroeconomic, demographic, and institutional features. It is measured as a percentage of GDP.
Tax compliance	Tax compliance relates to the situation in which taxpayers abide by the tax law, declare all their income, file a return, and pay the tax due on time.
Tax culture	Tax culture relates to the entirety of all relevant formal and informal institutions and practices embedded within the country's culture, including the dependence on tax-funded programs and people's ongoing interaction with the tax authorities. It is also about citizens' awareness of taxation and that taxes pay for the public goods and services society needs and wants.

Tax effort	Tax effort is defined as an index of the ratio between the share of the actual tax collection in GDP and taxable capacity. The analysis provides broad guidance for tax reforms in countries with various levels of taxable capacity and revenue intake.
Tax fairness	Tax fairness is a concept that stipulates that a government's tax would apply to all citizens, businesses, and residents equitably and broadly, based on the ability to pay.
Tax gap	Tax gap is the difference between the estimated tax liability for a tax year and the tax revenue collected on time. It accounts for non-filing, underreporting, and underpayment.
Tax policy	Tax policy is about a government's decisions on what taxes to levy, in what amounts, and on whom. A country's tax regime is a crucial policy instrument that may negatively or positively influence the country's economic growth and prosperity.
Tax self-assessment	Tax self-assessment relates to a system whereby each taxpayer estimates their income and tax liabilities and pays the estimated taxes on time.

EXECUTIVE SUMMARY

The primary business of government is strengthening the conditions that enhance the quality of life of all citizens. To effectively achieve this goal, government policymakers must answer the following questions:

- What matters for quality of life?
- What are the baseline conditions, and how much should they aim to improve citizens' living standards starting from the baseline over the next 10 to 20 years?
- How should improvements in the quality of life of citizens be measured? What key performance indicators (KPIs) are monitored and assessed to measure progress in improving citizens' quality of life?
- How should the government collaborate with citizens, businesses, residents, and development partners to identify and improve the conditions that enhance citizens' quality of life?
- How should the government raise funds to finance the programs that strengthen the conditions that enhance citizens' quality of life?

Citizens' quality of life and living standards are inextricably linked to the quantity and quality of, and access to, education, healthcare services, clean water, sanitation, agriculture and nutritious food supplies, peace, justice and security, transportation, and communication infrastructures, including roads, bridges, telecommunications, and internet connectivity, among others. Quality of life and living standards depend on citizens' income-generating abilities and national income equality. These factors must be analyzed, programmed, funded, and implemented to improve citizens' living conditions. They may require massive amounts of investments and funds. A significant source of funds is tax revenue collected from citizens, businesses, and residents. Countries like Ethiopia that do not have substantial natural resources such as oil, minerals, and precious metals depend heavily on tax revenues.

Taxes are imposed by law. We all remit taxes to the government to pay for the public goods and services we all need, want, and get from our government. The law delineates who pays tax, how much, on what, and how often. The law also determines who has the mandate to draft the tax policy, pass tax laws, enforce the laws, and collect the levied taxes from citizens, businesses, and residents. The Ministry of Finance and Economic Cooperation (MOFEC) drafts the tax policy in Ethiopia.

Ideally, MOFEC, in collaboration with Civil Society Organizations (CSOs), civic groups, such as labor organizations, professional associations, business leaders, academicians, the Chambers of Commerce, bilateral and multilateral development partners, and regional and international trade partners, drafts the tax policy and presents the draft tax policy to the Council of Ministers (COM). The COM discusses the draft tax policy in detail concerning the underlying rationale and assumptions and the tax policy's social, political, and economic implications and then makes adjustments and changes as necessary.

The final draft tax policy is presented to Parliament through the prime minister's office (PMO). Parliament, in turn, reviews, discusses, and debates the draft tax policy and, if necessary, requests amendments or changes, votes, and ratifies the final draft tax policy. Once endorsed by Parliament, the tax policy is published in the Negarit Gazetta and becomes law. The regional state governments follow similar processes and procedures.

The tax policy drafting process should begin with studying and understanding the baseline conditions linking the tax revenue collected and invested in the prior tax year and the development outcomes achieved. These studies are distributed and discussed with the relevant stakeholders as part of the tax policy drafting process. Before the tax policy is drafted, the following questions are discussed and clarified within the current Ethiopian and international context.

1. Given that the business of government is to develop, implement, and strengthen the conditions that enhance and strengthen citizens' living conditions, what are the **baseline conditions**? The factors that improve citizens' living conditions and quality of life include access to quality education, healthcare, clean water, sanitation, and hygiene; regenerative agriculture that supplies healthy and life-sustaining foods; clean environment and housing conditions; transportation infrastructure, including roads, bridges, railway networks, and airports; communication infrastructure; internet connectivity; and peace, security, and justice. To develop a robust development strategy, we must identify the current status of these enabling conditions, for example, the quality, quantity, and access to (a) primary, secondary, and tertiary education systems; (b) healthcare; (c) water, sanitation, and hygiene; and (d) security and justice. We must also identify and discuss how our living conditions and quality of life compare to neighboring countries and internationally.

2. How do we improve on these baseline conditions? What do we need to improve? What must we do to accelerate the improvement of citizens' standard of living, eliminate poverty, and attain a middle-income country status by 2030, as set by the prime minister's 10-year homegrown prosperity plan? Current baseline conditions are miserably low. A complete transformation is necessary. The education and healthcare systems need a complete change in quality, quantity, and reach. More qualified teachers, school administrators, nurses, doctors, and public health officers are required. The water, sanitation, and hygiene (WASH) sector must also transform and improve significantly. The country

needs to move from subsistent farming to regenerative mechanized agriculture that increases crop yield per hectare while protecting the soil and water systems and positively impacting climate change. Roads accessible year-round that connect rural communities to urban areas and markets must be built. What programs and activities must be implemented immediately to push the needle upward in the intermediate and long run? At the same time, improvement targets are established, monitored, and measured to ensure that government and community investments produce the intended outputs and improve citizens' living standards.

3. How much would it cost to invest in activities that accelerate improvements in the living standards of citizens and catapult Ethiopia into a middle-income country? The relevant government actors must develop a coherent development plan. They must review the baseline conditions, and identify the necessary programs and activities that must be implemented to achieve the goals set in the development plan. They must also develop a 10-year prosperity budget and break it down by budget year, programs, and activities. The Prime Minister must facilitate the process through a **National Tax Policy Convention (NTPC)** that engages all stakeholders.

An NTPC would be an excellent forum for the government to explain to citizens and businesses the challenges and opportunities the nation faces to make tangible improvements in people's living conditions and achieve a middle-income country status by 2030. The convention can facilitate gathering feedback and suggestions from various convention participants on what to invest in and how to raise the necessary funding, including an optimal tax policy. By building understanding and consensus on the national development plan priorities, objectives, performance measures, and funding needs, citizens' and businesses' voluntary tax compliance can be significantly enhanced. Partnerships between government, businesses, and communities can be forged to invest in programs that augment development activities funded by tax revenues. Citizens and businesses can also oversee the government's performance to help improve it and eliminate corruption.

4. The development program planners must also understand how the informal or shadow economy affects the country's economic and social development. In Ethiopia, the informal sector, or the shadow economy, is enormous. It accounts for 35% to 45% of the economy measured by Gross Domestic Product (GDP). Informality results in lower tax revenues that hinder the government's spending on social programs and infrastructure. The tax revenue loss is estimated to equal 8% to 11% of the GDP. Beyond lost tax revenues, the longer the situation continues, the more undermined the fairness and credibility of the tax system become. The NTPC can accelerate the formalization process by explicitly identifying and communicating the benefits and incentives foregone by the people and businesses operating in the informal sector. Formalization must provide training, micro-loans and grants, and marketing support along the value chain. These benefits can entice more informal traders and merchants to formalize. A rigorous study to identify the informal market players would isolate the criminal elements hiding in the informal sector and engaging in illicit trade and money laundering.

5. The development program planners must estimate the tax revenue collected to fund planned programs and activities together with existing programs. MOFEC must calculate how much tax revenue can reasonably be collected from citizens, businesses, and residents under current conditions. It must also explore other available sources of funding to augment tax revenues.

The Ministry of Revenue (MOR), the Ethiopian Customs Commission (ECC), and the regional state revenue bureaus (RSRBs) enforce the tax laws and collect tax revenues from citizens, businesses, and residents.

While we all need the essential public goods and services produced and delivered by the government, some citizens, businesses, and residents do not like to pay taxes. There are many free riders. Thus, a key responsibility of tax administrators is to clarify the tax law and educate, encourage, and persuade taxpayers to comply with it. Taxpayers are audited randomly to determine if (a) the tax returns of citizens, businesses, and residents include all income sources, and (b) taxpayers are declaring and paying their fair share of taxes on time. Tax returns are selected for review using risk-based auditee selection methods. All other things equal, risk-based selection uncovers and efficiently yields more tax revenue.

In Ethiopia, there is significant resource leakage and waste through corrupt procurement and contracting and inadequate project planning, implementation, management, and evaluation. Controlling this waste through mechanisms that enhance organizations' effectiveness, and efficiency and eliminate corruption would save resources. Additional tax revenues can be obtained by managing and controlling tax incentives, transfer pricing schemes, profit shifting, and money laundering. The tax revenue gain could be as much as 7% to 9% of GDP.

The government must formalize the shadow market as quickly as possible and unlock the tax potential from the shadow economy by strategically bringing as many businesses as possible into the tax net. Identifying traders operating in the shadow economy requires collecting data from various sources, such as the Domestic Tax Directorate, the ECC, other third parties, and field intelligence and observation. In addition, performing data matching would identify the leading shadow market players and allow the government to take action to bring them into tax compliance.

Furthermore, political-party–owned or –affiliated enterprises and state-owned businesses must be taxed to the fullest. According to the Ethiopian Chambers of Commerce 2018 survey, about 60% of small, medium, and large companies operating in Ethiopia are political-party–owned or –affiliated, paying minimal tax. The government should prohibit political parties or officials from owning or operating any business enterprise. All state-owned enterprises (SOEs) must be audited rigorously as the law requires.[1] Those SOEs determined to be unprofitable should be privatized or liquidated immediately. However, most SOEs have not been audited and were unprofitable due to corruption. Also, Tigray Peoples Liberation Front (TPLF) officials exploited these enterprises for personal gains and the political party's benefit.

Many types of taxes are imposed on citizens, businesses, and residents. In addition to funding the provision of public goods and services that enhance citizens' standard of living, the taxation system and the government fiscal policy must encourage business expansion and growth, employment creation, and provide for the elderly and those unable to participate in the workforce due to disabilities and health problems. It should also discourage the production, marketing, and consumption of goods and services harmful to human health, the environment, and society.

Government openness, transparency, and performance are critical elements that promote voluntary tax compliance. The government must monitor, measure, and communicate to citizens, businesses, and residents the development outcome and how it has spent the tax revenue it collected from society. The collaborative learning process among the key stakeholders would further increase tax compliance and improve governance and government transparency and performance. In addition, making the learning and adaptive approach transparent would help citizens, businesses, and residents change their belief that the tax system is unfair and inequitable. Exempting particular political-party–affiliated companies, as well as small and medium enterprises, from paying their fair share of taxes has been pointed out as an example of the unfairness of the tax system.

Developing and expanding the internet and digitizing taxpayers' information will significantly improve taxpayer information and tax

---

1   Proclamation No. 1/1995, Proclamation of the Constitution of the Federal Democratic Republic of Ethiopia, Article 96 (2) and Article 97 (7).

administration. A robust information and communication technology (ICT) sector, with widespread internet usage for tax administration service delivery, underpinning e-filing, and e-pay, would increase tax compliance and collection. Expanded internet usage with fewer in-person activities and manual data entry would reduce costs, enhance tax administration performance, and improve tax compliance. The robustness of government policies, regulations, and tax policy formulation and administration require increasing the technical capabilities of tax policymakers, tax administrators, program planners, and implementors.

CHAPTER 1

INTRODUCTION

This book is about taxation. Taxation relates to the policies, regulations, and processes involved in deciding how much each citizen, resident, and business should contribute to funding government activities (i.e., tax policy). It is also about how these contributions should be collected from citizens, residents, and businesses (i.e., tax administration). It also discusses how society ensures that each citizen, resident, and business contribute their fair share as determined by the policies and regulations set by the government. Taxes fund the government's operations, programs, and activities (i.e., fiscal policy). In this context, the government's primary business is delivering public goods, services, infrastructure, and security that improve people's living conditions.

Tax is the mandatory contributions we all make to the government monthly, quarterly, or annually as the law mandates. The amount of tax we pay is not based on the value of the public goods and services we receive from the government. Instead, it is based on citizens', residents', and businesses' incomes, wealth, asset value, and the mandated tax rate for each type of income source.

We all want a safe, secure, and quality life. Essential government services improve our living conditions and quality of life. The government provides vital services such as electricity, transportation, telecommunication, healthcare, education, community policing, and national defense to make our lives better and more secure. Where does the government, as an embodiment of society, get the resources needed to pay for these services? In many developed and developing countries, the government's primary revenue source to fund the provision of these essential goods and services is taxes paid by citizens, residents, and businesses.

This book discusses tax policy, its processes, tax fairness and equity, and tax administration and compliance. It highlights how a tax policy should be developed. It also outlines how tax policy must be made and how tax revenues are collected, managed, and invested by the government. The central focus is on the Ethiopian tax system, with examples drawn from developed and developing countries.

Development specialists agree that countries that mobilize and use domestic resources have a better chance of achieving their economic and social development goals. For example, to achieve the United Nations' Sustainable Development Goals (SDGs),[1] the Addis Ababa Action Agenda of 2015[2] called on governments to step up their efforts for more effective domestic resource mobilization. Domestic resources include tax revenues, service fees, investment profits from state-owned enterprises, and domestic borrowing.

Arriving at an optimal tax policy requires understanding, first, the implications of the tax policy on household savings, private enterprise investment, and its effect on the country's equitable economic and social

---

1   The Sustainable Development Goals are 17 interlinked global goals designed to be a "blueprint for achieving a better and more sustainable future for all." These SDGs were set up in 2015 by the United Nations General Assembly and are intended to be achieved by 2030.

2   United Nations (2015a). Addis Ababa Action Agenda. Third International Conference on Financing for Development, Outcome Document. New York, NY: United Nations. Available at: http://www.un.org/esa/ffd/wp-content/uploads/2015/08/AAAA_Outcome.pdf

development. Second, fair and efficient tax systems generate more tax revenues. Third, quality service delivery to citizens and taxpayers, governance transparency, transparent public finance management, and accountability help build trust in government, make taxpayers more tax compliant, and strengthen the social contract between citizens and the government.

Besides funding essential services such as education, healthcare, water and sanitation, and other infrastructure, taxes impact society and the economy in many ways. First, taxes influence businesses, households, and individuals' investment, saving, and employment decisions. Second, taxes affect the population's health and economic well-being, the environment's sustainability, political stability, and economic security and prosperity of individuals and communities. The government's overarching objective must be to strengthen the conditions for improved living conditions for people. The levying and collecting of tax revenues from citizens, businesses, and residents should be for these purposes alone.

For countries lacking a steady stream of revenue from natural resources, such as oil, minerals, and precious metals, tax revenues are the primary resources for funding the delivery of public goods and services to citizens. While receiving foreign aid from development partners can augment tax revenues, it is an unreliable source of revenue for many reasons. First, it comes with strings attached: it is often spent on the priority projects and programs of the donor country. And it is often dependent on the donor country's foreign policy agenda. Indeed, Madeleine Albright, Secretary of the United States Department of State in 1999, indicated that the United States would use its foreign aid as a political tool for rewarding friendly governments and punishing unfriendly ones. Donor countries can withhold or withdraw their support from a country for any reason that does not fit their foreign policy agenda.

Second, a sizable portion of the aid linked to the implementation of specific projects and programs goes toward paying the wages, transportation, and accommodation expenses of the so-called "experts" hired by the donor, often resulting in little, if any, tangible transfer of knowledge or capabilities to the host country. For example, on both the Tax, Audit, and Ant-Corruption (TAUT) program and the Tax Systems Transformation Program (TSTP) funded by the United Kingdom's Department for International Development (DFID), where I served as Deputy Team Leader, a slew of Her Majesty's Revenue and Customs (HMRC) personnel were paid out of the pot of money donated to the Government of Ethiopia (GOE). Most were redundant to the technical experts on our teams, and their technical contribution was not apparent to the GOE or us.

Foreign aid also has been a job and wealth creation program for those international non-governmental organizations (INGOs) engaged in delivering aid to famine and disaster-affected populations. They never graduate the assisted communities from emergency assistance to self-reliance. But their staff members live a comfortable life with maids and guards.

Third, foreign aid has declined over the past couple of decades as global economic growth has slowed with globalization and recurring financial crises and shocks. Further decline and shrinkage are expected as the COVID-19 pandemic and its variants ravage the health and wealth of the citizens of the donor countries. The war between Ukraine and Russia and climate change also affect these donor countries with accelerated and devastating forest fires, floods, and inflation.

Many countries borrow money from multinational banks such as the World Bank, regional development banks, and sovereign and private banks to augment domestic revenues. However, as history has shown, excess external debt can slow a country's development. The annual principal and interest payments associated with external debt drain a country's resources and severely hamper a country's economic development and social growth.

Ethiopia has reached its debt limit. Over the past three decades, the Tigray People Liberation Front (TPLF)-led government borrowed heavily from the World Bank and regional development banks.[3] Having reached its debt limit and facing diminishing foreign aid, Ethiopia has to rely more on tax revenue. In the fiscal year 2020/21, tax revenue covered about 70% of the government's budget, including civil servants' salaries and wage expenses (Figure 1.1). Also, the tax-to-GDP ratio is critically low. In 2019, tax revenue to Gross

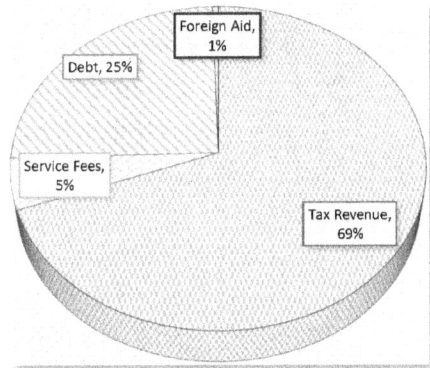

Figure 1.1: FDRE 2020/21 Budget (389 Billion Birr) Funding Sources

Domestic Product (GDP) was only 6.7%[4] in real terms. This is below the average for sub-Saharan African (SSA) countries. It is also below the required minimum (i.e., 15% of GDP) to sustain the country's current social and economic development needs. That means tax revenue must increase substantially.

Ethiopia is aiming to become a lower-middle-income country by 2030.[5] To that end, the government has developed a homegrown 10-year prosperity plan. The goal is to eliminate poverty, reduce inequalities, deliver quality public services, and build the infrastructure for inclusive

---

3   There are allegations that some of the money ended up in TPLF officials bank accounts in the US, Europe and other countries.

4   The International Monetary Fund, Government Finance Statistics Yearbook and data files, and World Bank and OECD GDP estimates.

5   According to the World Bank, middle-income countries (MICs) are defined as economies with annual per capita Gross National Income (GNI) between $1,026 and $12,475. MICs are broken up into lower and upper-middle-income economies. Lower-middle-income economies have per capita GNIs between $1,026 and $3,955, while upper-middle economies have per capita GNIs between $3,956 and $12,475. GNI is the total amount of money earned by a nation's people and businesses. GNI is used for measuring and tracking a nation's wealth from year to year. GNI includes income from foreign sources. Ethiopia's current per capita GNI is about $790. The World Bank, "The World Bank in Middle Income Countries", December 2020

and broad-based economic growth and prosperity. The government also wants to industrialize the country. It has constructed several industrial parks and has provided incentives to attract foreign direct investment (FDI). However, from Ethiopia's current position, unless fundamental social, political, governance, and economic transformations occur quickly, achieving a lower-middle-income country status by 2030 would be incredibly challenging, if not impossible.

To make matters worse, Ethiopians have low-tax culture. Without building a tax culture, rooting out systemic state and private-sector corruption, simplifying the tax code, reforming tax administration, providing clear guidance and technology-assisted support to taxpayers, enhancing tax compliance, and increasing tax revenue from current levels would be challenging.

The government must demonstrate to citizens that their tax money is spent and invested in programs that benefit everyone. Citizens should see paying taxes as an integral aspect of their relationship with the government and as part of their civic and patriotic duty.

Also, all foreign and domestic businesses must comply with the country's tax laws. Our observation has been that most foreign companies do not pay taxes. In addition, some domestic companies do not pay their fair share of taxes because of their direct and indirect ties to the ruling party and government officials. These include companies owned by the ruling party—the TPLF.

The Ethiopian tax code is complicated for most taxpayers, as most ordinary traders and merchants are semi-literate. Also, the numerous internal directives on interpreting and applying the tax code, which are not readily available to taxpayers, muddle the tax policy. To simplify the country's tax policy, these internal directives and the long arms of high-level government officials must be eliminated. The tax information available to taxpayers must be the same information used by tax officers.

The main objectives of the tax policy administration should be promoting self-assessment, incentivizing household savings and private-sector investment, and accelerating economic growth. The American Institute of Certified Public Accountants (AICPA) suggests that sound tax policy must meet the ten criteria in Table 1.1.[6] Currently, the Ethiopian tax system fails on most of these criteria.

---

6   The American Institute of Certified Public Accountants (October 2009). *Tax Reform Alternatives for the 21st Century.* New York, NY. https://www.aicpa. org/Advocacy/Tax/DownloadableDocuments/TPCS%204%20-%20principles%20for%20tax%20equity%20and%20fairness.doc.

Table 1.1: Criteria for Sound Tax Policy

Criteria	Effect
1. Simplicity	Simple tax laws enable taxpayers to understand the rules that apply to their situations and comply with them correctly and cost-effectively. Simplicity reduces the number of tax liability estimation errors, tax filing costs, reviews, and audits; improves compliance; and increases trust and respect for the system.
2. Fairness	Fairness dictates that similarly situated taxpayers are taxed similarly. Fairness must also meet the following criteria. a. *Exchange equity and fairness.* Over the long run, taxpayers receive appropriate value for the taxes they pay. b. *Process equity and fairness.* Taxpayers have a voice in the tax system; their voices are heard and treated with respect. c. *Horizontal equity and fairness.* Similarly situated taxpayers are taxed equally. d. *Vertical equity and fairness.* Taxes are based on the ability to pay. e. *Time-related equity and fairness.* Taxes are not distorted when income or wealth levels fluctuate over time. f. *Intergroup equity and fairness.* No group of taxpayers is favored to the detriment of others without worthy cause. g. *Compliance equity and fairness.* All taxpayers pay what they owe on a timely basis.
3. Economic Growth & Efficiency	A tax system should facilitate economic growth, capital formation, and international competitiveness. Also, it must not favor one industry or type of investment at the expense of others.
4. Neutrality	The tax system must be neutral in m**easuring** income, the appropriate tax rate, and taxpayers' ability to pay. A neutral tax system neither encourages nor discourages taxpayers from engaging in certain activities.

5. Transparency	Taxpayers should know that several types of taxes exist and how and when they will be imposed. Transparency lets taxpayers know the total cost of transactions and helps them better understand the tax system's impact and how to comply.
6. Minimizing Noncompliance	Minimize the tax gap, measured as the difference between the potential tax owed and the amount of tax collected, by increasing the ease of compliance, decreasing the incentives to avoid compliance, and using appropriate procedural rules and enforcement measures, including penalties.
7. Cost-Effective Collection	Minimize tax collection costs and compliance to both the tax administrators and taxpayers. Consider setting up convenient tax collection/payment points and the time for processing tax filings.
8. Impact on Government Revenues	The government should determine, with reasonable certainty, the amount and timing of tax collections. Policymakers need to achieve the desired level of revenue predictably and reliably within a reasonable range. A tax system that collects revenue from various tax sources will generate more stable tax revenue. For example, rising unemployment leads to reduced income tax collections, but property and sales taxes might be less affected; therefore, total revenues would be less volatile than if the government relied solely on employment income tax.
9. Certainty	Taxpayers need to be able to calculate their tax liability with confidence. Tax rules should specify how to determine the amount owed and when and how it is paid. When taxpayers lack confidence in their knowledge of (1) what their tax obligations are, (2) whether their calculations are correct, and (3) if their returns are correctly filed, compliance rates fall, and collection costs rise.
10. Payment Conveniences	Making the tax payment process convenient helps ensure compliance. The most appropriate payment mechanism would consider the liability amount, the best tax collection point, and the collection frequency.

1.1 THE ETHIOPIAN CONTEXT

With an estimated population of 112 million, Ethiopia is the second-most populous country in Africa, next to Nigeria. Youth below the age of 25 account for more than 60% of the population, 54% of whom are female. Also, 80% of the population lives in rural areas and is engaged in agriculture-related activities. This demographic topography presents opportunities and challenges for a country struggling to eliminate abject poverty, enhance its citizens' quality of life and economic prosperity, and join the ranks of lower-middle-income countries by 2030. The government must quickly address several socioeconomic issues left behind by the TPLF-led government.

1.1.1 The TPLF Era

Between 1992 and 2018, Ethiopia's economy grew faster, starting from a low base bolstered by a developmental state economic development strategy. For example, the gross domestic product rose from $10.5 billion in 1992 to $80 billion in 2018.[7] The average annual growth rate of the economy registered at between 8% and 11% of GDP.[8] Although Ethiopia is one of Africa's fastest-growing economies, it is still one of the poorest. With an estimated GDP per capita of only $783 in 2019, the TPLF-led government policies created colossal income inequalities. The Tigrayan elites wallowed in enormous wealth while more than 93% of the population lived in poverty and poor health.

Over the past 20 years, economic activities have remained buoyant despite obstacles to economic growth (drought, ethnopolitical tensions, internal displacement, migrations, and rapid population growth). The country was able to attract foreign direct investment, which helped accelerate the country's economic growth. The government continued

---

7   World Bank Group, Metadata 2018.
8   World Bank (2017). Country Partnership Framework: For the Federal Democratic Republic of Ethiopia, FY 2018–FY2022: Country Management Unit, AFC G3, Africa Region, May 22, 2017.

developing physical infrastructure through public investment projects by implementing the second phase of the Growth and Transformation Plan (GTP II), which ran out in the fiscal year 2019/20. It also sought to transform Ethiopia into a manufacturing hub by constructing several industrial parks in various parts of the country.

While government expansion of physical infrastructure (e.g., roads and highrise buildings) provided employment, the government's developmental state model suppressed the role of the private sector in the economy. For example, private-sector credit accounts for 9% of GDP, compared to more than 20% in SSA countries.[9] The private sector's development and growth were suppressed by TPLF-owned enterprises. Enterprises, such as the Endowment Fund for the Rehabilitation of Tigray (EFFORT) and other businesses controlled by TPLF, enjoyed several privileges not available to private enterprises. For example, TPLF enterprises can readily access bank loans, foreign currency, investment incentives, and tax holidays, enabling them to dominate all productive economic sectors and stifle competition from other enterprises.[10]

Rationed credit and foreign exchange allocation disproportionately benefited public and political party investments.[11] State and TPLF-allied enterprises dominated the import and export sectors, wholesale and

---

9   Ibid, p. 10.

10   The predominance of political party–owned companies referred to as parastatals that control the strategic income-generating sectors such as agriculture, industry, banking, mining, import-export, transportation, construction, insurance, and communications is bitterly resented by private entrepreneurs as well as the general population, which views it as a deliberate ethnic-based and systemic economic exploitation. TPLF-owned enterprises also enjoy preferential access to contracts, capital, foreign currency, physical infrastructure, administrative services, tax breaks, and other politically motivated and privileged supports. Since 1995, the TPLF has been using the parastatals under EFFORT as a "cash cow" to accumulate immense wealth to pursue Ethiopia's ethnically motivated political and economic domination.

11   Incidentally, non-TPLF political parties were blocked by regulation from engaging in income-generating business activities.

retail businesses, and the construction sector. At the same time, the law restricted other political parties in the country from owning or operating commercial enterprises.

The growth and competitiveness of the private sector were also hampered by the absence of reliable energy, telecommunication, and internet services;[12] efficient trade logistics; and exporting based on a more neutral exchange rate. Because the electric power supply was unreliable, all manufacturing and processing plants, office buildings, embassies, and diplomatic residences relied on diesel or gasoline-fueled generators at a high cost. On top of that, there were frequent shortages of the diesel and gasoline needed to run the generators.

Also, TPLF officials persuaded foreign investors to partner with select individuals to enrich themselves and siphon money out of the country. Most Chinese, Turkish, Middle Eastern, South African, Indian, Israeli, European, and American companies operating in Ethiopia have silent partners, mostly government or party officials or family members of the politicians. Consequently, special privileges and tax holidays were bestowed on these firms, and they did not have to pay taxes.

The Ethiopian Chambers of Commerce research also indicates that TPLF-controlled micro, small, medium, and large businesses accounted for more than 65% of the formal private economy in 2017. These businesses received special incentives and protections through internal directives outside the law and regulations governing business activities. For example, most paid lower rents for business premises owned by the

---

12 As reported by the World Bank, the ICT Development Index of the International Telecommunications Union ranked Ethiopia 162nd out of 166 countries in 2016 (34th out of 38 sub-Sahara Africa [SSA] countries); the Network Readiness Index of the World Economic Forum ranked Ethiopia 130th out of 143 countries in 2015 (24th out of 32 SSA countries); and the web index of the World Wide Web Foundation ranked Ethiopia 86th out of 86 countries in 2014 (21st out of 21 SSA countries). See World Bank Ethiopia Country Partnership Framework 2017, p. 11.

government. They also did not pay their fair share of taxes. Although the Ethiopian Constitution mandates the Office of the Federal Auditor General (OFAG) to audit parastatals and state-owned enterprises (SOEs), the TPLF-led government shielded these enterprises from all audits and reviews.

The Federal Democratic Republic of Ethiopia (FDRE) provided numerous tax incentives and holidays to attract foreign direct investment and stimulate domestic manufacturing and processing. The objective was to increase job creation, reduce import dependence, and increase national income through industrialization. However, these incentives were grossly abused, and the expected quality jobs, technology, and knowledge transfers never materialized. One scheme used by foreign companies to avoid paying taxes has been importing used equipment for manufacturing and processing plants from their home countries as new and replacing the equipment every five years. By this means, the tax holiday never expires.

As noted above, TPLF elites became silent partners to domestic and foreign investors to enrich themselves and siphon resources to TPLF coffers. They enabled tax fraud and evasion. The tax holiday incentive provided to foreign and domestic investors was used to defraud the government tax revenue and destabilize the domestic market. Under the TPLF's watch, illicit trade, money laundering, and financial fraud thrived.

The decline in the value of the Ethiopian currency (ETB) relative to the U.S. dollar harmed consumers' purchasing power and the productivity of manufacturers and processors. For example, an overall price increase on every market item following the 15% devaluation[13] of the ETB in July 2017 put pressure on household consumption. Because of the lack of foreign exchange and the dollar underground economy aside, many private manufacturing plants temporarily suspended production due to their inability to import raw materials and intermediate goods from abroad. It

---

13   World Bank (2017). Ethiopia: Impact of the Birr Devaluation on Inflation, Addis Ababa, November 8, 2017.

slowed down construction activities, and many people were laid off. The prices of goods soared, significantly hurting consumers, local investors, and home builders.

Nevertheless, the ETB's devaluation should have improved the competitiveness of Ethiopia's exports. The opening of several industrial parks, including in Addis Ababa, Hawassa, and Mekele, should have allowed the country to increase its leather, footwear, and textile exports.

According to the Growth and Transformation Plan II, public investment was expected to remain stable, particularly in the transportation, telecommunications, and energy sectors. However, progress on the Renaissance Dam, designed to generate 6,000 megawatts of electric power, was slow. The death of the general manager of the Renaissance Dam construction in 2018[14] revealed that the slowdown in the construction of the dam was primarily due to the massive embezzlement of funds and theft of construction materials by TPLF-associated individuals.

Under the GTP, the government had also planned to expand social infrastructures, such as hospitals and schools, and increase the quality and availability of essential public services. However, GTP failed to achieve its objectives due to *state technical incompetencies* and *systemic state corruption.*[15]

Since 2005, foreign investments in specific sectors, such as garment manufacturing and state-led infrastructure investments, have been driven by foreign investments. The country ran up a sizeable current account deficit, which reached 8.2% of GDP in the fiscal year (FY) 2017.

---

14 Arab News, Manager of Ethiopia's $4bl Nile Dam project committed suicide, September 22, 2018.

15 Resources siphoned out of Ethiopia have been invested outside the country to the extent where Ethiopian investors, mostly Tigrayans, ranked as the seventh-largest investors in Dubai. EFFORT, the TPLF-owned enterprise, has considerable investments in Dubai, the United Kingdom, Europe, the United States, and China.

Ethiopia's current account deficit was mainly funded through external borrowing. Over the years, Ethiopia built up significant external debt due to the borrowing associated with its large-scale infrastructure projects. Ethiopia's external debt is low as a percentage of GDP (31.9% of GDP in FY 2017). However, it is significantly higher than its current account receipts (233.4% of current account receipts in FY 2017), reflecting Ethiopia's weak export position.[16] The slowdown in export receipts in FY 2017, combined with the high external debt, led the International Monetary Fund (IMF) to classify Ethiopia at a high-risk level of debt distress in its debt sustainability analysis.[17] The TPLF-controlled enterprises dominated the primary foreign currency earners, such as coffee, flower exports, and garments. Consequently, the foreign currency earnings from these exports went directly to the TPLF coffers in foreign bank accounts.

Furthermore, the state-centric ethnopolitical model promoted and fostered by the Tigrayan-led FDRE narrowed the political space for public discourses, social action campaigns, and civil society engagement. Social action campaigns were prohibited, and community organizers and political activists were arrested, jailed, and beaten or killed. Consequently, there were few mechanisms for community self-help development activities and ensuring state accountability to citizens.

The divide between the public sector, civil society, and the business community and the strictures placed on civil society, citizen engagement and participation, and the media led to the stagnation of reform processes, increased state corruption, and political tension. We can characterize the Tigrayan-controlled government as a government for a specific group of politicians and political actors instead of a government for ordinary citizens. The door was widely opened for massive systemic corruption by TPLF-favored officials at subnational and national government levels. There were no opposition parties. The parties representing the different

---

16 World Bank (2018). External Debt to GDP.

17 Sky News, African nations at risk of economy-crippling debt, IMF warns. May 9, 2018.

ethnic groups in the ruling party coalition were creations of TPLF. These parties were soft opposition parties. After the 2005 election, which saw the ruling party lose the national and local elections in many parts of the country, ballot boxes were half full before citizens cast their ballots for national and local candidates to ensure TPLF-associated candidates won the elections. The winners were predetermined.

TPLF had control over all levels of government, from village-level governments to the national level. It controlled the movements and thoughts of citizens and civil servants through a cell arrangement called "five-to-one," which restricted the gathering of citizens to five people. Of those five, one acted as a team leader and reported on the other four members' thoughts, observations, and opinions to a higher cell. In effect, "big brother" watched over all citizens and residents. People did not trust family members or their neighbors—this impeded economic growth and prosperity. Prosperity requires an open and collaborative society.

Moreover, the Ethiopian armed forces were dominated by Tigrayans. Eighty percent of the high- and middle-ranking officers were Tigrayans. The elite troops were mainly composed of the Tigrayan ethnic people. Since the 1998 conflict with Eritrea, 80% of the armament, including tanks, trucks, and missiles, was moved to different military camps in Tigray to defend the region from Eritrean aggression.

The FDRE has five government levels, including the Kebele, the Woreda (or district), the Zonal, the regional state, and the federal (see Figure 1.2). The FDRE 1995 Constitution (Article 47) organized the country into autonomous ethnic regional states with the promise of equitable economic and social development. Today there are 11 ethnic regional states, including the newly formed Sidama and South Eastern Peoples regional states, a break away from the Southern Nations Nationality People (SNNP) regional state, and two city administrations—Addis Ababa and Dire Dawa.

Figure 1.2 shows that the regional states are further segmented into zonal administrations. The powers and functions of zones vary from region to region. In SNNP and Amhara regional states, zones play intermediary roles between the regional government and Woredas. In the other regional states, zones play an oversight role over Woreda administrations. Because of their ethnic diversity and to ensure all ethnic groups have equal access to essential public goods and services, there are also nationality zones and Liyu (i.e., Special) Woredas in five regions: Afar, Amhara, SNNPR, Benishangul-Gumuz, and Gambella. According to the Central Statistical Agency's (CSA's) December 2018 census, there were 120 zones, 1,064 Woredas, 27,723 Kebeles, and 18,966,145 households across all regional states and city administrations of Addis Ababa and Dire Dawa (see Table 1.2).

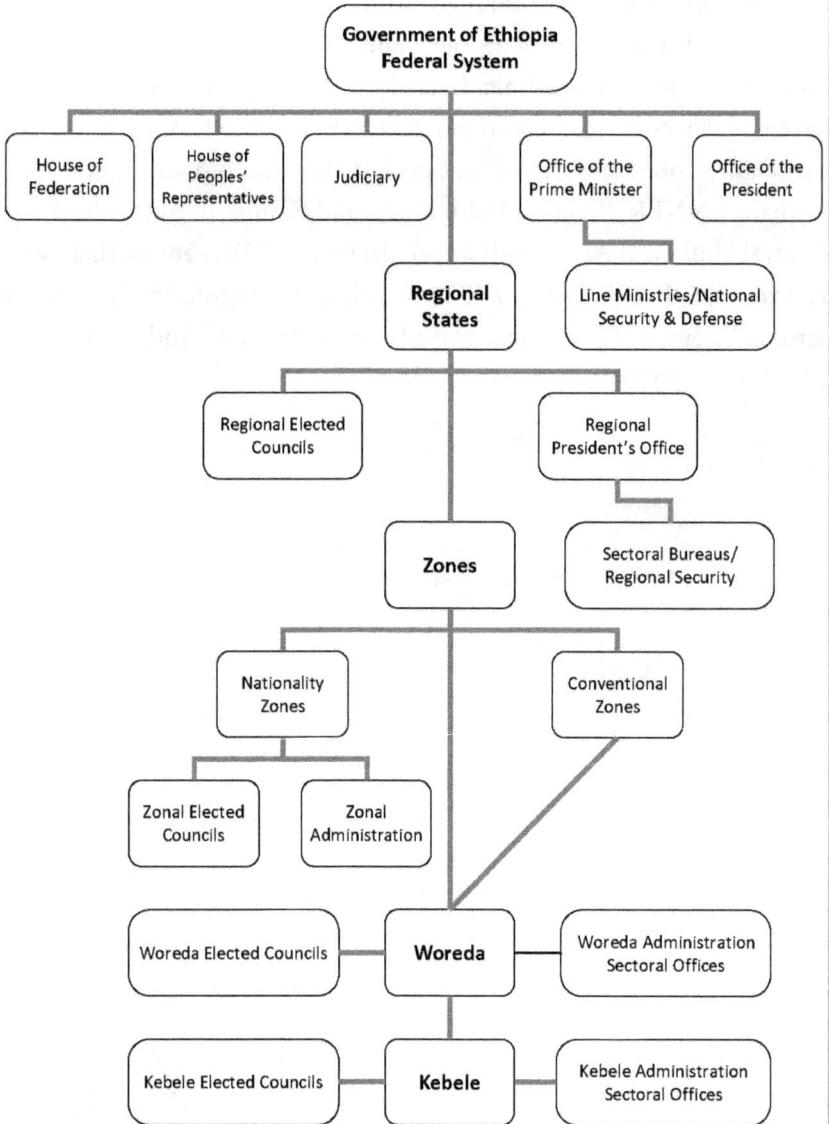

Figure 1.2: FDRE Decentralized Governance Structure

Table 1.2: Subnational Governments Under Ethiopia's Federal Structure

CSA December 6, 2018, Census Result

Regions	Zones		Woredas	Kebeles	Number of Households
	Conventional Zones	Nationality Zones			
Tigray	7	0	52	2,084	1,176,439
Afar	6	0	34	335	184,837
Amhara	12	4	207	7,107	4,845,582
Oromia	38	1	338	10,869	6,793,462
Somale	11	0	100	1,284	908,923
Bennishangul	3	1	22	333	233,072
Sidama	1	0	29	1,107	797,823
SNNP	13	5	143	4,315	2,838,980
Gambella	4	0	14	163	83,356
Harari	1	0	9	9	59,624
Dire Dawa	1	0	1	1	93,138
Addis Ababa	11	0	11	115	950,909
Total	**109**	**11**	**1,064**	**27,723**	**18,966,145**

While regional states have elected councils, conventional zones do not have councils. Woredas and Kebeles do have elected councils. Conventional zones do not have a legally recognized tier of government with constitutionally mandated powers and structure as a self-governing entity. However, they have coordinating and supervisory authority over Woreda administrations on behalf of the regional state administration.

On the other hand, nationality (or special) zonal administrations established for regional minority ethnic groups are recognized as the highest political organ of the ethnic group. They are mandated to collect revenues, dictate the language used, and formulate laws and regulations. They can also ratify the laws and regulations they prepare through their elected councils.

While the FDRE 1995 Constitution devolves decision-making powers to subnational governments, lower-level tiers cannot make independent decisions. The TPLF-led Ethiopian Peoples' Revolutionary Democratic Front (EPRDF) formed a coalition ruling party. This party approves all regional and local decisions. The centralized partisan structure of the EPRDF had penetrated to the local level. Consequently, the sub-national governments did not have complete control over their affairs. The central government could interfere in its administrative affairs through the party apparatuses. In effect, decentralization was not an effective and efficient public service delivery mechanism to citizens nor did it lead to effective and balanced regional development. Instead, it was a tool for strengthening the TPLF's grip on power and sustaining its hegemony.

EPRDF controlled all branches of government at the national level, as well as the entire constituent regions and local and grassroots administrative units of government. The affiliated ethnic-based regional parties facilitated political control of EPRDF within their jurisdictions.

The security apparatus was deployed in every community. I remember an incident in Harrar regional state. My team and I met the chairman of a beneficiary, Kebele, to discuss his understanding and opinion regarding the World Bank's social accountability project implemented in his community. Throughout the interview and discussion, the security officer responded to our questions. Finally, when we asked the Kebele chairman why he was not answering our questions or talking, he said, "The security guys have stolen my mouth!" In other words, he cannot give his opinion on the subject of government accountability to communities. The donor community forced the project on the government to protect essential services delivery to communities that did not vote for the ruling party during the 2005 national election. The donors feared the EPRDF would cut off funding for essential service delivery, particularly in districts that did not elect the ruling party.

Moreover, the 2009 civil society registration legislation prevented civil society organizations (CSOs) from playing a watchdog or civil liberties advocacy role.[18] The law restricted and undermined the role of INGOs, civic groups, and civil society organizations in the political arena.

1.1.2 The Coming of Prime Minister Dr. Abiy Ahmed

On February 15, 2018, Prime Minister Hailemariam Desalegn resigned from power. He had been prime minister since the death of Prime Minister Meles Zenawi in 2012. His resignation was triggered by a series of political protests and unrest all around the country. Protesters were demanding inclusion in the political and governance processes, relaxation of security restrictions, adherence to the rule of law, and the end of the ruling Tigrayan elite's dominance. While the Tigrayans represented only 6% of the population, they dominated the Ethiopian political space and the economic and investment arenas over three decades. They amassed great wealth while displacing and impoverishing non-Tigrayan citizens.

One month after Prime Minister Hailemariam Desalegn resigned, Dr. Abiy Ahmed was appointed by Parliament as Ethiopia's caretaker prime minister until the next national election. Soon after he became the interim prime minister, Dr. Abiy Ahmed announced a series of reforms and initiatives. Prime Minister Abiy announced that he would shift to a private-sector-led economic development and growth model, with the state continuing to play a significant role in the economy. He announced plans to privatize a series of SOEs exploited by the TPLF elites.

Once in office, Prime Minister Abiy Ahmed began freeing up the political space. He pardoned opposition political leaders and released hundreds of thousands of political prisoners held by the TPLF-led government in various government and private prisons. The prime minister opened the door for all political parties to campaign in the upcoming national, regional, and local elections. He welcomed the return of the diaspora that had left the country because of political prosecutions. The prime minister also expressed his intention to shift away from the TPLF-constructed

---

18   Proclamation No. 621/2009. Proclamation to provide for the Registration and Regulation of Charities and Societies.

ethnopolitical arrangement to a united Ethiopian political model. The prime minister also established peace and friendship with Eritrea. Dr. Abiy and Esaias Afewerki, president of Eretria, agreed to work together strategically to develop the economies of both countries.

The 2009 Civil Society Registration Proclamation was amended to open up the political space for CSOs and civic groups. The new Organizations of Civil Societies Proclamation No. 1113/2019 changed most of the restrictive rules of the 2009 proclamation.[19] The proclamation distinguished between domestic and foreign CSOs. Domestic CSOs are organizations formed according to Ethiopian laws, either by Ethiopians or foreigners who reside in Ethiopia. Although some of the restrictions in the 2009 legislation were removed, the continued ethnocentric political arrangement continues to limit CSOs' advocacy and oversight roles broadly.

Dr. Abiy also issued the homegrown 10-year prosperity plan. The plan intends to foster quality-based economic growth, increased productivity, and competitiveness; build a green and climate-resilient economy; bring about institutional transformation; ensure fair and equitable opportunities for women and youth and guarantee private-sector-led economic growth.[20] In the 2021 national election, Dr. Abiy Ahmed was elected Ethiopia's prime minister by a wide margin.

The 2020/2021 government budget was increased by 30% from the previous fiscal year. The increase was earmarked for capital expenditures. Foreign loans and grants financed 18% of the budget deficit. The Ministry of Finance and Economic Cooperation (MOFEC) expects tax revenues to increase with GDP growth and stabilize the budget deficit. However,

---

19 Proclamation No. 1113/2019, Organizations of Civil Societies Proclamation, March 7, 2019.

20 Office of the Prime Minister (2019). A Homegrown Economic Reform Agenda: A Pathway to Prosperity, September 2019; Fana Broadcasting. Addis Ababa, June 11, 2020 (FBC)—Ethiopia has unveiled its 10-year development plan with the theme "Ethiopia: An African Beacon of Prosperity."

tax revenues are only 6.7% of GDP, compared with a low average of around 20% in sub-Saharan Africa. Because of the economic effects of COVID-19 and the conflict in the Tigray regional state, the expected GDP growth may also not materialize as expected.

Although economic growth, driven by physical infrastructure investment, led to reduced poverty and improved service delivery, the challenges faced by Prime Minister Abiy's government are substantial. Most of the youth population, which makes up more than 60% of the country's population, are undereducated, unskilled, and unemployed. Thus, both an increase in domestic revenue generation and transparency are required to educate and skill up the youth and effectively reduce poverty. Also, increased domestic revenue generation and transparent service delivery are crucial to achieving the UN Sustainable Development Goals and the national development objectives.

Moreover, gender equity remains a severe challenge, particularly in traditional and Islamic communities. While women make up more than 54% of the population, fewer women are in decision-making positions on the supply side. Prime Minister Abiy's decision to appoint women to key cabinet positions partially addresses the gender disparity. Close to half of the cabinet-level posts are held by women. However, women experience unequal opportunities and access to information and services on the demand side. For example, most women entrepreneurs run micro, small, and medium businesses in the informal sector. Informal sector actors miss critical forms of support from the government and the donor community. They miss out on credit assistance and skills training, which can enable them to grow, improve, and expand their enterprises and, in the process, generate jobs and income for themselves and others.

Female business owners do not formalize their businesses because social norms make dealing with male service providers difficult. Additionally, government processes do not cater to women's specific needs. In Ethiopia, the low participation of women in the formal business sector is related to sexual harassment, lack of education, family responsibilities, and lack of access to information.[21] In a focus group discussion on March 16, 2017, in Sebeta City, Oromia, many women indicated one must be a prostitute to succeed in this male-dominated corrupted society. Everybody wants either sexual favors or monetary payment to provide any form of government service.

Prime Minister Abiy's ambitious reform agenda requires significant citizen engagement and participation as well as public oversight and accountability. For the country to generate more tax revenue to finance its social services and development activities, we must transform citizens' mindsets and attitudes and the Ethiopian tax system.

Tax revenue collection is currently below expectations for several reasons, including taxpayers' non-compliance arising from their perceptions that the tax system is unfair and that everybody is cheating on their taxes, hostility between taxpayers and tax officials, and negative attitudes toward the tax system.[22][23] These negative attitudes emanate from the belief that the tax system is not equitable and that tax officials are corrupt and inept. Over the past three decades, political–party–owned and favored enterprises—which often have a turnover of thousands, millions, and billions of ETB annually—have been exempted from paying taxes.

The Ministry of Revenue (MOR), the Ethiopian Customs Commission, and the MOFEC are critical to increasing tax revenues by simplifying the tax law and broadening the tax base. For example, pulling in and

21 Samuel Taddesse (2011). Women's Entrepreneurship Development & Gender Equity (WEDGE), 2009/2010 Performance Report, February 2011, Contract No.: 40065609/0, International Labor Organization (ILO), Geneva, Switzerland.

22 Neway Gobachew, Kenenisa Lemie Debela, and Woldemicael Shibiru (2017). "Determinants of Tax Revenue in Ethiopia." *Economics*. Vol. 6, No. 1, 2018, pp. 58–64. doi: 10.11648/j.eco.20170606.11.

23 Tadele Bayu (2015). "Analysis of Tax Buoyancy and Its Determinants in Ethiopia (Cointegration Approach)." *Journal of Economics and Sustainable Development* Vol. 6, No. 3, ISSN 2222-1700 (Paper); ISSN 2222-2855 (Online). www.iiste.org.

formalizing the informal sector, revisiting and adjusting the policies and regulations governing tax exemptions and investment incentives, and improving tax administration processes and systems would generate significant tax revenue.

However, the tax gap remains high, and tax effort is low, signifying that many challenges remain. According to a recent IMF study, the government collected only 63% of the potential tax revenues, resulting in a 5% shortfall in GDP.[24] The tax system is costly, costing more than $2.20 to collect $100, compared to the worldwide average of only about $1.00. The burden of merely paying taxes is also sky-high, as indicated by the country's ranking (133 out of 190) in the World Bank's "Doing Business: Paying Taxes" rating.[25] In short, tax rates are high, revenues low, and tax collection and compliance costs high.

Taxpayers' noncompliance and informality increased with the high tax burden on non-TPLF-affiliated small and medium enterprises. This also resulted in a reduction in VAT revenue collection. VAT was introduced in 2003. Initially, VAT revenue was high. Subsequently, it began to decline. Consumers began to avoid paying the 15% VAT on their purchases, and merchants refused to issue VAT receipts to their customers to hide their sales revenues.

Moreover, there is a lack of understanding of VAT taxation principles. The inconsistency and confusion in implementing tax assessments further contribute to poor tax compliance. Tax penalties and interest on taxes owed are outrageously high, prompting small- and medium-sized businesses to close shop or shift to the informal sector.

The MOR also faces the challenge of access to an aggregation of the relevant data required to improve tax administration effectiveness and efficiency. MOR employees have not been trained sufficiently in the

---

24 Ricardo Fenochietto and Carola Pessino (2013). Understanding Countries' Tax Effort. IMF Working Paper. WP/13/244.

25 World Bank (2018). Ethiopia Doing Business: Reforming to Create Jobs, p.4.

Standard Integrated Government Tax Administration System (SIGTAS), data sourcing, and data matching. Moreover, the Enterprise Information and Communication Infrastructure (ICT) suffers from inherent architectural problems and data entry backlogs. It does not automatically generate aggregated data on tax collection or taxpayer registration, nor does it automatically calculate interest penalties for late payments.

MOR is affected by many organizational issues as well. The staff lacks specialized data verification, tax auditing, and compliance skills. They require in-depth, on-the-job training. Other significant challenges include general managerial skills and organizational development, effective performance management, and human resources management skills. Ethnic-based, rather than merit-based, hiring and promotion have weakened the Ministry. Trained and knowledgeable MOR staff get hired by large taxpayers offering attractive salaries and benefits to lower their tax exposure.

When an employee leaves a post, there is no mechanism or enforceable corporate policy for transferring the incumbents' information, skills, and knowledge to the new replacements. The incumbent's experience, knowledge, and talent are lost once an employee leaves the organization.

MOR is not a learning organization.[26] For example, directors hold their knowledge and skills close to their chests. Their information, experience, and expertise are not shared with subordinates. Each directorate is regimented, and staff morale is incredibly low. Thus, employees cannot be creative even if it would benefit the organization.

---

26 Learning organizations are organizations where leaders share information and expertise that enable their employees system-wide to continually expand their capacity to work collaboratively to generate the desired results and outcomes, where new and expansive patterns of thinking are nurtured, where collective aspiration is set free, and where people are continually learning to see the whole together.

Learning organizations are characterized as organizations that proactively make efforts in the form of investment and encouragement to educate their employees to adapt to the rapidly changing technology and business environment. In addition to educating, a learning organization encourages employees to take risks with innovative and creative ideas. In this way, they inculcate creative thinking and learning from experience in their employees. They encourage their employees to provide quality service to taxpayers while generating the highest tax revenue without stressing those taxpayers.[27] Managers of learning organizations also share important policy decisions and other information with their employees so everyone working there is on the same page. This has the effect of making each employee feel that they are an essential member of the organization.

The MOR's counterparts, the Regional Revenue Bureaus (RRBs), face similar tax collection challenges. The RRBs are plagued by problems of VAT compliance and a large informal sector, high staff turnover, and scarcity of qualified personnel.

The MOFEC oversees economic and fiscal policy, development planning, and budgeting. MOFEC successfully revised Ethiopia's tax regime in 2001. However, it is severely challenged by capacity gaps. For example, MOFEC's Macroeconomic Policy and Management Directorate (MPMD) is understaffed. The lack of specialized skills, such as macroeconomic modeling, microsimulations, and policy impact assessment, undermines the organization's effectiveness.

The complicated tax system, limited tax policy, and administrative capacities negatively affect businesses and the economy. Apart from constraining government revenue potential and economic performance, their combined impacts create unnecessary trade, investment, and economic efficiency barriers and open the door for corruption. They slow down

---

27 Peter M. Senge (1990). *The Fifth Discipline: The Art & Practice of The Learning Organization.* Penguin Random House.

business responsiveness to marketplace opportunities, divert resources away from productive investments, hamper entry to markets, reduce innovation and job creation, and discourage entrepreneurship. The current structure and application of tax incentives and tax holidays deny the government substantial tax revenue with no benefit to justify these incentives. Beneficiaries of these incentives, in effect, undermine smaller businesses and monopolize the market at an inflated cost to consumers.

A well-thought-out tax policy and spending plan are needed to put the government on a sustainable long-term fiscal path and ensure the achievement of its prosperity objectives in an inclusive manner. It must generate sufficient tax revenue to meet Ethiopia's security, economic, and social development needs

> Taxation is not a new phenomenon. In Ethiopia, before 1940, taxes were used to support ruling classes and feudal lords, raise armies and build defenses against foreign enemies. Often, the authority to tax stemmed from the divine or supernatural rights of the kings and emperors.

and preserve flexibility to address unforeseen events, including disease epidemics, natural disasters and emergencies, and war and conflict. It must also work to reverse the drastic devaluation of the Ethiopian Birr. It is a poison pill planted by the TPLF that will devastate the Ethiopian economy in the long run. Ethiopia must learn to invest and live within her means, as was the case before the coming of the TPLF regime. Ethiopia can be food self-sufficient with a sound agricultural policy and strategy and does not need to import food items. It has sufficient resources to produce chemical as well as natural fertilizers domestically. Ethiopia can also manufacture most of the drugs, medicines, and metal works the country needs.

1.2 STRUCTURE OF THE BOOK

In the rest of the book, my goal is to explain how we can reform the tax regime and generate sufficient domestic revenue to achieve Prime Minister Abiy's prosperity objectives. I will attempt to be as systematic as possible.

For example, in Chapter 2, I will discuss taxation issues. Taxes are involuntary contributions citizens and businesses must make for the goods and services they collectively provide for themselves and others. The annual contribution amount is set by agreement through a legislative process. Fair and equitable tax policies are often established through dialogue and collaboration between civil society, the private sector, and the government based on what goods and services the government must deliver. For example, engaging and educating citizens/taxpayers and their government counterparts in a social accountability setting can help to strengthen feelings of responsibility and identity to the government. It persuades government officials to deliver better and more public goods and services transparently, cost-effectively, and equitably. The government must regard taxpaying citizens as partners rather than merely people who hold obligations toward them. Dialogue and a consultative approach between citizens, the private sector, and the government are more necessary now than ever, given the tax administration's tarnished image and history as a repressive and corrupt government agency.

As our demand for better quality public goods and services increases, the price of those services rises. Thus, we must pay more taxes and pay in full and on time. In this sense, effective taxation would require connecting tax compliance to citizenship rights and obligations and upholding collective responsibility and collaboration values. It is equally important to discuss tax fraud and corruption's detrimental effects on society. Corruption is a cancer that deprives government entities of the resources required for delivering quality services and denies improvements in citizens' quality of life.

Chapter 3 is about who has the mandate for making tax and fiscal policies and the capacities required for effective and efficient fiscal and tax policies. In Ethiopia, the tax policy is drafted and presented to the Council of Ministers by the MOFEC. MOFEC is responsible for preparing sound tax and fiscal policies in collaboration with all the relevant stakeholders, including the MOR, the Ethiopian Investment Commission, the Ministry of Trade and Industry, and civil society.

Chapter 4 discusses the types of taxes imposed on citizens, residents, and businesses. These taxes are also classified into direct and indirect taxes. The chapter also outlines the various sources of taxable income and commercial transactions.

Chapter 5 is about tax administration. Tax administration is about enforcing the tax laws and collecting tax revenues from citizens, residents, and businesses effectively, fairly, and efficiently with minimum tax compliance costs to taxpayers[28].

The Ethiopian MOR is currently working on a restructuring plan to simplify its business processes, reduce tax administration and collection costs, stem system-wide fraud and corruption, and reduce taxpayers' compliance costs. Business process redesign is yet at a diagnostic stage and would take several years to complete. Shifting to merit-based hiring and promotion would require political accommodation as we change from an ethnocentric to an ethnic-blind Ethiopia paradigm. Citizens also expect their government to do good with their tax money with minimum waste. The issue is about government transparency and accountability to ordinary citizens.

The MOR needs to shift Ethiopians' tax culture through tax awareness campaigns and taxpayer educational programs. It must use a multifaceted approach to educate and raise Ethiopians' tax culture and increase tax compliance. For example, the Ministry's Tax Fairness Cooperation

---

28 Mattijs Alink and Victor van Kommer (2016). Handbook on Tax Administration (second Revised Edition), IBFD, Amsterdam, The Netherlands;

Project (TFCP), implemented by Cowater International and the MOR, worked in Merkato, one of the biggest open markets in Africa. It delivered tax awareness training to the traders and merchants operating in Merkato. MOR has also started working with the Ministry of Education and local universities to introduce tax education in elementary and secondary schools and universities to reach future taxpayers. MOR frequently broadcasts radio and televised messages to educate citizens about its work and encourage voluntary tax compliance. Tax education activities must continue.

In Chapter 6, we discuss taxpayers' obligations and rights. The MOR has begun to communicate these obligations and rights to taxpayers. It has also started recognizing and giving awards to compliant taxpayers, linking taxpaying to good citizenship to increase tax compliance and improve the tax culture. However, we have found that some taxpayers selected as 'good taxpayers' are tax non-compliant. The MOR needs to revise its 'good taxpayers' selection criteria.

Chapter 7 is about the tax audit process. It lays out the tax audit selection processes, tax auditors' obligations, and the rights of auditees. It also outlines and discusses the avenues available to taxpayers to appeal tax audit findings if they object. Chapter 8 summarizes taxpayers' beliefs about the current Ethiopian tax system's equity and fairness.

CHAPTER 2
TAXATION AND THE TAX-POLICY– MAKING PROCESS

Taxation is the government's imposition of a levy on the incomes and commercial transactions of citizens, residents, and businesses. Tax is a compulsory payment made to federal, regional, or local governments based on income and profit earned, the appreciations in the value of assets owned, and commercial transactions. *Tax is the price we all pay for the goods and services we collectively provide to ourselves and others in our communities through our government.*[1] Tax is inextricably linked to the government's capacity to deliver public goods and services and protect the security and safety of citizens.

According to Schumpeter, in a democratic society, taxation finances the state's (government) capacity to deliver essential public goods and

---

1   This definition of taxation is based on the assumption that the government is created/organized by the people for the people. Some forms of governments are dictatorial, and all decisions are made by the leader without regard for what the people need and want.

services we all need.[2] Different government levels use the tax revenue collected to pay for public sector goods and services, as defined in Box 2.1, provided to citizens, residents, and businesses.

Box 2.1: Definition of Public Goods & Services

Public goods & services are available to all people, whether they pay taxes or not. Furthermore, consumption by some people does not reduce the consumption by others. Because it is difficult to charge for the benefit of these public goods, and because people cannot be excluded for not paying for them, there is no incentive for private firms to supply these public goods. For these reasons, these goods and services are provided by the government. Examples of public goods include national defense, community policing, and street lighting.

The government also supplies **public sector goods & services** that benefit society and are excludable. Public sector goods and services include education, healthcare, potable water, electricity, roads, public transportation, and telecommunications. These goods and services can be produced and supplied by private firms for the paying public. That is why we have private schools, private healthcare facilities, private toll roads, private transportation services, and private telecommunications. However, these private goods and services providers can exclude nonpaying members of society. The government, therefore, must serve those members of society who cannot afford to pay.

Public goods are available to all people, whether they pay taxes or not. Furthermore, consumption by some people does not reduce the consumption by others. Because it is difficult to charge for the benefit of these public goods, and because people cannot be excluded for not paying for them, there is no incentive for private firms to supply these public goods. Therefore, these goods and services are provided by the government. Examples of public goods include national defense, community policing, and street lighting.

The government also supplies **public sector goods** that benefit society and are excludable. Public sector goods and services include education, healthcare,

---

2   Joseph Alois Schumpeter (1918). "The Crisis of the Tax State." In Richard Swedberg (ed.), *The Economics and Sociology of Capitalism*, 1991. Princeton: Princeton University Press.

potable water, electricity, telecommunications, roads, and public transport. These goods and services can be produced and supplied by private firms for the paying public. That is why we have private schools, private healthcare facilities, private roads, private public transport services, and private telecommunications. However, these private goods and service providers can exclude non-paying members of society. The government, therefore, must serve those members of society that cannot afford to pay.

Since ancient times, the idea of taxation has been around and supported several types of public goods and services. Soon after people settled in large communities, collective action was needed to obtain the things everyone in the community required, which no individual family could provide independently. People paid taxes through labor. Others paid taxes by delivering a portion of their farm crops, livestock, and other valuables. Over time, legal tender replaced all forms of tax payments, and a modern tax system was born. Although societies have become more complex now, the basic idea of tax and taxation has remained the same. Tax is a compulsory levy on individuals' and residents' earned income, consumption and personal property values, business profits and property values, and commercial transactions. And society uses the tax to provide the public goods and services and security and justice services it needs.

Taxation is based on law and is not a payment for services directly received by individual citizens, residents, or businesses from the government. It does not require taxpayers' consent. It is a compulsory contribution to federal, state, and local government budgets to deliver public goods and services to citizens, residents, and businesses. Imagine trying to buy a piece of your country's national defense. That would be impossible. Yet, in practice, tax policy developed in consultation with citizens, residents, and businesses can expand the tax culture and voluntary tax compliance, reduce the cost of tax administration, and positively influence infrastructure development, economic growth, and government accountability (see Figure 2.1).

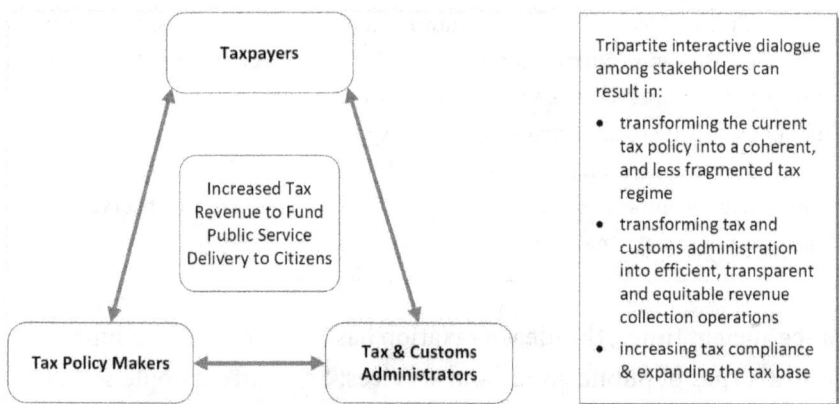

Figure 2.1: Why Does Consulting with Taxpayers Matter?

On the one hand, a high tax rate can discourage private-sector investment and household savings. Conversely, a low tax rate reduces the resources available to the government to provide essential public goods and services that we all need. There should be a balance between what citizens want and expect and what the government can produce and supply with the available resources.

The taxation conversation is crucial to recognize synergies between what a government does in infrastructure development, household purchasing power, business investment, and economic growth. Employment, households' purchasing power, and private sector investments increase with government investment in infrastructure. Explaining these synergies to taxpayers and using evidence for why the tax rate should be raised or lowered can build taxpayers' trust in their government and enhance tax compliance (see Box 2.2 for tax compliance definition).

Box 2.2: What Is Tax Compliance?

Tax compliance is about taxpayers' willingness to pay taxes. The definition of tax compliance has two essential elements, as follows:

- **Administrative compliance** is related to compliance with the administrative rules of tax filing and the timely payment of tax liabilities.

It encompasses compliance with reporting requirements, procedural compliance, and regulatory compliance.

- **Technical compliance** involves the calculation of tax liabilities according to the technical requirements of tax law, or when taxpayers pay their share of tax following the tax code provisions.

Income tax laws are not clear cut. Ambiguity exists on three levels:[*]

- in the precise meaning of statutory language;
- in the application of how the law applies in a specific factual situation; and
- in the type of evidence sufficient to establish the facts.

Thus, measuring technical compliance must begin with determining the correct amount of tax payable. Given some *ambiguity* in the interpretation and application of the tax law, estimating the correct amount of tax can differ widely, depending in part on the taxpayer's background, biases, and skill levels. Ambiguity in the tax law is a significant problem for taxpayers. Long and Swingen assert any ambiguities that lead a taxpayer to a different interpretation from that of the tax administration's (assumedly inclusive of a tax administration's interpretation developed and promulgated well after filing the tax return) are traditionally considered by administrations to represent noncompliance.[*] In short, voluntary compliance is the taxpayer's willingness to comply with the tax authority's directives and regulations.

[*]Susan B. Long and Judyth A. Swingen (1991). "Taxpayer Compliance: Setting New Agendas for Research." *Law & Society Review, Volume 25, Number 3 (1991)*, pp. 637–683.

The question remains: how should the government decide on the tax levy level, and who should pay tax? The tax levy level depends on the cost of government service delivery, infrastructure development, construction and maintenance, social and economic development needs and goals, and taxpayers' ability to pay. More and better-quality public service delivery to citizens translates into higher government spending. All other things being equal, higher government costs mean more tax revenue is needed and requires raising tax levy levels.

In most developed and democratic countries, taxation is based on consultation and dialogue with the taxpaying public and businesses, academicians, citizen representatives, and parliamentarians (see Figure 2.2). The taxation dialogue with civil society, businesses, and special interest groups tying taxes with public finance management, quality and quantity of public goods and services delivered, and government accountability and service delivery performance increase voluntary tax compliance.

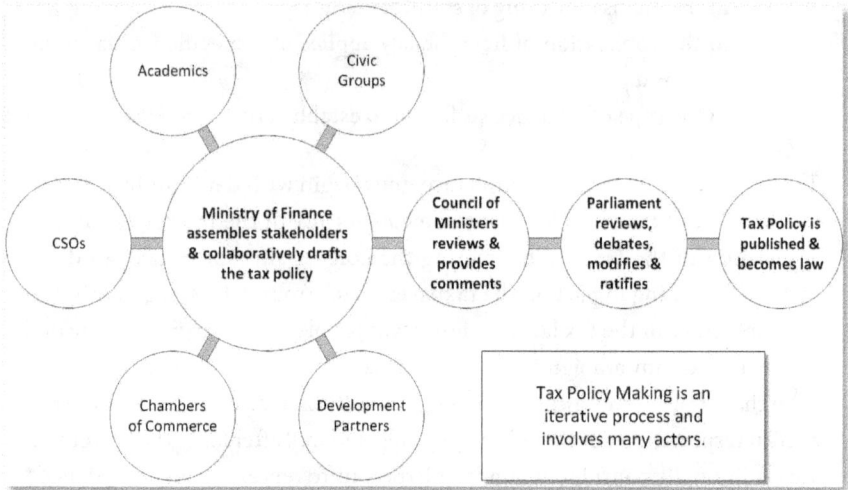

Figure 2.2: The Tax-Policy–Making Process

As noted by Moore, the tax-policy–making process should first involve political negotiations among the stakeholders.[3] Second, bargaining over the why, nature, and level of taxes is central to building accountability relations between the government and the taxpayers based on obligations and rights. Tax policies developed consensually with taxpayers and implemented transparently are considered fair and equitable. Third, for taxation to positively affect accountability, most citizens, residents, and businesses must share the tax burden. Tax issues must be prominent on the political agenda. Taxation is linked to the government's budget

---

3   Mick Moore (2008). "Between Coercion and Contract: Competing Narratives Around Taxations and Governance." In D. Brautigen, O-H Fjeldstad and M. Moore (eds). *Taxation and State-Building in Developing Countries: Capacity and Consent.* Cambridge: Cambridge University Press.

and performance regarding essential public service delivery, including defense and security, and progress toward economic, social, and infrastructure development goals.

Furthermore, constructive dialogue and consultation are instructive and cultivate a taxpaying culture (Fjeldstad and Heggstad 2012a).[4] They also ensure that taxation and tax compliance determine the government's legitimacy. Government legitimacy is crucial. Government legitimacy is defined by (a) how it consults and works with citizens, residents, and businesses; (b) how it collects and uses the tax money to improve citizens' living conditions; and (c) how its programs and activities are inclusive, fair, and equitable with no group left behind. It also depends on how the government interacts with the constellation of stakeholders in tax-policy–making (see Figure 2.3). In this regard, one key challenge is strengthening accountability between the government and the taxpayers.

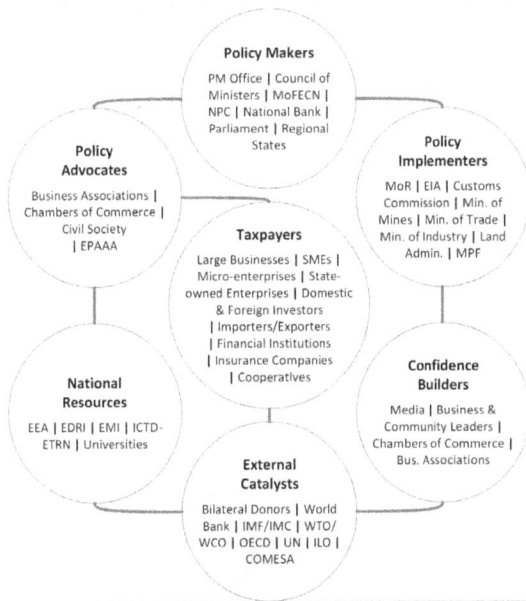

Figure 2.3: The Constellation of Stakeholders

---

4   Odd-Helge Fjeldstad and Kari Heggstad (2012a). Building Taxpayer Culture in Mozambique, Tanzania and Zambia: Achievements, Challenges and Policy Recommendation. CMI Report R 2012: 1 Berger: Chr. Michelin Institute.

In much of the world, the channels through which governments hold themselves accountable to citizens and citizens communicate their demands for better government performance are weak, resulting in conflict, massive citizen resistance, demonstrations, and riots. In most countries, the wealthy and the political and religious elites have stifled meaningful political discourse and restricted citizen participation in policymaking. For example, in the United States, the rich have politicians in their pockets and ensure the government policies are in their favor. The rich ensure their control over government policymaking through sizeable political campaign contributions, constant lobbying, and wining and dining with the politicians. The middle class has lost its voice over time. Politicians have stopped fighting for the needs of the poor and the middle class in America and other countries. In Ethiopia, we also don't see politicians advocating and ensuring their constituents' basic needs are met.

In most countries, one form of communicating demands is mass protests by marching to government offices and holding signs. Over the past 30 years, when citizens marched peacefully to relay their grievances and demand redress from the government in Ethiopia, demonstrators were bitten by the police, and some were killed. Others were imprisoned in jails built in the middle of deserts without due process. Prime Minister Abiy's government must urgently address how it deals with protesters, listen to their grievances, and respond appropriately. Open and constructive dialogue and communication with the constellations of stakeholders can build trust in government, foster citizen and government collaborations, and avert street protests.

The government must develop systems and procedures for collecting citizens' and businesses' feedback regarding the existing tax policy and its administration and use. That feedback should then be processed, categorized, and addressed. If necessary, the fiscal and tax policies and administration systems must be reformed. The government must demonstrate to citizens and businesses how their complaints and feedback are addressed in tax policy and administration reforms and how it invests their tax money. Such a process would strengthen the social contract between taxpayers and the government.

2.1 TAX POLICY SETTING FOR
SUSTAINED PROSPERITY

All other things being equal, governments collect and use tax revenues to create, expand, and strengthen the conditions that enhance citizens' living conditions. Before governments set tax and fiscal policies, they must understand and articulate society's current living conditions and where they should be in 10 to 20 years. Such a long-range vision should guide society's economic, social, and infrastructure investment needs and determine the nation's concurrent tax and fiscal policies.

The first question that needs answering revolves around where political leaders and citizens want their country's economic and human development worldwide ranking to be 10 to 20 years from now. It should begin by laying out a well-considered strategy and program to enhance citizens' standard of living (SOL) and quality of life (QOL). The development strategy must identify the determinants of quality of life and the mutually supporting programs and activities that must be implemented to achieve the desired level of QOL (see Figure 2.4). For example, Prime Minister Abiy Ahmed of Ethiopia wants his country's economic standing to rise to a middle-income country status within the next ten years, with the ultimate goal of eliminating poverty and raising the standard of living of all Ethiopians. But what does that mean, and how does it happen?

Before answering the question, we must define "middle-income country" status. The world's middle-income countries (MICs) are diverse by landmass, population, and income level—the World Bank groups MICs into lower– and upper-middle-income countries.[5] Countries with per capita gross national income (GNI) between US$1,036 and $4,045 are classified as lower-middle-income countries. On the other

---

5   World Bank (2020). World Development Report 2020; and Umar Serjuddin and Nada Hamadeh (2020). New World Bank Country Classification by Income Level: 2020–2021. World Bank Blog, July 1, 2020.

hand, countries with per capita GNI between $4,046 and $12,535 are grouped as upper-middle-income nations. According to the World Bank, middle-income countries are home to 75% of the world's population and 62% of the world's poor. Simultaneously, MICs represent about one-third of the global gross domestic product (GDP) and are major engines of global growth.

Given this definition of MICs, where does Prime Minister Abiy want Ethiopia to be in 10 to 20 years? For Ethiopia, a per capita GNI jump from the current $800 to the median MIC per capita income of $2,000 in 10 years would represent a tremendous accomplishment.

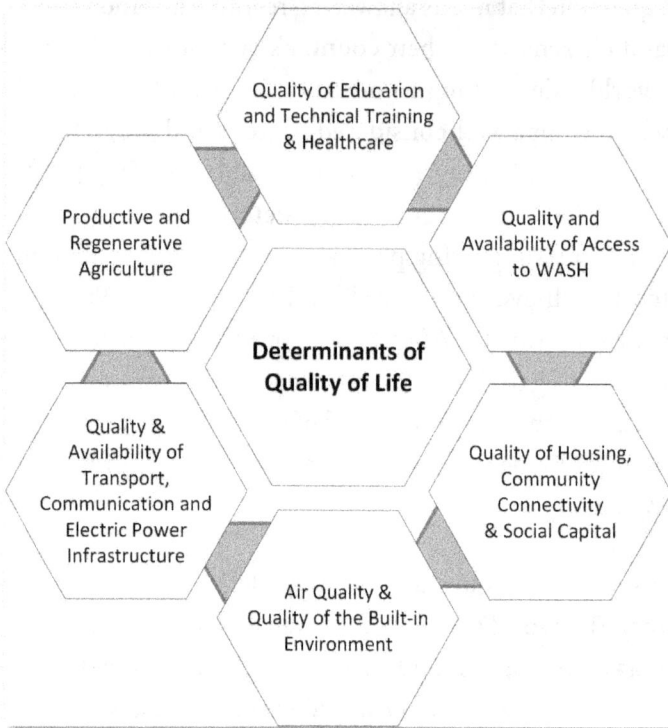

Figure 2.4: Determinants of the Quality of Life

GNI is the total income earned by a nation's people and businesses.[6] GNI equals GDP[7] plus income earned by citizens working abroad minus income earned by nonresidents.[8] In other words,

GNI = GDP + money flowing in from foreign countries – money flowing out to foreign countries

While GNI is a better measure of a nation's prosperity than GDP, it does not tell us if citizens' economic well-being and standard of living have improved. For example, a per capita GNI of $2,000 does not mean that each citizen earns that amount. It is a mathematical value obtained by dividing the total GNI by the population number. In many countries, 1% of the population controls a significant proportion of the country's wealth and income. For example, in the 1990s, when I was working in Nicaragua, thirteen families owned 90% of the country's wealth. In

Box 2.3: Definition of Social Capital

Social capital pertains to the norms and networks that enable collective action. It encompasses institutions, relationships, and customs that shape the quality and quantity of a society's social interactions. Social capital is critical for communities to prosper economically and sustain development. High levels of social capital reflect the abilities of community members to work together to address their everyday needs, fostering greater inclusion and cohesion, and increasing transparency and accountability.

---

6   GNI is considered a better measure of a nation's wealth than GDP. M. P. Todaro and S. C. Smith (2011). *Economic Development* 11. Addison-Wesley, Pearson, 10, 0–13.

7   GDP is the total market value of the goods and services produced by a country's economy during a specified period. It includes all final goods and services that are produced by the economy. The final users of goods and services are divided into three main groups: households, businesses, and the government. One-way GDP is calculated—known as the expenditure approach— by adding the expenditures made by those three groups of users. Accordingly, GDP = Consumption + Investment + Government Spending + Net Exports.

8   Michael P. Todaro and Stephen C. Smith (2011). *Economic Development* 11. Addison-Wesley, Pearson, 10, 0–13.

the United States, 1% of the population controls close to 95% of the country's wealth.

Thus, GNI does not provide information on citizens' well-being or other components of a nation's wealth, such as air quality, housing, road and transportation conditions, the overall health of the people, life span, community life, gender equality, income opportunities, access to quality education and healthcare, community safety, security, good governance, or the health of communities' social capital. See Box 2.3 for a definition of social capital.

Considering GNI as an insufficient measure of citizens' quality of life, the Organization for Economic Cooperation and Development (OECD) created the Better Life Index (BLI). The BLI comprises eleven variables: housing, income, jobs, community, education, environment, civic engagement, health, life satisfaction, safety, and work-life balance.[9] Still, according to some economists, the BLI uses a limited subset of indicators compared to other measures, such as the Gross National Well-Being Index, Sustainable Society Index,[10] and Bhutan Gross National Happiness and Social Progress Index. Many social scientists argue that, while a better measure than GNI per capita, the eleven dimensions of BLI do not fully capture what is tremendously vital to citizens. For example, the BLI does not include social networks and social capital that sustain human relationships and enable collaborative problem-solving and freedom of movement and speech. Others have pointed out that the BLI does not include such factors as poverty, purchasing power, economic

---

9   OECD (2020). *How's Life? 2020: Measuring Well-Being*, OECD Publishing: Paris.

10   International Institute of Management (IIM). Gross National Happiness and Well-Being (GNH/GNW), A Policy White Paper, Working Paper V1.0, June 4, 2005, Updated June 2018. The Gross National Well-Being Index has 21 indicators including: sufficient food, safe sanitation, education, healthy life, gender equality, income distribution, population growth, good governance, biodiversity, renewable water resources, consumption, energy use, energy savings, greenhouse gases, renewable energy use, organic farming, genuine savings, GDP, employment, and public debt.

inequality, access to health insurance, and environmental pollution, all of which affect citizens' well-being and living conditions.[11]

Taxation must improve people's well-being and quality of life. Improving the living conditions of citizens must be the government's primary objective. Concerning the United States, for example, in 1811, Thomas Jefferson, the third president of the United States (1801–1809), in his letter to Thaddeus Kosciusko, wrote, "The happiness and prosperity of our citizens... is the only legitimate objective of the government and the first duty of governors."[12]

In 2016, the prime minister of the United Arab Emirates (UAE), Sheikh Mohammed bin Rashid Al Maktoum declared that making citizens happy is the business of the government. He indicated that he "wants his people to be happy now"; consequently, he doubled civil servants' salaries and opened the Ministry of Happiness for business.[13]

The Kingdom of Bhutan decided that government business is creating the enabling conditions for citizens' happiness. The Kingdom of Bhutan's 2015 Gross National Happiness report stated, "We all know that our country belongs to a stream of civilization where the explicit purpose of the government is to create enabling conditions for our citizens to pursue happiness."[14] The report also indicated that the Bhutan Constitution stipulates, "The State shall strive to promote those conditions that will enable the pursuit of Gross National Happiness." The United Nations Human Development Index (HDI) emphasizes "enhancing citizens' well-being" as the government's primary business.[15]

---

11 Stephen Krason (September 2, 2014). "A 'Better Life Index' that Ignores What Makes for a Better Life". *Crisis*. Retrieved February 10, 2018.

12 As recorded in writings of Thomas Jefferson (1903–1904) Memorial Edition (ME) 13:41.

13 UAE Vision 2021.

14 Centre for Bhutan Studies & GNH Research, A Compass Towards a Just and Harmonious Society, 2015 GNH Survey Report, published in 2016.

15 United Nations Development Programme, Human Development Report, 2016.

In America, "life, liberty, and the pursuit of happiness" is enshrined in the Declaration of Independence, drafted and adopted in 1776.[16] The framers of the Declaration of Independence also ensured that the government's primary duties are to preserve and protect citizens' unalienable rights to life, liberty, and the pursuit of happiness. Moreover, installing checks and balances ensured that federal and state government institutions did not impinge on these citizens' rights.

The 2017 World Happiness Report, published by the United Nations Sustainable Development Solution Network (SDSN),[17] puts citizens' happiness at the center of government business. The OECD also recommended that "citizens' well-being should be at the center of government efforts."[18] There is thus a broad consensus that the business of government is *"creating, strengthening, and sustaining the enabling conditions that enhance and increase the quality of life, the standard of living, and happiness of citizens."* Annex 2.1 provides a detailed description of QOL, SOL, and Happiness matters.

For low-income countries, i.e., those with per capita GNI less than $1,035 in the 2021 ranking, ascending to a prosperous middle-income country would be an enormous struggle. In these countries, most people's living standards are low. Economic growth and infrastructure development are sluggish. Development of the electric power generation and connectivity to the electric grid, access to telecommunication and the internet, and road and transportation networks are in poor condition. However, the rest of the world is moving into the digital economy. Developing countries must leapfrog, adapting the latest philosophy, thinking, and technology to catch up. They would need robust mindset changes and

---

16 The United States of America, The Declaration of Independence, 1776, Amendment 14 of the Constitution of the United States, Citizens Rights ratified July 9, 1868.

17 Sustainable Development Solutions Network, World Happiness Report 2017, United Nations.

18 OECD (2016). Strategic Orientation of the Secretary-General: For 2016 and beyond, Meeting of the OECD Council of Ministerial Level Paris, June 1–2, 2016.

achieve peace, security, justice, and social action campaigns to build their economy and livelihoods as a cohesive society.

As noted above, catapulting Ethiopia to a middle-income country by 2030, i.e., raising per capita GNI from $800 to $2,000 or $3,000—at a minimum—would be challenging. The prime minister's strategic vision would need to consider several factors, including

- Ethiopia's current economic global standing,
- the rapid rate of population growth in both urban and rural communities,
- the demographic of the population,
- the rapid decline in the purchasing power of citizens,
- the effects of climate change,
- the frequency of natural and human-caused hazards and emergencies,
- the ethnic unrest and political instability, and insecurity,
- citizens' mindsets, and
- impacts of worldwide technological advances in the private sector and governmental functions.

Indeed, Ethiopia is far behind the rest of the world in adopting information and communication technology (ICT) in government, businesses, and educational institutions. For example, in 2019, Ethiopia ranked 137 out of 141 countries regarding ICT utilization in the government and the private sector. Despite recent advances in ICT infrastructure provision, the scope for further expanding access to a stable and high-speed internet remains enormous.[19]

According to the 2019 World Population Review, Ethiopia had an estimated population of 112 million, with a median age of 17.9 years and over 60% of the population under 24.[20] The majority of this co-

---

19 World Bank (2020). World Development Report 2020: Trading for Development in the Age of Global Value Chains.

20 United Nations (2020). World Population Prospects 2019. Department of Economics and Social Affairs: Population Dynamics.

hort is low-skilled and under-educated. According to the 2019 Global Competitiveness Index, Ethiopia ranked 137 out of 141 countries in education and human capital.[21] Ethiopia ranks 173 out of 189 countries in the 2019 HDI. According to the 2020 Legatum Prosperity Index, Ethiopia ranked 150 out of 167 countries.[22]

Over the past decade, wrong-headed policies and high-level corruption across all institutions ravaged and impoverished the nation, undermined the country's economic development potential, and decelerated the improvement of the quality of life for most citizens. The Tigray Peoples Liberation Front, in power between 1991 and 2017, engineered and implemented policies that kept non-Tigrayan citizens less educated and less productive. While the Tigrayan political elites amassed great wealth, the rest of the citizenry became poorer and polarized, entangled in ethnic politics. Furthermore, the nation's social capital was kept in tatters. The five-to-one security cell arrangement implemented by the Tigrayan-led national government destroyed trust among neighbors and friends. It encouraged spying among neighbors, friends, and colleagues, stifling freedom of speech and open expressions of views and opinions. It created divisive historical events that never occurred to sow hate among the ethnic groups. For example, it erected a statue in Arrusi depicting the cutting of women's breasts by Emperor Menelik's soldiers in the eighteenth century. An act that never happened. There was no conflict or war in that region of Ethiopia during Menelik's reign. This was done purposely to incite hate and conflict between the Oromo and Amhara ethnic groups.

According to the UN HDI, Ethiopia also ranked near the bottom regarding educational attainment. While educational attainment has been improving, overall academic competencies remained low, and there are substantial gender and rural-urban disparities. Nearly 32% of men and 51% of women ages ten and older were illiterate in 2013; only 1.8% had

---

21 Klaus Schwab (2019). The Global Competitiveness Report. The World Economic Forum 2019.

22 Legatum Institute (2020). The Legatum Prosperity Index: A Tool for Transformation. www.prosperity.com.

completed secondary education. Education spending remained high, yet learning outcomes remained low.[23] The situation continued to worsen.

The availability of healthcare in Ethiopia is also deficient, with only 52% of the population having access to medical services of any kind. Infant mortality is 58 per 1,000 live births.[24] One in every eight children does not survive until their fifth birthday. The leading public health problems include HIV/AIDS, malaria, respiratory infections, perinatal conditions, alcohol and drug addictions, and dysfunctional families. In both urban and rural areas, curable diseases remain significant killers. Tetanus, diphtheria, measles, and diarrhea often cause death, particularly among children. Polio, whooping cough, malaria, and other endemic diseases are features of everyday life. Providing a comprehensive health service accessible to all rural and urban communities is beyond the Ethiopian government's scope. The high infant mortality rate also indicates the mediocre quality of public health services.

Widespread poverty and low-income levels, low education levels (especially among women), inadequate access to clean water and sanitation facilities, poor access to health services, and traditional practices have contributed to the high ill-health burden. The average life expectancy at birth is relatively low at 60 years and is declining with rising HIV/AIDS infections. One in four persons is an HIV/AIDS carrier in urban areas. Furthermore, 60% to 80% of non-HIV infectious diseases are attributed to limited access to safe water and inadequate sanitation and hygiene.

Also, an estimated 50% of the consequences of malnutrition are caused by environmental factors that include limited access to potable water and poor hygiene and sanitation. According to healthcare specialists, there are strong links between sanitation and stunting. Open defecation has

---

23 United Nations Development Program, Ethiopia National Human Development Report 2018: Industrialization with a Human Face, UNDP Country Office, Addis Ababa, Ethiopia.

24 World Health Organization (2018). World Health Statistics 2018: Monitoring Health for the SDGs, Sustainable Development Goals.

led to fecal-oral diseases such as diarrhea, which can cause and worsen malnutrition. Only 65% of households have access to improved water sources, and only 6.3% can access improved sanitation.[25]

According to the World Bank, in 2018, only 45% of the population had access to electricity, and Ethiopia is dependent on hydropower.[26] Consequently, there are frequent electric power outages when the rainfall is low. Since the changes and upgrading of equipment in the mid-2000s, the telecommunication network is frequently out or overloaded; callers using landlines and mobile networks cannot connect. The situation is made worse by inclement weather. The Ethiopian Telecommunication Corporation (ETC) has not publicly addressed its failures nor admitted that the coverage and quality of services are below what they should be.

Indeed, the 2020 World Economic Forum Global Competitiveness Report ranked Ethiopia's overall telecommunication infrastructure as 136 out of 153 countries.[27] Mobile telephone subscriptions and fixed telephone lines per one hundred people are particularly low, rated at 141 out of 141 countries. Internet access is ranked 136 out of 141 countries. Ethiopia's telecommunication sector has the lowest internet and mobile telephone penetration rates globally. Mobile phone penetration is about 25% in Ethiopia, whereas the sub-Saharan Africa average is 70%. Access to the internet is also low at 2.5% compared to 40% in Kenya. The capacity to provide services is deficient because the government monopolizes the sector, constraining competition. However, the telecommunication sector's liberalization is essential for Ethiopia's accession to the World Trade Organization (WTO).

The 2020 World Happiness Report ranks Ethiopia 136 out of 153 countries with a score of 4.186.[28] The low ranking indicates that most

---

25   UNICEF (2020). Water, Sanitation and Hygiene (WASH) Ethiopia.
26   World Bank (2018). World Development Index.
27   World Economic Forum, Global Competitiveness Report 2020.
28   World Happiness Report 2020. New York: Sustainable Development Solutions Network.

Ethiopians are unhappy with their living conditions. People's living standards remain stagnant or are declining with the rising cost of living and the ethnic and religious tensions planted and nurtured by the Tigray People Liberation Front-led government.

Thus, achieving and sustaining prosperity for all Ethiopians is a tall order. It would require the government and its citizens to invest heavily in peacebuilding and ethnic harmony,[29] education, healthcare, and agriculture, on which 80% of the population depends for their livelihoods. It also requires transforming the physical and economic infrastructure to generate quality employment opportunities, increase productivity, put Ethiopia into a competitive position with the rest of the world, and shift the country from a raw material supplier to a producer and trader of finished quality specialized goods and services. Agricultural productivity must be increased to ensure food and nutrition self-sufficiency. We must also expand and improve irrigated and regenerative agriculture.

Most of all, Ethiopians need a complete mindset change and to begin deploying their creativity for developing Ethiopian-accented products and services. Ethiopians have a lot to offer to the outside world regarding agricultural products, unique pharmaceutical products, clothing, and household utensils and products. Ethiopians must find their comparative advantage to compete with the rest of the world. Ethiopia must quickly draft her Vision 2040 and work on achieving the objectives set in there. Countries that have changed their mindset and looked inward to build prosperity have been more successful than countries trying to westernize their economies.[30]

In addition, Ethiopians must transform their mindset and perspective in several areas. They must believe in **ethnic unity and oneness in purpose**

---

29 Achieving ethnic harmony should not be difficult as 80% of the population has for centuries intermarried and is of mixed ethnicity. The issue is more on achieving balanced economic development across regions and communities.

30 Eric Kacou (2010). *Entrepreneurial Solutions for Prosperity in BoP Markets: Strategies for Business and Economic Transformation.* The Wharton School of Business: Philadelphia.

and collective actions to quickly solve the social and economic problems facing them and to rapidly improve their quality of life and standard of living. They must abandon the TPLF-planted ethnic division, a poison that eats away at communities' social capital and forever keeps all Ethiopians in poverty, despair, and ignorance. They must begin to believe that they can prosper and improve their living standards and quality of life through **honest hard work**. They must cast away the belief that they can amass wealth through corruption, shady business practices, and cheating, which over the past 30 years, the TPLF had cultivated into a culture.

Ethiopians must **believe that a lifestyle change is good**. There are many good and some bad conventional cultures practiced around the country. Those good traditional ways must be enhanced and modernized. At the same time, they must abandon the wrong traditional ways of life born out of despair. For example, sorcery and witchcraft widely practiced in urban and rural communities must be debunked, ridiculed, and left behind. It is a form of emotional and material exploitation of despairing people without any good outcome.

Most Ethiopians are stubborn and take offense at people who do not accept or agree with their opinions or points of view. They must develop an **open mindset to listen to other people's ideas and beliefs, even if they differ from theirs**. They must learn to reconcile and incorporate others' thoughts and suggestions in decision-making or opinion-forming processes. There is no shame in admitting ignorance or changing one's position based on the informed opinion of others. For this, we must believe that the observations and opinions of others are as valid as ours, and we must learn to negotiate in good faith and reach consensual decisions and actions. At the same time, we must learn to **question and research issues** before taking a position or forming an opinion. We must research for tangible and factual evidence rather than jumping to conclusions and taking action based on someone's fake or malicious stories. Citizens must become inquisitive and examine what they hear and read for truth and facts. They must learn to be open to debate and learn from others' experiences.

Many Ethiopians have lost self-confidence and respect for themselves and others because of the disorderly governance practiced by the TPLF-led government over the past three decades. Ethiopians must begin respecting themselves and others **and believe in goodness, sharing, and kindness**. Over the past three decades, most Ethiopians were directly and indirectly taught to avoid, suspect or look down on people from a different ethnic group or political party. Trust in our neighbors and friends to do good must be restored regardless of political views or ethnicity.

Over the past 2,000 years, Christianity has played a significant role in community life. At the same time, it has held back Ethiopia's economic, technological, and political development and progress. In the 1930s and 1940s, the Coptic Church vehemently resisted the government's attempt to introduce modern education. The Ethiopian Coptic Orthodox Church must transform and modernize and reform its teachings. The old Egypto-Ethiopian Orthodox Christianity ingrained in people's minds the tradition of begging and not doing productive work on Saint days. There are more than 300 Saint days in a calendar year. Eking a life through begging on the street corner has become a profession for many.

The church must discourage its followers from begging and teach them to believe in earning their living through honest hard work. Begging on street corners or near churches should be banned and made a sin. Also, people who want to help the poor must be told not to give to street beggars. Instead, they should be encouraged to donate to charities organized to help the needy. The Orthodox Christian Church must preach and transform the mindsets of its followers, saying *God loves and rewards hard work*, not beggary. It should also encourage its followers to work on farm and off-farm regardless of Saint days, except for Sunday, which is a day of rest, and thanksgiving.

Over the past 50 years, morality and respect for other members of society have been dimensioned by communism and other factors. Schools must start to teach **ethics** to students. They must also teach students that **honesty, hard work, academic excellence, and creativity** are the only means to eradicate poverty and seed and grow prosperity. To motivate other students, communities must recognize and celebrate the top achievers in their respective communities and award them prizes for their academic performance and inventions.

Citizens must stop being dependent on food aid from abroad. Since international NGOs came to Ethiopia to deliver emergency assistance, they have stayed longer than needed, creating aid dependency in many communities. Our surveys show that farmers produce enough food to last 4 to 6 months because of their dependence on foreign aid. Ethiopians, as much as possible, must be **self-reliant**. They must revert to collective social action to produce sufficient food and feed themselves and the needy in their communities. Moreover, collaborating with the government and the private sector, they must prepare their communities to withstand natural and human-caused disasters by stockpiling essential goods for emergency responses.

Communities and citizens must stop depending on the government to solve every small problem in their communities. They should use their problem-solving and creative mindset to solve their communities' issues collectively. They should forge community–business-government partnerships to solve the most pressing needs in their communities. For example, they could organize and establish neighborhood watches to fight crime in their community. They should also take collective action and build culverts to divert stormwater from destroying homes in their communities and build access roads, community clinics and schools, and so on. They can make their community look beautiful and environmentally healthy. They can plant trees, flowers, and vegetables and keep their villages green while producing edible plants.

Furthermore, to address the deficiencies and constraints mentioned above, since 2019, all government institutions have adopted the homegrown 10-year prosperity plan. All government institutions have been synchronizing their vision, mission, and objectives to enhance people's standard of living and bring them in line with middle-income countries.

In this process, each sector would need overhauling and transformation. Each sector would require a new and revolutionary strategy to achieve the goals set by the 10-year homegrown prosperity plan. Each budget holder must identify what needs to be done to transform its business processes and improve citizens' outcomes. It must identify its key stakeholders and strategically collaborate to achieve targeted outputs and results efficiently and effectively.

More may need to be done in addition to what has been specified in the prime minister's prosperity plan to catapult Ethiopia to middle-income country status. The subsequent section will discuss what needs to be done in selected service and economic sectors. As noted in Figure 2.4 above, determinants of Quality of Life, among others, include the following:

- Quality of Education and Technical Training & Healthcare
- Quality, Availability, and Access to WASH
- Quality of Housing, Community Connectivity & Social Capital
- Air Quality, Green Areas in Cities, Towns, and Villages & Quality of the Built-In Environment
- Quality & Availability of Transportation, Communication, and Electric Power Infrastructure
- Productive and Regenerative Agriculture

A. Transforming the Education Delivery System

One government objective is to produce a competent and productive workforce to support the country's economic and social development to achieve a middle-income-country status by 2030. To this end, what would the government need to do to transform the country's education and training systems? This question can be answered only by first reviewing and understanding the country's current education system's status and establishing baselines. It would also require an explicit and standardized definition of quality education. Box 2.4 describes quality education, and Figure 2.5 shows the determinants of quality education.

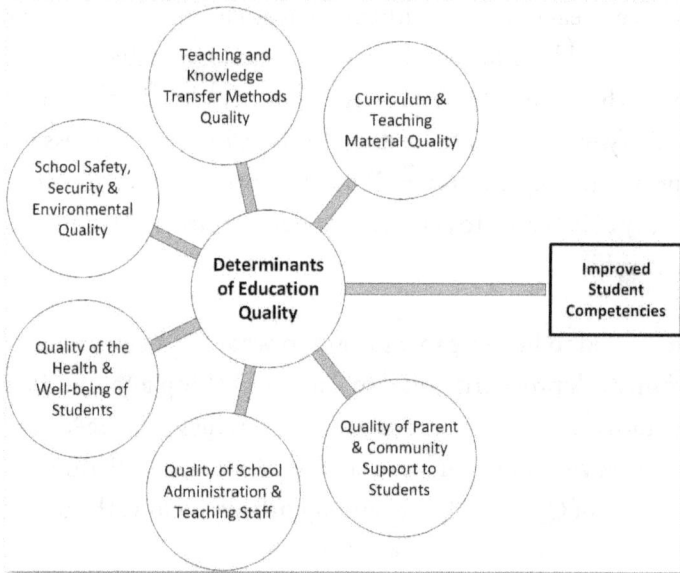

Figure 2.5: Determinants of Quality Education

The second step analyzes the challenges and opportunities of creating a quality education system and ensuring equitable access for boys and girls in urban and rural communities. And the third step is identifying the programs, activities, and resources required to transform and reorientate the academic, Technical, and Vocational Education and Training (TVET) systems to deliver quality education and produce highly competent graduates. As defined in Box 2.4 and shown in Figure 2.5, providing quality education would require

- reviewing, upgrading, and changing the current school curriculum to be better quality and future-oriented to support a technology-driven economy,
- training and fielding better-qualified teachers, upskilling the existing teaching workforce, and changing and improving the quality of the current teaching and learning approaches and methods to capture the interest and attention, intuition, and stimulating the creativity and innovativeness of students,
- updating and replacing the existing textbooks and teaching materials, bringing in new ones, and

- expanding school-based research and innovation (R&I) laboratories so that students and teachers can connect theory with practice and also experiment with their ideas, and upgrading the school environment and management. The school environment must instill confidence, responsibility, continuous discovery, learning, and problem-solving in students, teachers, and community members.

Box 2.4: Definition of Quality Education

According to the United Nations Sustainable Development Goals, quality education relates to an educational system designed to help all children reach their full potential and enter society as full and productive citizens. Quality education is not measured purely by a test score or by how many words per minute a 5-year-old can read. Quality education focuses on the *whole* child—the social, emotional, mental, physical, and cognitive development of each student regardless of gender, race, ethnicity, socioeconomic status, or geographic location. It prepares the child for life, not just for national exams.

A quality education provides resources and directs policy to ensure that each child enters school healthy and learns about and practices a healthy lifestyle; learns in an environment that is physically and emotionally safe for both students and adults; is actively engaged in learning and is connected to the school and broader community; has access to personalized learning and is supported by qualified, caring adults; and is challenged academically and prepared for success in college or further study and employment and participation in a global environment. A quality education system allows schools to align and integrate fully with their communities and access a range of services across sectors to support their students' educational development. At minimum, a quality education system ensures access to quality teachers, quality learning tools and professional development, and safe and supportive quality learning environments.

See also, UNICEF (2000). *Defining Quality in Education*, a paper presented by UNICEF at the meeting of the International Working Group on Education, Florence, Italy, June 2000.

As noted in Chapter 1, the Federal Democratic Republic of Ethiopia (FDRE) is organized into ethnic-based regional states and two administrative cities. Consequently, the Tigrayan-led government introduced ethnic language-based teaching and learning without developing the appropriate teaching material and textbooks. This has limited the competencies and mobility of school system graduates in most parts of the country, particularly in the Oromia and SNNP regional states. For example, students use their local language up to grade eight, and when they enter high school, they learn science and math in English. The low English language proficiency has prevented many students from achieving their learning goals; many drop out of school after their first year of high school. Education in the ethnic mother tongue has created a language barrier as well. Also, as mandated by the FDRE Constitution, the working language for the federal government is Amharic. In effect, the Amharic language proficiency requirement has locked out most school graduates from federal government employment. Most Tigrayans are proficient in Amharic and hold most federal government jobs.

To attract Foreign Direct Investment, support domestic industrial growth, and quickly move the country to middle-income-country status, Ethiopia needs capable and motivated graduates with the proper employability skills. Employability skills are as critical as academic competencies. Annex 2.2 identifies and defines the various elements of employability skills. Currently, most graduates entering the labor market lack primary employability skills.

The challenges of transforming the quality of the Ethiopian education system are enormous. There are significant increases in school-age children yearly, yet most rural and urban schools are overcrowded. New schools and classrooms would need to be built and furnished to house the new students. Moreover, the existing schools are aging, with roofs leaking and walls crumbling. They also do not have sufficient potable water. Most schools do not have adequate science laboratories. They have to be fitted with well-stocked science laboratories at each grade level. The quality of the teaching staff is also low, their teaching methods archaic, and their subject matter knowledge shallow. School management and administration are unqualified to manage quality education systems. Interaction between the school system and the surrounding community is weak to nonexistent.[31] There needs to be a collaborative relationship between the schools and the community.

Furthermore, there is a severe shortage of trained teachers and school administrators. The school day is short as there are up to three shifts. An extended school day is necessary to engage and instruct young students properly. It would also require parental support and supervision. However, most parents are illiterate and cannot review and help correct their student's homework or answer questions on a specific topic.

Moreover, a twenty-first-century school environment would need strong telecommunication, information technology, water and sanitation, and electric power infrastructure. It also requires a robust and up-to-date public health service and a clean water supply. Healthy students are productive and competent.

Also, hunger and malnutrition are significant constraints to quality learning. They need addressing. Schools in America, Europe, and many other countries have student feeding programs to supplement what students eat at home. As events in America, Nigeria, and other countries have shown, school safety and security are essential elements of a quality school environment. Strong community policing and protection are integral elements of quality schools. Hooligans should not harass female students as they travel back and forth from school to their homes or live away from their parents in colleges around the country. They need protection, and the community can provide it. Schools must be safe from terrorist attacks as well.

Though families play a crucial role in meeting children's needs, communities are responsible for supporting children's healthy development.

---

31 Samuel Taddesse, Abebe Berhanu, Gebeyehu Woldaregay, and Joyce Wolf (2007). Basic Education Strategic Objective (BESO) II-Basic Education Program, Final Evaluation, January 2007.

Parent and community members' involvement is critical to developing and cultivating a peaceful, safe, and problem-solving–oriented learning environment for boys and girls. The school must have separate boys' and girls' bathrooms and playgrounds. In addition, it should have a girls' clubhouse, headed by a female teacher, to educate and assist young girls that come of age or menarche.

As practiced across Ethiopia, the ethnic quota-based promotion and hiring system must be replaced entirely by ethnic-blind merit and performance-based systems. Employment opportunities and services must be accessible and offer competitive living wages. A multilingual learning environment would expand employment opportunities for school graduates. Internship programs with area businesses would further impart basic workplace skills. School-based activities focused on unity and one Ethiopia would, over time, cleanse the toxic ethnic tension left behind by the TPLF-led ruling party of the past three decades.

Heavy investment is required to switch over to a twenty-first-century education delivery system. We must invest in new schools, additional classrooms, and R&I laboratories. We must upgrade and replace the current textbooks and teaching materials and enhance the school environment with playgrounds and other amenities. Simultaneously, we must establish a robust school-based public health system and link schools and communities to telecommunications, the internet, electric power, road infrastructure, and a potable water supply.

Teacher training institutions must be upgraded and funded to produce high-quality schoolteachers and administrators. Elementary and secondary schools should be staffed with high-quality and experienced teachers to build our students' critical academic and educational foundation.[32] *The aim is to build a capable workforce to accelerate industrialization and domestic economic growth and create entrepreneurs and initiative-takers.*

---

32 Currently, most primary schools are staffed with tenth-grade graduates. A tenth-grade graduate has very little knowledge or wisdom to part to students.

Partnering with the business community would be essential to identify the skills needed in the future. The education curriculum must be drafted with civil society, business leaders, community leaders, and development partners. The adequacy of tertiary education to meet employment needs is currently low, with a score of 37 out of 100, and would need drastic improvement. The goal is to enable graduates from the Ethiopian education system to compete for and win good-paying jobs in any part of the world or have the capability to create and build income-generating enterprises.

B. Transforming the Healthcare System

Ethiopia must address its high health burden as quickly as possible. Currently, access to a quality public healthcare system is unavailable for most citizens. Many people living in peri-urban, urban, and rural communities depend on traditional healthcare systems, including witch doctors, midwives, herbalists, traditional bonesetters (or ወጅ), and holy water. Some treatments are harmful and ineffective against killer diseases like HIV/AIDS, coronavirus, tuberculosis (TB), malaria, respiratory infection, diarrhea, childhood diseases, and other diseases and disorders. There is also an increase in noninfectious diseases such as cancer, diabetes, heart diseases, hepatitis B&C, and high blood pressure. Mental health and eye problems are also becoming prevalent.

Over the past three decades, the government has significantly invested in the public health sector to improve health outcomes. As shown in Figure 2.6, Ethiopia has a three-tier health system. The secondary and tertiary levels comprise general and specialized hospitals. The number of people served increased by tier level. The Woreda (district) health offices and the regional state health bureaus are responsible for managing, coordinating, and distributing technical support at each level of government. However, policymaking is in the hands of the Federal Ministry of Health (MOH). In 2019, for a population of 107 million people, there were[33]

---

33 United States Department of Commerce: Privacy Shield Framework—Ethiopia Country Commercial Guide—Ethiopia-Healthcare.

- 17,154 health posts available and 438 under construction,
- 4,063 health centers available and 68 under construction,
- 338 hospitals available and 218 under construction, and
- 3,867 private clinics and 43 private hospitals.

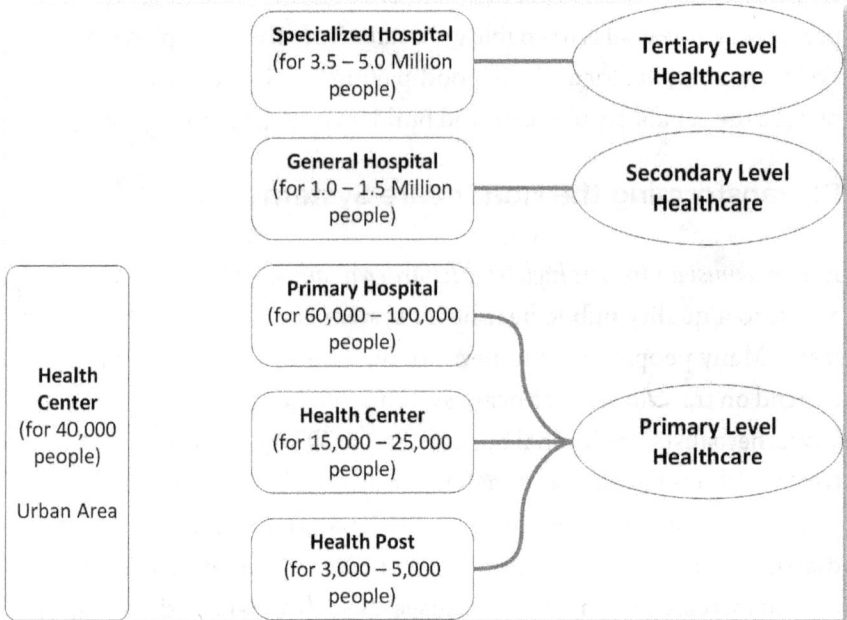

Figure 2.6: Ethiopia's Healthcare System

Primary care is established at the Woreda level. It includes a primary care hospital, local health centers, and rural health posts. There are also private clinics and hospitals in urban areas that augment public health facilities. However, these private-sector healthcare services are out of the reach of ordinary citizens because of cost. They are relatively expensive compared to government healthcare services.

Since 2004, health extension workers (HEW) employed by Woreda health offices have facilitated patient referrals to health centers or the primary hospital for more severe health issues. Community extension workers (CEWs) also monitor health and disease epidemics locally. They educate citizens about sanitation and avoiding the spread of contagious diseases. They instruct families about childcare, nutrition, and family planning and provide essential primary care services like contraceptive use, immunizations, and treatment for common childhood illnesses.[34]

Each health center coordinates five health posts, with two health extension workers and one health post per community. The health extension program uses task-shifting and "community ownership" to provide essential healthcare services at the grassroots level.[35] Since 2003, 40,000 and 50,000 HEWs have been recruited, trained, and deployed with development partners' assistance, including the United Nations, the United States Agency for International Development (USAID), Irish Aid, and the European Union. Since the program's implementation, maternal and child health has improved. However, coverage and the performance of the HEWs vary by region.

Despite government efforts to increase healthcare coverage, recurring drought, conflict, disease outbreaks, internal displacement and migrations, and systemic corruption have hampered progress toward providing accessible and quality health services to all citizens. Furthermore, high fertility rates and low contraceptive use continue to drive rapid population growth and the spread of sexually transmitted diseases, straining the healthcare system.

Moreover, in many areas of the country, patients must travel several miles to reach the nearest health center. Because of distance and cost, health services are not accessible or affordable for many citizens, particularly the most vulnerable, including mothers and children.

---

34 Yibeltal Assefa, Yalemzewod Assefa Gelaw, Peter S. Hill, Belaynew Wassie Taye, and Wim Van Damme (2019). Community Health Extension Program in Ethiopia, 2003–2018: Success and Challenges Toward Universal Coverage for Healthcare Services. Globalization and Health, https://doi,org/10.1186/s12992-019-0470-1.

35 Netsanet W. Workie and Gandham NV Ramana (2013). The Health Extension Program in Ethiopia: UNICO Studies Series 10. The World Bank, Washington DC, January 2013.

In some parts of the country, women do not seek government healthcare services because of the fear of being given the wrong medicines and treatments. There have been allegations that many women in the Amhara regional state were sterilized without their knowledge. This was because the TPLF-led government wanted to control the growth of the Amhara population. Other reasons for not seeking medical care include healthcare costs and difficulty reaching a healthcare facility—nearly 80% of Ethiopian women live in rural communities.

For most rural women, finding transportation and the distance to a health center are barriers to accessing healthcare services. Many are concerned about arriving at a health center to find no health worker or the drugs they need. Finally, the road infrastructure in the remotest villages either doesn't exist or is in poor condition. Women are often frightened to go alone due to the high rates of rape and abductions. Drug use, sex trafficking, and prostitution are some of the nefarious weapons used by the TPLF to weaken the morale and dignity of Ethiopians while amassing wealth.

Also, with the growing number of noncommunicable diseases, the Ethiopian healthcare system is faced with tremendous challenges. Most noncommunicable illnesses can be prevented at a low cost. Still, the treatment is significantly more expensive than infectious diseases.[36] This puts pressure on the resources of the healthcare system. Other challenges faced by the healthcare system include

- lack of transparent and accountable pharmaceutical and logistics management systems,
- shortage of foreign currency hindering timely procurement of medical equipment, supplies, and pharmaceuticals from abroad,
- delays in the procurement bidding processes,
- poor data management and reporting for proper evidence-based decision-making and early warning systems,

---

36 Anton Fubstetter (2016). Health Systems in Ethiopia: Challenges and Opportunities, Policy Brief. The World Bank Group, June 2016.

- shortage of human resources, lack of capacity, and disinterest in working in rural communities, and
- systemic corruption within and outside government.

We must invest in various areas to enhance the quality, availability, and access to the healthcare system. We must build the skills and capabilities of healthcare professionals and extension workers to deliver quality healthcare to all citizens with integrity, regardless of ethnicity, religion, or creed. Many healthcare managers, doctors, and nurses need extensive on-the-job training. We must also ensure they are resourced with adequate medical equipment and supplies.[37]

The existing national and subnational medical schools and training institutions need a complete overhaul to produce more competent healthcare workers. The curriculum needs upgrading and refocusing to include diagnosing and treating infectious and noncommunicable diseases like heart attacks, kidney failures, and diabetes. Facilities must be refurbished, expanded, and appropriately equipped and staffed with qualified medical doctors, public health officers, nurses, and health extension workers.

Hospitals, health clinics, and health centers need robust digital health information systems to

- improve health data accuracy to support effective and efficient decision-making regarding the deployment of health personnel and the production or procurement of appropriate and effective pharmaceuticals and health products for patients, tracking health outcomes of patients, and
- provide data for early warning and medical emergency preparedness.

---

37 The 2021 theft of medical equipment and pharmaceuticals and the destruction of health facilities by the TPLF terrorists are expected to add more pressure on the Amhara and Afar health systems over the next three years.

Under the second Growth and Transformation Plan (GTP II), the MOH implemented various changes to the healthcare system. The MOH improved health services to reduce health-related burdens.[38] For example, cancer has become one of the fastest-growing healthcare challenges. The MOH has been working to establish cancer diagnosis centers in hospitals and expand radiation therapy programs and access to chemotherapy services to address this tremendous health burden. Cancer chemotherapy services are provided only in four health centers. MOH has decentralized the service into twelve hospitals in different regional states.

Other priority programs identified by MOH include

- implementing drone technology to deliver vaccines, blood, and other health-related commodities in hard-to-reach rural communities,
- improving the management of human and infrastructural resources,
- increasing and expanding the capabilities and competencies of healthcare workers, including doctors, public health officers, nurses, and health extension workers,
- improving research and evidence-based decision-making and enhancing the adaptation and use of technology and innovation,
- facilitating the procurement of drugs, medical supplies, and equipment and ensuring the timely availability of essential medicines at the health centers,
- increasing patient satisfaction, stemming corruption, and strengthening good governance,
- working on an early warning system, risk assessment, and multi-sectoral coordination mechanisms that can improve response time for epidemics and disease outbreaks,
- procurement of quality medical equipment with after-sales maintenance service, and
- developing a system for checking the efficacy and effectiveness of imported drugs and medicines before entering the country.

---

38   Ministry of Health Website www.moh.gov.et/.

As part of addressing the above priority areas, the MOH is reforming agencies such as the Ethiopian Food and Drug Administration (EFDA) and the Ethiopian Pharmaceutical Supply Agency (EPSA). EFDA Proclamation No. 661/2009 and the Food and Medicine Administration (FMA) Proclamation No.1112/2019 mandate EFDA and FMA, respectively, to ensure the efficacy and currentness of imported and domestically produced medicines. Other responsibilities of the EFDA and FMA include

- promoting and protecting public health by ensuring the safety, efficacy, and quality of health and health-related products and services through product quality assessment and registration,
- licensing and regular recertification of health professionals, health institutions, pharmaceutical, food processing plants, bakeries, and other food establishments, and
- provisioning up-to-date regulatory information while promoting proper health and health-related products and services, including appropriate and efficacious medicines.

Ensuring 100% availability of efficacious-essential drugs at all healthcare facilities without stock shortages and consistently using established procurement and delivery procedures would require reforming the EFDA. EFDA must be transformed into a corruption-free, more effective, and efficient organization. EFDA implements a "zero backlogs" strategy for medicine registration and licensing activities. The EFDA has digitized the importation and registration of health commodities using[39]

- *i-Register,* which is a digital platform used by importers to apply for market authorization and product registration, and
- *i-Import,* which is a digital online application platform for importers to apply for and receive permits to import all health commodities.

---

39 Ethiopia Food and Drug Authority website.

These digital platforms need updating to expand access and generate timely reports for decision-makers. Both i-Register and i-Import must be required universally without exemption.

The EPSA is the public procurement agency responsible for purchasing pharmaceuticals, medical supplies, and equipment. It is responsible for Ethiopia's supply chain management of public health commodities. The agency has nineteen branch warehouses serving more than 3,800 health facilities in nine regional and two administrative states.[40] The EPSA has developed digital applications to ensure EPSA distribution hubs to health facilities across Ethiopia and establish efficient inventory, fleet, and information management systems. These improvements ensure the availability of health commodities throughout the health system at all times. Digital platforms developed and implemented by the EPSA include the following:[41]

- *Vitas* is a platform designed to support logistics management information, warehouse management, and inventory control. Currently, Vitas is implemented at the central warehouse and eighteen regional hubs across Ethiopia.
- *Dagu* is a platform that supports logistics management information and inventory control at service delivery points using systematic record-keeping. This application provides service at more than 700 sites all over the country.
- *mBrana is* a platform integrated with Vitas and other PSA programs to manage inventory from beginning to end.

40 USAID Global Health Supply Chain Program (2020). Ethiopian Pharmaceuticals Supply Agency Network Analysis: Optimizing Commodity Delivery to Remote Health Facilities and the Communities They Serve. Technical Brief, May 2020.

41 Federal Democratic Republic of Ethiopia (2018). Pharmaceutical Supply Agency—Pharmaceutical Transformation Strategic Plan (PSTP) for 2018 to 2020, September 2018.

However, systemic corruption throughout the system has undermined the Ethiopian MOH's efforts to transform, modernize, and expand healthcare coverage over the past three decades. Most of the drugs entering the country are either expired or fake. Also, there are shortages throughout the country due to underground-economy trading and drug smuggling. Frequent internet and electric power outages also hampered the various healthcare system digital platforms. Timely and accurate reporting for decision-makers and the public are lacking. There are severe deficiencies in accountability.

Ethiopia aims to reduce its dependence on imported drugs, medical supplies, and equipment. To that end, Ethiopia must modernize and expand the existing pharmaceutical manufacturing plants. It must also invest in new medical supplies and equipment manufacturing plants, expand research and development efforts, and reduce imports significantly.

To share the cost burden, the government must begin working with the private sector through public-private partnerships (PPPs) and government and community partnerships (GCP). It must also establish other mechanisms to reduce its cost burden. Also, the government's Productive Safety Net Program (PSNP) must include health insurance for vulnerable people. All these transformative changes require significant investment, funding, and leadership.

C. Transforming the Water and Sanitation Systems

Undoubtedly, water is a precious commodity. Clean water is a critical ingredient in human life. Clean water and waterborne diseases and sanitation control are intertwined with human health. Water is also essential for food production, manufacturing, and industrial processes. Without water, humanity cannot survive.

In Ethiopia, we believe water cleanses our sins and embeds good spirits in our souls. The Coptic Christian Orthodox Church has holy water. They give people holy water to drink to heal themselves, wash away their sins, and sprinkle in their homes to get rid of evil spirits. Ethiopia has 13 months of sunshine. Twelve months have 30 days each and the 13th month has 5 or 6 days, depending on whether it is a leap year or not. On the thirteenth month of the year, which happens to fall between September 4 and 10 on the Gregorian calendar, the rain is considered blessed by God. As children, we used to run naked in the rain to make us good and blessed children. Some adults did the same.

Clean water is necessary for human and animal sustenance. The United Nations Sustainable Development Goals define "safely managed water" as water available on-premises when needed and free from contamination.[42] In Ethiopia, only 60% of urban dwellers and 5% of the rural population have access to the on-premises water supply. However, nearly 80% of the population lives in rural and peri-urban areas. Potable water is in short supply.

Also, Ethiopia depends on rainfed subsistence agriculture resulting in food shortages, particularly during low rainfall seasons. As Ethiopians shift to commercial agriculture, they need large amounts of water for irrigated agriculture.

Water is also essential for well-managed sanitation and hygiene systems. In Addis Ababa and other cities, as the number of people living in high-rise buildings has risen, water demand has increased astronomically. Water is needed for cooking, cleaning, washing, bathing, flushing, and cleaning toilets. But the reservoirs feeding the water supply are affected by climate change, and their levels are falling rapidly. Residents of Addis Ababa and other cities and towns are being rationed water, and water may not be available for several days. Consequently, toilets in office buildings, restaurants, and apartment buildings stink of human waste and are unhealthy.

---

42 United Nations (2015). 70/1 Transforming Our World: The 2030 Agenda for Sustainable Development, Resolution adopted by the General Assembly on September 25, 2015, Seventieth Session Agenda items 15 and 116.

Despite the high need for clean water, we have continued disrespecting our rivers and waterways. We dump garbage and sewage in our rivers and defecate in them. We continue to disrespect our rivers by dumping industrial and agricultural toxic waste in them.

The lakes around the country, including Tana and the Rift Valley lakes, are becoming shallow and choked with silt and weeds. Furthermore, many Rift Valley lakes have become toxic from industrial waste. Deforestation has also reduced the rainfall in many parts of the country. The rainforests have disappeared. The Bonga rain forest in southern Ethiopia is in imminent danger of disappearing with heavy illegal logging.

Incidentally, people living in rural areas, for example, in Gojjam and Begemedr in the Amhara regional state, don't know about underground water. They marvel when someone digs a borehole and obtains water. For many years people were kept ignorant about boreholes by the Coptic church to protect the water flowing into the Blue Nile that goes to Egypt. Until 1954, the Ethiopian Coptic Christian Orthodox Church's patriarchs were Egyptians from Alexandria, Egypt. They had a personal stake in protecting and preventing the use of the lakes, rivers, and streams feeding the Nile River. Over the centuries, many kings and emperors were deposed from power for trying to use the water from Lake Tana and the Nile River for irrigated agriculture.

Latrines with safely managed fecal waste are in short supply. The Federal MOH's 2011 Community-Led Total Sanitation and Hygiene (CLTSH) Programme rapidly increased rural access to low-technology latrines.[43] However, many rural communities still practice open defecation in the bushes near streams and rivers, contaminating water sources. The downstream population thus suffers from waterborne diseases. Residents also suffer from airborne contagious diseases as the wind blows the dried fecal waste in the air.

---

43 UNICEF (2017). Progress on CLTSH in Ethiopia: Findings from a National Review. WASH Field Notes, FN/01/2017.

In the 1950s and 1960s, many rural and urban communities suffered from diseases such as typhoid, cholera, malaria, yellow fever, leishmaniasis of the skin, bubonic, and diarrhea. Their bodies were infested with tapeworms, roundworms, and other parasites from eating raw meat and untreated or unboiled water. These parasites cause malnutrition in children.

In an article I published in the *Ethiopian Herald* in 1962, I indicate that many of these diseases were spread by house flies, mosquitos, sandflies, lice, bedbugs, fleas, and rats.[44] The primary problem was the lack of good sanitation practices and the widespread open defecation close to human habitats, which became the breeding ground for insects that spread many diseases. I suggested boiling, once a week, clothing and bedding material to kill lice, bedbugs, and fleas, bathing, washing, and cleaning oneself thoroughly with boiled water. We must use pit latrines and drain standing water near people's homes. Standing water is a breeding ground for insects, particularly mosquitos. Avoiding eating inadequately cooked meat will reduce tapeworm infection drastically. Unfortunately, feasting on raw meat is a tradition in many parts of the country.

According to the World Bank, in 2019, open defecation was practiced by 32% of the rural population and 7% of urban households.[45] Handwashing facilities are limited, particularly in rural areas, lacking adequate fecal sludge management. Developing and expanding city-wide holistic sanitation services and off-site sanitation infrastructure in rural areas will be necessary to reach the SDG 6 goal of "sustainable and safely managed sanitation." Planning for water supply and toilet construction, water security, and solid and liquid waste management is essential.

---

44 Samuel Taddesse (1962). "Fight Against Enemies of Health." *The Ethiopian Herald*, Sunday, August 11, 1962.

45 World Bank (2019). Water and Sanitation in Ethiopia—Building Blocks of Progress, April 30, 2019.

Over the past twenty years, ponds, wells, streams, and lakes have become shallow. Many people collect water from these shallow sources, often contaminated with human, animal, and industrial waste. During months and sometimes years of drought, diseases run rampant through small villages and towns. Frequently there is not enough water for people to bathe, leading to infections and sickness in children. Waterborne illnesses, such as cholera or diarrhea caused by fecal contamination, are the leading causes of death in children under five.

According to the 2017 UN-Water Annual Report, only 11% of the population used a safely managed drinking water service on their premises.[46] Another 30% used a "basic service" (less than 30 minutes round trip for water collection). Others relied on "limited service" (more than 30 minutes travel to fetch water) from "unimproved sources" (such as unprotected dug wells or springs) or surface water. In most communities that lack access to water on or near their premises, young girls and women bear the burden of fetching water.

Regarding sanitation, in 2017, only 7% of the population used a safely managed sanitation service, and 7% had "limited service" (latrines shared with other households). Another 63% had to rely on a simple pit or a bucket, with 22% defecating in the open.[47] [48]

Regional water bureaus and Woreda water desks are in charge of investment planning, monitoring, and technical assistance to water service providers. Their capacity to fulfill these tasks is low. According to a research report funded by the United Kingdom's Department for International Development (DFID), the community-managed service delivery approach in rural areas "has bypassed local government authorities and

---

46 UN-Water Annual Report 2017.

47 SDG 6 Monitoring. "Ethiopia." *UN Water.* Retrieved November 29, 2020.

48 Seleshi Bekele Awulachew, Aster Denekew Yilma, Makonnen Loulseged, Willibald Loiskandl, Mekonnen Ayana, and Tena Alamirew (2007). Water Resources and Irrigation Development in Ethiopia, Working Paper 123, International Water Management Institute.

reduced their ownership. However, these actors are needed if rural services are to be sustainable and scalable."[49]

The Addis Ababa Water and Sewer Authority provide water and sewer services. Town water boards are responsible for service provision in other cities and towns. They are expected to contract out service provisions to private operators. Community water and sanitation committees operate water systems and promote sanitation in rural areas through social action campaigns. However, not all the local committees are registered, which is a prerequisite to opening a bank account to collect funds from users.[50]

A lot can be done to conserve and increase the water supply. First, the reforestation program started by Prime Minister Abiy must be expanded and accelerated. To ensure the survival of the newly planted trees, communities must take ownership and nurture and protect these trees from drying and dying or being stamped or eaten by livestock.

Second, non-native plants must be removed from the banks of creeks and rivers. This will increase the creek and river water flow. In South Africa, eliminating such plants using community actions increased the river and stream water volume and flow within a few years.

Third, communities should harvest and store rainwater for home use and livestock during the rainy season. Some communities are already gathering and using rainwater, but water harvesting must be expanded. We found that many communities in southern Ethiopia practice rainwater

---

49 Getnet Alemu and David Thomas (May 2009). "Financing in the Water, Sanitation and Hygiene (WASH) Sector in Ethiopia: May 2009 Evidence From Benishangul-Gumuz Regional State." *Research-Inspired Policy and Practice Learning in Ethiopia and the Nile region (RiPPLE) / DFID*. pp. vi–vii. Retrieved August 21, 2011.

50 Seleshi Bekele Awulachew, Aster Denekew Yilma, Makonnen Loulseged, Willibald Loiskandl, Mekonnen Ayana, and Tena Alamirew (2007). Water Resources and Irrigation Development in Ethiopia, Working Paper 123, International Water Management Institute. See also, Water supply and sanitation in Ethiopia, Wikipedia.

harvesting. With the help of Non-Governmental Organizations (NGOs), some communities have built underground large-capacity cement water tanks.

A simple canal is constructed to redirect the water from the hill's side. Different-sized pebbles are placed in the canal to catch and remove the debris from the water. The filtered water enters the concrete water tank. Because the concrete tank is enclosed, the water does not evaporate and lasts for an extended time. After collecting water from the concrete water tank using a bucket tied to a rope, the outlet is closed. Other communities harvest rainwater from corrugated tin roofs in schools and other structures. The water accumulates in huge water tanks, and villagers collect water. The tank has conveniently placed faucets for villagers to use. These water storage tanks are owned and managed by the respective community. The community ensures that there are fences around these water tanks to keep the area around the storage tank clean of animal waste and other garbage. An assigned person opens the gate and allows people to collect water at a scheduled time.

As suggested by the National Academies of Sciences, stormwater and gray water can also be harvested and treated to add to the water supply in urban areas.[51] Cities and densely populated areas produce lots of gray water. Gray water is wastewater from bathroom sinks, showers, bathtubs, cloth washers, and laundry sinks. It does not include water from toilets or kitchens.[52] However, the gray water is treated by filtration and chlorination, with the goal of not detecting fecal coliform bacteria. Ethiopians need to adopt these rainwater and wastewater harvesting techniques to maximize water availability in urban communities for agriculture and toilet flushing.

---

51 National Academies of Sciences, Engineering, and Medicine (2016). *Using Graywater and Stormwater to Enhance Local Water Supplies: An Assessment of Risks, Costs, and Benefits.* Washington, DC: The National Academies Press. doi: 10.17226/21866.

52 Ibid.

Fourth, the government must excavate and remove the silt and weed from the bottom of existing lakes and water reservoirs. Most recently, volunteers from all parts of the country helped remove the weed and plant growth from the bottom of Lake Tana. The silt must also be excavated and removed to increase the lake's depth and water volume.

Fifth, many rivers and streams overflow during the rainy season. For example, in the town of Tefki, the Awash River overflows and floods the surrounding area every rainy season. Artificial lakes and dams could be constructed to capture the overflowing water. These lakes can be a water source for irrigated agriculture during the dry season.

Sixth, the government must take urgent action to control and prevent the dumping of waste and garbage in rivers and streams. It must manage the disposal of toxic agricultural and industrial waste. For example, Lake Zewai, one of the pristine lakes in the Rift Valley, is contaminated by toxic waste from the surrounding flowers, strawberries, vegetable farms and tanneries, and other manufacturing and processing plants. The fish and fowl are dying, and the people living around the lake are unhealthy. Incidentally, Lake Zewai has an island that was the resting place of the Ark of the Covenant during the Italian occupation from 1935 to 1940. Now the Ark sits in Axum. The government must ask citizens, residents, and businesses to respect the rivers, streams, and lakes.

Seventh, Ethiopia should adopt innovative toilets that conserve water and convert solid waste into fuel or compost. For example, under a Bill & Melinda Gates Foundation grant in the United States, RTI International developed a novel human waste treatment system.[53] The newly designed and developed toilet operates as a closed-loop, with technology to treat and reuse liquids and generate power via a chemical-free combustion process. The toilet works without piped-in water, a sewer connection, or outside electricity—and converts human waste into burnable fuel,

---

53 RTI International, Reinventing the Toilet, https://www.rti.org/impact/reinventing-toilet.

stored energy, disinfected, and nonpotable water. As it stands now, the system runs on the equivalent of two car batteries; a solar panel can also power it. The toilet contributes to water savings through low flush volume and using recycled and disinfected liquid for flush water. The toilet also incorporates women's sanitation needs into the design. These toilets could be installed on street corners for public use, in restaurants, and shared community spaces. They can replace unsafe and odoriferous pit latrines.

Eighth, sewage treatment plants must be modernized, and the improved technology spread to other cities and towns around the country. Dumping sewage into streams and rivers has had dire health consequences for downstream populations. Also, flooding vegetable farms with untreated sewage harms human health. A USAID-funded project implemented a sewage treatment plant in Lebanon that separated the water from the sludge. The water was treated, stored in a water tank, and piped to farmers. The sludge was treated and dried in the sun and used as fertilizer. Ethiopia needs to adopt such sewage treatment plants in cities and towns.

Ninth, in geographic areas where underground water has not been exploited, like in Gojjam and Begemedr, hand-dug wells should be introduced for community use.

Transforming the water and sanitation sector would require massive investment. Communities and responsible government agencies at the federal and local levels must collaborate to bring about meaningful change. Communities must contribute their time, labor, and resources. At the same time, the government must invest in transformational infrastructure. The water distribution networks in cities and towns need upgrading and fixing to conserve water and prevent water loss through broken water distribution pipes. Culverts and the water drainage spouts must be reconstructed, and the runoff water must be channeled to water storage tanks.

D. Transforming Agriculture

The agriculture sector is vital in most Ethiopians' lives and livelihoods. About 14 million smallholder farmer households account for an estimated 95% of agricultural output. Agriculture contributes 44% to the country's GDP and 85% to the country's export earnings. Furthermore, the sector employs 85% of the population (women constitute 49.5%). Between 2004 and 2014, agricultural output grew by 7.6% per year on average.[54] Driving this increase were public investments in the adoption of chemical fertilizers and improved seed varieties. Yet, severe food shortages exist, and the arable land continues to shrink.

Although a foreign currency earner, livestock production is declining and becoming expensive due to the shortage of fodder, grazing land, and escalating animal feed prices. The livestock sector contributes up to 16% of GDP. Ethiopia's livestock production systems can be categorized into crop-livestock mixed systems, pastoral and agro-pastoral systems, and urban and peri-urban production systems. It plays a crucial role in the overall Ethiopian farming system. Livestock is a source of draught power for plowing and tilling the land. It also supplies farm families with milk, meat, and manure, serves as a source of cash income, and plays significantly in Ethiopian society's sociocultural values. Many rural households use livestock manure as fuel for cooking and organic fertilizer.

In the 1950s and 1960s, wealth was measured in terms of the number of heads of cattle owned by a household. In 1961, when I was a teacher in Chencha, Gamu Goffa, in the southern part of Ethiopia, I noticed that some farmers had 3,000 to 5,000 heads of cattle.

When I left Ethiopia in 1968 for graduate school in America, the population of Ethiopia was nearly 18 million. On the other hand, the livestock population was recorded at over 96 million. Many households had two

---

54 Fantu N. Bachewe, Guush Berhane, Bart Minten, and Alemayehu S. Tafesse (2018). "Agricultural Transformation in Africa? Assessing the Evidence in Ethiopia," *World Development*, Elsevier, vol. 105(C), pp. 286–298.

to ten cows and bulls in their backyard, in addition to small ruminants. Now the livestock population has declined drastically. The grazing land has shrunk.

In pastoral areas, livestock production has underpinned the population's livelihood for centuries. However, pastoralists are severely affected by climate change and conflict. Their ability to move their animals to better watering and grazing land during bad times is becoming narrow due to ethnic strife. Despite the livestock sector's importance to farmers, pastoralist populations, and the national economy, it has remained underdeveloped and underutilized.[55]

The Ethiopian government has formulated policies, strategies, and programs to promote agricultural development to achieve food and nutrition security and build resilience. The government of Ethiopia's (GOE's) agricultural sector transformation objectives focuses on improving agricultural production and productivity, commercialization, reducing natural resource degradation, reducing vulnerability to natural disasters, and building disaster mitigation capabilities by ensuring food security. But it does not include an explicit strategy for soil rejuvenation and protection or increasing farm households' incomes.

Indeed, the agricultural industry requires a substantial transformation to sustain economic growth, reduce poverty, and ensure food security. To this end, the GOE established the National Agricultural Transformation Agency (ATA) in 2011 to identify systemic constraints to agricultural development and growth and provide solutions. ATA established the Ethiopian Soil Information System (EthioSIS), a digital soil fertility map covering 90% of the country, realizing that healthier soils are a prerequisite for healthier plants and that soil needs vary across agroecological zones. Informed by this data, ATA published

---

55 Azage Tegegne, Berhanu Gebremedhin, and Dirk Hoekstra (2010). Livestock Input Supply and Service Provision in Ethiopia: Challenges and Opportunities for Market-Oriented Development. IPMS Working Paper 20. Nairobi (Kenya): ILRI.

soil-based fertilizer recommendations used by the Ethiopian Institute of Agricultural Research (EIAR) to develop crop-specific fertilizer recommendations for farmers.

ATA also developed a hotline for smallholder farmers with interactive voice response and short message service (IVR/SMS) capabilities. The number is easy to remember: **8028**. It's toll-free and provides farmers with seasonally pertinent information: when and how to plant different crops and identify and treat diseases like Wheat Rust and Fall Armyworm.

The Ethiopian Agricultural Businesses Corporation (EABC), a state enterprise, imports ATA-recommended fertilizers. However, the EABC's corrupt practices along the fertilizer supply chain resulted in high transaction costs for the government and farmers. Smallholder farmers paid twice as much as they should for inputs like urea and DAP (diammonium phosphate).[56] Except for the political elites' shell companies, EABC's monopoly power crowded out the private sector. The private sector plays a minor role in fertilizer importation and distribution—corruption in fertilizer importation and the distribution chain rendered ATA's efforts to enhance agricultural production useless.

ATA has reported significant increases in agricultural productivity based on the number of farmers using improved seeds, organic and inorganic fertilizers, and modern farming methods. However, the sector has been slow in using mechanized farming. And the government program failed to build resilience among smallholder farmers to shocks stemming from climate change.

Most agricultural production in Ethiopia is rainfed. Only 6% of the farmland is irrigated, and overall crop yields are low with high post-harvest losses. Despite ATA's efforts, market linkages are weak, and the use of improved seeds, fertilizers, pesticides, and chemicals for controlling

---

56   Johanes U.I. Agbahey, Harold Grethe, and Workneh Negatu (2015). "Fertilizer Supply Chain in Ethiopia: Structure, Performance, and Policy Analysis." *Afrika Focus*, Volume 28, Nr. 1. 2015, pp. 81–101.

crop-destroying rodents, insects, and birds remains limited. Increased agricultural investment is needed to enhance the value chain competitiveness for crops such as maize, wheat, barley, coffee, sesame, chickpea, fava beans, honey, potato, livestock, small ruminants, goats, sheep, and poultry.[57]

In the livestock sector, a lot needs to happen. The experience so far has been the limited supply of improved animal genetic resources for dairy development, sheep production (meat and wool), improved poultry (broiler and egg production), supply of bee colonies, provision of forage seeds and planting material, dairy goats, supply of processing equipment and utensils (dairy, apiculture), drug supply, and vaccination services.[58] Donor-financed projects and government programs supply these services. The private sector's contribution to livestock input has been limited to providing veterinary drugs and services, roughage and concentrate feed, and processing equipment and utensils. Due to shortages of skilled human capital and financial resources, agriculture extension services' impact on the livestock sector has been limited.

The Woreda Office of Agriculture and Rural Development Engagements with farmers are limited. There is a gap in coordination and basing livestock development interventions on scientific knowledge with the value chain in mind. The extension system must be re-oriented to respond to the increasing demand for improved and market-oriented livestock development. This would ensure farmers, pastoralists, and private commercial producers benefit themselves and contribute to the development of the national economy.[59]

---

57   The cost of small ruminants to consumers has skyrocketed. An egg, which used to cost just ETB 1.00 about 10 years ago, is now ETB 8.00. Sheep, which used to cost about ETB 1,000.00 10 years ago, now cost more than ETB 4,500.00.

58   Azage Tegegne, Berhanu Gebremedhin, and Dirk Hoekstra (2010). Livestock Input Supply and Service Provision in Ethiopia: Challenges and Opportunities for Market-Oriented Development. IPMS Working Paper 20. Nairobi (Kenya): ILRI.

59   Ibid.

In collaboration with development partners, the GOE invested in the PSNP to build the resilience capacity of chronically food-insecure communities. The PSNP's objective is to prevent the depletion of household assets, stimulate market activities, improve access to services, and rehabilitate and enhance the natural environment through labor-based public works.[60] It is an ongoing program and targets more than ten million beneficiaries across Ethiopia. However, more resources are required to expand and continue the program as more communities are affected by drought conditions and locust infestations. The program also needs reconstruction to graduate program beneficiaries to self-reliance.

Our evaluation of the USAID-supported public works program, such as building retaining walls on hillsides and constructing culverts and other structures, has created a dependency on food aid.[61] Some farm communities complained that these programs are making day laborers of farmers. Others have said they are not working hard on their farms as they know food aid from America and Canada is available. They only produce crops sufficient to feed them for 3 to 6 months. Also, farmers are not investing much in the land as it does not belong to them. According to the FDRE Constitution Article 40, Sub-Article 3, all land belongs to the government. Thus, the government can remove farmers from their land, which has happened in different parts of the country.

Despite all efforts, the agricultural community is under stress. First, the landholding of smallholder farmers is small, averaging two hectares per farm household. At the same time, the family size keeps growing, and the family is continuously food insecure. Also, the price obtained for surplus production is insufficient to pay for farm inputs and household

---

60 Guush Berhane, John Hoddinott, Neha Kumar, and Alemayehu Seyoum Tafesse (2012). Ethiopia's Productive Safety Net and Household Asset Building Programs (2006–10). Policy Brief, USAID/Ethiopia, January 2012.

61 Sharon Benoliel, Samuel Taddesse, Roberta van Hoeften, Mamo Weldeberhan, Laura Williams, and Astaire Zewdie (1998). Assessment of the Impact of USAID PL 480 and Title II Food Aid on Vulnerable Communities in Ethiopia, USAID, Africa Bureau.

consumption. Rural farmers also lack access to markets. Access roads are very rough, and consolidators cannot reach the farmers.

Furthermore, numerous factors affect farmer incomes, including the unpredictability of crop yields and external factors such as too much rain or insufficient rain or longer or shorter rainy season, input availability and cost, farmers' health and productivity, market price volatility, and political insecurity. Farm cooperatives established to provide greater market power to smallholder farmers have failed to produce the expected results because of the board members' greed, corruption, and political interference. Ruling party operatives have infiltrated farm cooperatives and sit on the board.

Transformation of the agricultural sector requires massive investment in infrastructure. We must invest in irrigation schemes and post-harvest storage systems to reduce post-harvest losses and build access roads to link farm communities to markets. Work is required to strengthen marketing and value chains to enhance smallholder farmers' productivity and incomes. Sound policies and institutional arrangements are necessary to regulate and manage the sector, including revitalizing farmers' cooperatives and the agriculture supply chains. The agriculture supply chains involve farm-to-intermediate silos, intermediate silos to processing plants, and consumer domestic and international markets.[62]

As noted above, the arable land is shrinking, and the soil conditions are deteriorating. Traditional slash-and-burn agriculture has caused tremendous damage to forest resources. Work is needed to reforest and reclaim the dead soil using organic matter. We need to expand regenerative farming and bring to health the soils we depend on for growing food crops.

---

62 Nicolas Denis, Valerio Dilda, Rami Kalouche, and Ruben Sabah (2020). *Agriculture Supply-Chain Optimization and Value Creation.* McKinsey & Company, May 2020.

But more fundamentally, the land must be privatized. According to the FDRE Constitution, the land belongs to the government.[63] There is no assurance that farmers or communities cannot be moved from the land they are tilling at any time.[64] Private land ownership would encourage farmers to invest more in land improvement and keep the soil alive. Also, buying and selling the land would enable productive farmers to expand their landholdings and produce more.

Furthermore, pastoralists must be settled and assisted in sustainable feeding and caring for their livestock. In Metahara, Oromia regional state, pastoralists have settled and are engaged in cash crops and livestock production. They use the water from the Awash River to irrigate their crops and water their livestock.

Investment in year-round accessible rural roads is needed to link farmers to markets and generate increased farm income. Road infrastructure is essential for connecting farm and rural communities to urban markets and changing living conditions. In 1996, my team and I drove to northern Mozambique's fertile plateau, Zambezi, to see how the farmers were doing. We found that most farmers produced similar crops, and the opportunity for bartering was minimal. Moreover, the surplus production was not reaching the market and was left to rot on the field. We suggested to USAID/Mozambique that they fund the construction of a road to connect that farm community to Maputo. At first, the proposed route went through no man's land and looked like a waste of resources.

After several meetings and discussions, the mission director approved the construction of the road. The road was built. Six months after the road's opening, my team and I rode along the new route to that farm community. Along the roadside, several towns and villages had popped up. Consolidators carried consumer goods to sell in the remote towns, bought

---

63 Article 40, Sub-Article (3), Proclamation No. 1/1995, Proclamation of the Constitution of the Federal Democratic Republic of Ethiopia, August 21, 1995, Addis Ababa, Ethiopia.

64 Article 40, Sub-Article (8) of Proclamation No. January 1995.

surplus produce, and brought it to Maputo. The farm communities had become more prosperous and encouraged to continue crop and vegetable production. We had a similar experience in Tanzania, the Roads project.

2.2. INJECTING NEW PROSPERITY IDEAS

Transforming and enhancing the living conditions of citizens and achieving "rapid broad-based and sustained economic growth and prosperity and ascendance to middle-income country status" would require transforming mindsets and providing ideas and resources for change. As noted above, in addition to developing robust communication and transportation systems, the education, health, water and sanitation, and agriculture sectors need overhauling and transforming. One approach for working directly with citizens and accelerating change in these and other sectors is launching a high-profile Ethiopian Prosperity Corps Program (EPCP). EPCP would penetrate all segments of society around the country and awaken, galvanize, and mobilize the population to attain broad-based prosperity. EPCP can be a catalyst for change. It can change the conversation and engage citizens in cleaning up their neighborhoods, improving their homes' construction and sanitary conditions, educating their children and themselves, and creating wealth and prosperity.

Prosperity Corps volunteers can motivate and spark the creativity and imagination of the vast majority of ordinary citizens and transform lives. These volunteers, composed of Ethiopian university senior class students and faculty, the diaspora, civil society organizations, professional associations and chambers of commerce, and volunteers from the international community, can inject new and innovative ideas into communities. They can promote and foster community collaborative problem-solving and collective action for a better quality of life. They can introduce neighborhood beautification programs.

The program would introduce new and innovative approaches to doing business and accelerate citizens' productivity. It would open avenues for the youth to learn new skills and knowledge and make them productive and responsible members of society while pursuing their education. By establishing micro-Research & Innovation (R&I) hubs across the country, the program could enable citizens to transform ideas into products and services and take them to market. These R&I hubs also serve as business incubators and training centers for entrepreneurship and artisanship. They provide access to technology and new production and business management methods. The R&I centers are open and accessible to the public.

Furthermore, through these R&I hubs, Prosperity Corps volunteers can help farmers restore degraded soils by applying better farming techniques and soil maintenance and introducing water conservation methods such as drip irrigation. The volunteers will train pastoralists with improved farming methods, livestock fattening, and fodder production towards zero-grazing. The volunteers will work with local communities to process, package, and bring products developed from oilseeds, coffee beans, hides and leather, cotton, wool, and other fibers to market. Volunteers will also train and upgrade the skills of the local carpenters, masons, plumbers, electricians, and builders. They will teach the potters, weavers, and dairy farmers to produce better quality and internationally competitive products. They will build, expand, and strengthen the supply chains from farm to market and workshops to market.

Also, the EPCP can help alleviate the poor state of education in urban and rural areas, recognizing education as the gateway to prosperity. As indicated elsewhere, the program could enhance public education quality by introducing a twenty-first-century curriculum, including artificial intelligence and training people in analytics and computer coding. It would mobilize and nudge families and community members to engage in their children's education. Parents must educate themselves through night school to engage with their students meaningfully.

A squad of eight to ten volunteers with complementary skill sets work with farmers, pastoralists, artisans, villagers, educators, and youth in a given Kebele.[65] One mission of these volunteers is to strengthen and grow existing livelihoods, create new ones, and accelerate community members' productivity and prosperity through collective actions.

In the 1950s and 1960s, the United States sent experts from the Department of Agriculture to work with farmers in the field through Point Four Program and later USAID. These experts showed the farmers how much and when to apply fertilizers and irrigate their crops using groundwater. Very soon, the productivity of farmers in the Ethiopian highlands grew fourfold. Crop yield per hectare increased on average five-fold. Intercropping, introduced in some parts of the country, increased the variety of crops and fruits produced and marketed. EPCP volunteers can obtain similar or better results.

The volunteers can accelerate policy changes as well. They will be encouraged to gather data on the institutional, policy, and legal constraints ordinary citizens, small businesses, and micro-enterprises face in urban and rural communities. They will work with grassroots associations, local authorities, chambers of commerce, and the regional and federal governments to resolve these constraints. A well-organized and implemented EPCP can play a critical catalytic role in the country's sustained economic and social development and transformation.

The premise for the urgency of organizing and implementing EPCP is that *delayed prosperity, joblessness, and increased poverty can fuel conflict and crimes and destabilize the country.* Under existing conditions, creating wealth for most Ethiopians over the next decade would be challenging without a Prosperity Corps program that galvanizes communities for

---

65 To be effective, the EPCP must be organized by sector. For example, to facilitate the transformation of the education system, volunteers must have expertise in curriculum development, education delivery systems, and school management and administration. Similarly, volunteers working in the healthcare sector must have expertise in the delivery of healthcare and the prevention and treatment of infectious and communicable diseases. The same would be true for those engaged in working in the agricultural sector.

collective action. Climate change affects agricultural productivity. It accelerates deforestation, reduces freshwater flow, shrinks the arable land, affects livestock production, and displaces millions of people. We need community members to brainstorm and create adaptive and resilient solutions to these climate-caused problems.

A properly implemented EPCP could usher in prosperity and accelerate wealth creation for all Ethiopians. Its benefits would include the following:

- Increased trust and understanding between local communities and private sector businesses through corporate social accountability initiatives
- New talents learned by community youth due to participation in the EPCP activities
- A more robust social capital that enables collaboration and social action for better living conditions and quality of life
- Increased understanding and trust between citizens and their national, regional, and local government leaders, resulting in a robust social contract and corruption-free partnership between citizens and the government
- Increased number of tax-compliant citizenries that pay their fair share of taxes to fund the delivery of quality public goods and services, including quality healthcare, education, and hard and soft infrastructure
- Increased use of alternative energy sources, forest management, and product development and production methods for a green economy

2.3 FUTURISTIC FISCAL AND TAX POLICY

A **futuristic fiscal and tax policy** would anticipate required organizational changes and the associated investment for transforming the critical social and economic sectors that enhance citizens' living conditions and quality of life. It also would anticipate the resources required to implement and progress on the to-be-drafted Ethiopian Vision 2040. As noted above, whole-of-society planning, budgeting, and activity implementation would help determine the level of monetary and other resources required to achieve sustained prosperity for all Ethiopians. That means all budget holders must develop their long-term and annualized budgets. The budgeting process must begin at the community level.

Aggregating the investment needs from the bottom up will provide a starting place for thinking further about the required level of investment and expenditure, given the absorption capacities of communities and government organizations. It will also consider public-private partnerships (PPPs) and government and community partnerships (GCPs). The process will determine how much of the development plan can be addressed through PPPs and GCPs. The balance will provide a baseline for direct government investment. The process will also estimate the funding required for social protection, emergency preparedness and response, and other contingencies.

Once all government institutions have drafted their strategic plans from the bottom up; laid out their expected outputs, result, and outcomes; and identified the various activities to be implemented, they develop their annualized budgets. Moreover, they will identify their strategic partners and collaborate and share resources to deliver better quality results to citizens. The next step is estimating how much revenue can be generated through taxation.

Current tax policies and administration practices must be reviewed, assessed, and adjusted to be fit for purpose. Even after exploring ways to maximize tax collection and the most effective and optimal use of the collected tax revenues, not all government activities can be funded through taxation. Nonetheless, before we resort to domestic or external borrowing, we must clean up and eliminate unproductive investment and tax incentives and programs. We must also sanitize government systems from corruption.

Currently, investment tax incentives are equivalent to 7% of GDP. Tax incentives are provided to attract Foreign Direct Investment, encourage domestic investment in the processing and production of essential goods, and invest in remote locations. While the policy's intent is noble, it has allowed firms to abuse the investment incentives grossly. It has encouraged tax evasion and tax avoidance. Tax incentives have also created horizontal inequities, introduced production and market inefficiencies, and compromised the quality of goods and services. They have also denied tax revenue to the government that could have been spent on essential public goods and services.

Countries provide investment tax incentives to speed up economic development and growth and improve citizens' living conditions. In most cases, investment tax incentives promote technology transfer and diffusion or employment creation in effective and efficient ways relative to alternative policies. Investors can be provided tax incentives to invest in remote locations, for example, to offset some of their transportation expenses. However, international organizations and economists have found tax incentives ineffective.

Also, the reluctance to scale back incentives, as evidenced in Ethiopia, may be symptomatic of vested interests, political inertia, and tax competition with other countries. It might also be that the overall benefits that incentives generate for society are overstated, for example, concerning employment creation, technology transfers, and impact on people's living conditions. The evidence supporting the manifestation of these benefits is weak.[66] The social benefits of investment tax incentives would depend on the following:[67]

---

66 Alexander Klemm and Stefan Van Parys (2009). Empirical Evidence on the Effectiveness of Tax Incentives, International Monetary Fund, Wp/09/136.

67 IMF, OECD, UN, and World Bank (2015). Options for Low Income Countries' Effective and Efficient Use of Tax Incentives, Report to the G-20 Development Working Group, October 2015.

- *The net investment size*: Corrected for redundancy effects (investments that would have occurred without the incentive) and displacement effects (i.e., the reduction in any other capital investment) to infer the net incremental increase in the invested capital due to the incentives.

- *The net impact of increased investment on jobs and wages*: New jobs can yield significant social benefits by reducing unemployment. However, suppose new jobs displace existing jobs. In that case, the social benefits depend on the productivity (and wage) differential and spillover effects between the new and old jobs and the net increase in total employment.

- *The productivity spillovers*: The extent the new investment boosts productivity elsewhere in the economy, such as supplying or competing firms through technology transfer or increasing the productivity of domestic firms (often seen as a particular benefit from inward FDI). This magnifies social benefits by raising income levels widely. But what is the net increase in income and wealth of citizens resulting from these incentives?

Similarly, the *social costs* of tax incentives must be assessed against the following:[68]

- *Net public revenue losses:* Tax revenue falls if tax incentives are redundant or create leakage and abuse. But additional net investment and jobs can recover some of the revenue loss.

- *Net increases in administrative and compliance costs*: i.e., complex tax incentives can increase enforcement and compliance costs and open up opportunities for rent-seeking and corruption.

- *Scarcity of public revenue*: the tax revenue losses and the social goods forgone against the private profits of those businesses that benefit from the investment tax incentives.

- *Resource allocation distortion:* Discrimination in favor of some and against other investments implies that taxes, rather than differences in productivity, quality of goods, and relative prices,

---

68 Ibid.

determine resource allocation. These resource allocation distortions reduce the overall productivity and wealth of a nation.

Tax incentives are generally inferior to nationwide tax reforms that indifferently tax all investment activities across all economic sectors.[69] All other things equal, broadening the tax base and lowering the tax rate for all is more effective in inducing economic activities and investments than investment tax incentives. The provisions of investment tax incentives for underserved regions and critical economic sectors to reduce dependence on imports would be necessary. The benefits may outweigh the cost. In such circumstances, policymakers should provide clear and transparent qualification criteria, the terms and duration of these incentives, and robust enforcement mechanisms, including monitoring, evaluation, and auditing.

Second, transfer pricing used by related companies needs to be addressed. A transfer price is paid on goods and services purchased from an associated company.[70] Transfer pricing is a legitimate and necessary feature of multinational enterprises' commercial activities. However, the transfer prices between the related companies often do not follow the market and international norms. They distort profit allocation among the countries where they operate. Transfer pricing artificially shifts earnings out of a country, denying essential tax revenue to the host country.

Profit shifting and base erosion through transfer pricing schemes can also have broader implications. Tax avoidance by high-profile corporate

---

69 Duanjie Chen (2015). The Framework for Assessing Tax Incentives: A Cost-Benefit Analysis Approach, Paper for Workshop on Tax Incentives and Base Protection, April 23–24, 2015, United Nations, New York, NY.

70 OECD (2017). Transfer Pricing Guidelines for Multinational Enterprises and Tax Administrations, July 10, 2017. https://www.oecd.org/tax/transfer-pricing/oecd-transfer-pricing-guidelines-for-multinational-enterprises-and-tax-administrations-20769717.htm. According to this OECD definition, enterprises are associated or related if an enterprise participates directly or indirectly in the management, control, or capital of another enterprise or (b) the same persons participate directly or indirectly in the management, control, or capital of two enterprises.

taxpayers using transfer pricing schemes is perceived as "unfair" by independent enterprises governed by market demand and supply forces. It undermines the overall tax system's legitimacy and credibility, thus discouraging tax compliance by other taxpayers. Moreover, enabling these companies to have artificial monopoly power in their economic sectors would suppress independent enterprises' incomes and profits. It would distort the market, further deny the government tax revenue, raise consumer costs, and fuel inflation.

Many countries have addressed the tax risks created by transfer pricing by introducing domestic tax rules based on the "arm's-length principle."[71] Most double tax treaties also incorporate the arm's-length principle as the basis for allocating profits (and thus taxes) between related enterprises.[72] The arm's-length principle provides broad parity of tax treatment for commercial transactions between associated companies and those between independent enterprises. There should be equal treatment between members of a group of companies (which may gain tax advantages through non–arm's-length transfer pricing) and independent enterprises. It also provides an objective standard that replicates market outcomes. Economists assert that the arm's-length principle helps reduce distortions to international trade and investment and maintains the domestic market's competitiveness and the integrity of the tax base.

According to the OECD transfer pricing guidelines, the related companies' tax liabilities in the countries where they operate should not undermine the market's competitiveness. Enterprises must be required to report taxable profits that would be expected if the related enterprises had adopted market prices (and other conditions) consistent with

---

71 At its most basic level, the arms-length principle states that the price charged in a transaction between two related businesses should be the same as the price charged in a comparable transaction between two unrelated enterprises.

72 OECD (2017). The Platform for Collaboration on Tax: A Toolkit for Addressing Difficulties in Accessing Comparable Data for Transfer Pricing Analysis. https://www.oecd.org/tax/discussion-draft-a-toolkit-for-addressing-difficulties-in-accessing-comparables-data-for-transfer-pricing-analyses.pdf.

those between independent enterprises in comparable circumstances. Typically, tax administrators have the authority to adjust taxable profit where related companies do not adopt an arm's-length condition in their transactions. To establish such prices and other circumstances, it is essential to compare the requirements of commercial transactions between the associated companies with those that exist between independent parties in comparable circumstances. Thus, comparability analysis must be conducted whenever the arm's-length principle is violated.

Enforcing the arm's-length principle would require collecting data from the market for specific goods and commodities and cross-matching the data. The prices paid by independent businesses are compared with related enterprises' transaction prices. Over the past 20 years, domestic and foreign companies have used transfer pricing schemes extensively, particularly in developing countries, to avoid paying taxes. Robust data-supported analytics is required to monitor, assess, and enforce the arm's-length principle. Over the past three decades, Ethiopia has lost tax revenue due to transfer pricing schemes practiced by foreign and domestic companies. A back-of-the-envelope estimate indicates that the tax revenue loss is more than 7% of GDP.

Third, as noted above, Ethiopia has a large informal sector. We must integrate the informal sector into the formal economy and the tax net using innovative approaches. The informal sector comprises numerous actors, including microenterprises, illicit traders seeking to avoid paying taxes, and traders engaged in contraband trade. It also includes those individuals and organized criminals involved in money laundering. In Ethiopia, the informal or shadow economy accounts for 35% to 45% of the country's economy. The shadow economy's potential tax revenue loss to the government is substantial, amounting to 8% to 11% of GDP,[73] a considerable tax revenue loss.

---

73 Emerta Asaminew (2010). The Underground Economy and Tax Evasion in Ethiopia: Implications for Tax Policy. Ethiopian Economic and Policy Research Institute (EEPRI) and Ethiopian Economic Association (EEA). October 2010.

Further analysis of the informal or shadow market shows that it includes businesses, manufacturers, exporters, importers, traders, retailers, merchants, and youth that

- fail to register correctly and, therefore, not in the tax net,
- operate without Taxpayer Identification Number (TIN) or a business license,
- have business licenses and TIN but opt to hide their incomes from the tax authorities,
- fail to issue Value-Added Tax (VAT) receipts to their customers, and
- operate on the street alongside formal merchants.[74]

The shadow economy in Ethiopia also thrives because of the cash economy. Both legal and illegal transactions are in cash, and the government has difficulty tracking these transactions.

Fourth, we need to determine how much tax revenue can be saved through allocational and operational efficiencies in government organizations. Although the government had gone through the business process reengineering once before, the real purpose then was to reassign the civil servants according to the ethnic makeup of the ethnically oriented regional states established by the EPDRF or the ruling party. That process displaced many professional career civil servants. It depleted the capable human resources of federal and regional state governments. What is needed now is to understand each organization's mandate and determine how effectively and efficiently it could execute its mandate. And then redesign and adjust the business processes and procedures of the organization to be fit for purpose.

During 2018 and 2019, Cowater implemented the Tax Systems Transformation Program funded by the DFID, which studied how to

---

74 These youths operate without business licenses and TIN and do not pay rent or taxes. They present unfair competition to the formal merchants, sometimes selling similar products and goods.

redesign the Ethiopian Ministry of Revenue's (MOR's) business processes. Many of its employees were playing with their mobile phones and not engaged in productive work. Employees are seen loafing around, gossiping, and not doing the people's business. The offices also do not look like professional organizations conducting the people's business. Redesigning business processes would not be sufficient until employees' needs are met. Because of ethnic-based hiring and promotion, many employees feel unappreciated or not valued. They have no motivation to work hard. That must change. A back-of-the-envelope calculation indicates that a significant amount of tax revenue, approximating 5% to 9% of GDP, can be saved by enhancing organizational effectiveness and efficiencies across all government organizations.

Fifth, corruption must be identified, controlled, and eliminated in all its forms. According to Transparency International, corruption lowers the tax-to-GDP ratio. It causes long-term damage to the economy by reducing the amount invested, increasing the size of the informal economy, distorting tax structures, and corrupting the tax morale of taxpayers. All of these, in turn, further reduce the long-term revenue-generating potential of the economy.[75]

According to a statistical estimate by Tanzi and Davoodi (2000), a one-point increase in the Corruption Perception Index is associated with a 2.7 percentage-point decline in the tax-to-GDP ratio.[76] Corruption has a wide-ranging effect on the development of a country. It retards private-sector investment and profitability, reduces the tax revenue available to the government, and results in shoddy infrastructure and poor-quality supplies and service delivery.

---

75 Transparency International (2010). Exploring the Relationships Between Corruption and Tax Revenue. U4 Expert Answer No. 228, U4 Anti-Corruption Resource Center, January 12, 2010.

76 Vito Tanzi and Hamid R. Davoodi (2000). Corruption, Growth and Public Finances. IMF Working Paper. WP/00/182, November 2000 http://www.imf.org/external/pubs/ft/wp/2000/wp00182.pdf.

Imagine, in the first place paying bribes out of your investment capital to speed up the permit and other processes. You now have less money to invest. So, you scale down your ambition and invest in a smaller project. If other investors do the same, the investment rate decreases, and economic growth slows down. The potential tax base has become smaller, and tax revenue is low. That is precisely what has happened in Ethiopia since 1995 due to systemic corruption in federal, regional, and local governments.

Corruption does not stop there. Imagine having corrupt employees who steal from your company. That harms your company's growth and profitability; if the theft continues, your company might even go bankrupt. That has happened to many small enterprises in the United States, Ethiopia, and other countries. While working at the Federal Reserve Bank of New York in downtown New York City, my friends and I used to go to a couple of restaurants for lunch. They had a good clientele base and were busy. But we noticed that in the afternoon, the cooks would steal the meat from the kitchen and sell it on the street corner out of their pickup trucks for a low price. Within a year, both restaurants went bankrupt.

Also, several coffee shops around Washington, DC, went bankrupt because workers would substitute their milk, coffee, and sugar and store receipts when the owners were not around. The revenue collected for the real owners was much lower when the owners were not there. Eventually, these coffee shops folded. The net effect of these types of corruption and crime is high unemployment, low economic growth, and less tax revenue for government programs.

In Ethiopia, another form of corruption is the formation of shell companies by government officials to bid for government contracts. These shell companies submit high bids yet win but deliver low-quality products and services. Low-quality infrastructure built through such shell companies was redone at a high cost to the government. Billions of ETB and foreign currency were squandered and stolen through such means. Eliminating corruption at all levels would generate significant tax revenue for the government without raising the tax rate.

2.4 TAX POLICY-MAKING

Tax policy-making is a challenging task. First, it is difficult to estimate how much tax revenue should be collected to pay for public goods and services that improve citizens' living conditions. It requires robust project design and appraisal capability. Second, it creates winners and losers. The losers often complain loudly, saying the tax system is unfair and may cause tax noncompliance to rise.[77] Third, the tax policy must be tailored to society's prosperity plan's objectives while synchronizing the tax policy to international competitiveness needs.

Thus, tax policy should be formulated in consultation with citizens, residents, businesses, and international trading partners. Tax policy made in a consultive process would succeed because all concerned understand the tax policy, its implication, and how it would affect them and others. It balances the interests of all concerned. A successful tax-policy–making process communicates the final tax policy and its administration to all stakeholders.

For Ethiopia, as the country begins a new era of governance, the prime minister should convene a tax policy convention. The convention must involve all stakeholders, including regional states leadership, civic groups, civil society organizations and academicians, community and business leaders, and development partners. According to the Tax Policy Convention Agenda, shown in Box 2.5, the convention organizers would first facilitate a discussion on where the country stands now and where it should be in the next decade. As mentioned earlier, in his 10-year homegrown prosperity plan, Prime Minister Abiy has set the goal of achieving a middle-income country status by 2030. All convention participants must discuss and understand the implications of this goal. The discussant must elaborate on what the nation must do to achieve that goal effectively and efficiently.

---

77 Carlo Cottarelli (2012). Structures, Processes, and Governance in Tax-Making, IMF Fiscal Affairs Department. Speech made in Said Business School, Oxford, March 8, 2012.

Second, the organizers should review each economic and social sector's baseline conditions or the starting point. They should highlight how each sector can be transformed and how the transformation will be financed. Throughout the convention, participants should be given opportunities to ask questions and express their views and suggestions in a series of roundtable discussions. The organizers should use participants' feedback to develop the expected outputs, results, and outcomes that lead to a middle-income country status and seek consensus from the convention participants.

To finance the development plan, taxation must be at the center of the financing discussion. The convention organizers must ensure that the tax debate addresses the need to protect the poor and the disadvantaged. The tax burden must be balanced and shared by all. The macro-level conversation must be replicated at the community level to ensure that all citizens are aware and invested in the prosperity plan of the country.

We must also ensure that the institutions responsible for drafting the

---

Box 2.5: Draft Agenda for a National Tax Policy Convention

- Welcome and Opening Remarks by the President of the National Government
- Introduction & Discussion of Objectives and Expected Outcomes of the Convention
- Introduction of the Purpose and Intent of the Homegrown Development Plan
- Presentation and Discussion of the Transformation Program
    o Education
    o Health
    o Water and Sanitation
    o Agriculture
    o Transportation & Road Infrastructure
    o ICT
    o Industry
- Presentation of Roundtable Discussions
    o Education
    o Health
    o Water and Sanitation
    o Agriculture
    o Transportation and Road Infrastructure
    o ICT
    o Industry
- Discussion on Transformation Program Implementation and Funding Needs
- Conference on Fair and Equitable Taxation
- Next Steps

fiscal and tax policies have sufficient capabilities and resources. The tax policy and administration system must be explicit, simple to interpret, economical to administer and comply with, and fair and equitable.[78]

The Ethiopian Ministry of Finance and Economic Cooperation (MOFEC) is responsible for drafting the tax policy at the federal level. And at the regional state level, the regional states' Finance & Economic Development Bureaus (RSFEDBs) have the mandate for the regional states' tax policies. The institutional capacities of these organizations must be strengthened, and their responsibilities aligned with the outcomes of the tax policy convention.

In the past, the Ethiopian tax policy formulation process involved sending a questionnaire to the Chambers of Commerce and their members to complete without having a healthy dialogue of giving and taking. The government also has held a taxpayers' forum to discuss draft tax legislation from time to time. However, the dialogue process is inadequate. It is a one-way communication channel, and the feedback mechanism and follow-up are weak or nonexistent. Feedback provided by the participating taxpayers is rarely addressed or adequately explained.

The tax policy dialogue requires a unique and transformative platform. For example, a social accountability project in Ethiopia served as a platform for bringing together local government essential service providers and communities.[79] In this platform, community members reviewed the service providers' performance relative to their needs and the quality and quantity of public goods and services received and challenged the service providers. A face-to-face dialogue between the frontline service providers and community members took place. Service delivery performance scores (i.e., **citizens' report cards**) were reviewed and reconciled against the service providers' **self-assessment scores**.

---

78   Adam Smith (1776). *The Wealth of Nations.*
79   Samuel Taddesse (2017). *Social Accountability in Ethiopia: A Guidebook.* Lulu Publishing Services: Raleigh, North Carolina, USA. www.samtaddesse.com.

Once agreement on the performance scores is reached, the service delivery deficits are identified and prioritized. Then, both sides drafted and signed a time-bound joint action plan (JAP) to resolve the service delivery deficits systematically and collaboratively. The respective civil society organization contracted to implement the social accountability project in the community moderates the face-to-face dialogue. The moderators ensure that the face-to-face discussion does not result in finger-pointing and steers it to be a constructive dialogue of giving and taking.

Service delivery deficiencies are often caused by the lack of resources, corruption, political interferences, and weaknesses in frontline public service providers' professionalism and capabilities. The JAPs prompt budget adjustments, additional resources contributions by community members, and frontline service providers' in-service training.

Lessons learned from the social accountability project can be applied to the taxation conversations. Tax compliance increases with constructive dialogue and discussions among public sector service providers, citizens, businesses, tax policy-makers, and tax collectors. Taxpayers must ask, and the government must respond on how it spends the tax revenue and why some public services are still inadequate. Such dialogues promote and foster government accountability to taxpayers.

Awareness and understanding of the linkages between public goods and services and taxes influence taxpayers' compliance. The tax authorities must explore how to convey the connections between taxes and public service delivery to citizens, residents, and businesses. Suppose people feel that the government collects tax revenues fairly and equitably and uses the tax revenue to deliver essential services that benefit citizens equally. In that case, citizens are more likely to pay their tax liabilities per the tax law willingly.[80]

---

80   Odd-Helge Fjeldstad (2004). "What's Trust Got to Do With It? Non-Payment of Service Charges in Local Authorities in South Africa." *The Journal of Modern African Studies* 42, 539–562.

Constructive dialogue among key stakeholders, as shown in Figure 2.7, would facilitate crafting an optimal tax policy that encourages private sector investments and business expansion while generating sufficient tax revenue for funding government economic and social infrastructure development programs. The tax-policy–making process must examine and understand the impact of taxation on economic growth, citizens' quality of life, and the business sector's development.

As noted elsewhere, national and subnational governments levy taxes to pay for various services they deliver to communities. The GOE uses the tax revenue collected for

- the construction of schools, the purchase of textbooks and school supplies, and for the training, hiring, and paying the salaries of teachers, school administrators, and other school staff,
- the construction of clinics and hospitals and for the training, engaging, and paying the wages of the nurses and doctors, and other hospital staff and for medical supplies and drugs,
- recruiting, training, hiring, and paying the salaries and equipping the armed forces to defend the country,
- recruiting, hiring, training, deploying, and paying the wages of the police force that provides safety and security to communities,
- building courthouses, prisons, and appointing and paying the salaries of judges, and
- the provision of potable water, roads, and bridges, among others.

It is critical to ensure that the tax revenue is spent strategically for a more meaningful impact on people's lives.[81] It is also vital to ensure that no resource leakages occur through corrupt contracting, procurement practices, or other means. According to Transparency International, citizens believe corruption is exceptionally high worldwide, including in Ethiopia. Ethiopia's corruption index of thirty-five ranks it 107 out of

---

81 Lucie Gadenne (2016). Tax Me, But Spend It Wisely? Sources of Public Finance and Government Accountability. Warwich Economic Research Papers, No:1131, October 2016.

180 countries.[82] As witnessed over the past three decades in several developing countries, systemic corruption can divert resources and impede economic and social development. Public officials' corruption and greed can create income and wealth inequalities and lead to political unrest.[83]

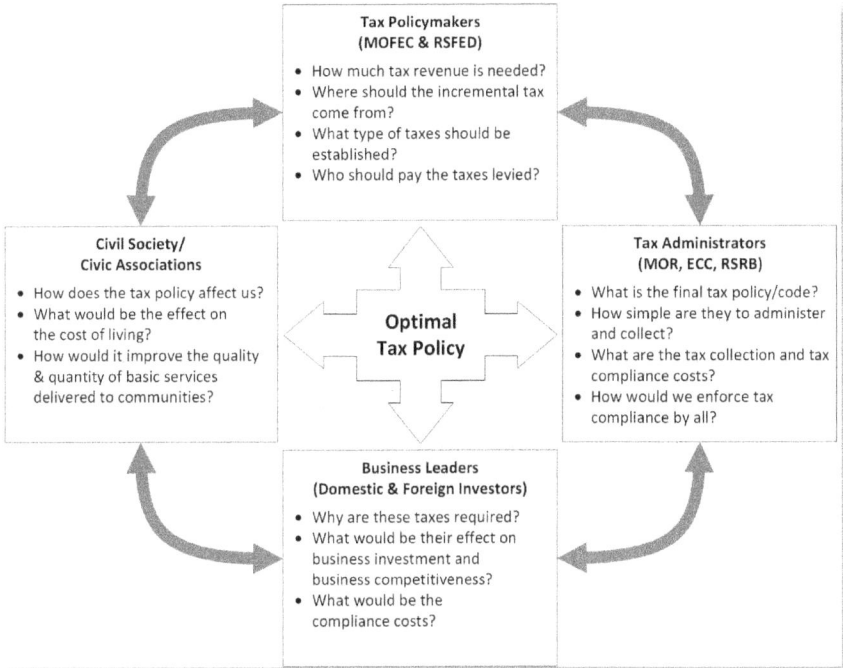

**Tax Policymakers
(MOFEC & RSFED)**

- How much tax revenue is needed?
- Where should the incremental tax come from?
- What type of taxes should be established?
- Who should pay the taxes levied?

**Civil Society/
Civic Associations**

- How does the tax policy affect us?
- What would be the effect on the cost of living?
- How would it improve the quality & quantity of basic services delivered to communities?

**Optimal
Tax Policy**

**Tax Administrators
(MOR, ECC, RSRB)**

- What is the final tax policy/code?
- How simple are they to administer and collect?
- What are the tax collection and tax compliance costs?
- How would we enforce tax compliance by all?

**Business Leaders
(Domestic & Foreign Investors)**

- Why are these taxes required?
- What would be their effect on business investment and business competitiveness?
- What would be the compliance costs?

Figure 2.7: Tax Policy-Making

Corruption in government procurement inhibits economic growth, distorts markets, and reduces trade competitiveness and foreign direct investment. Specific effects include[84]

---

82 Transparency International (2018). 2017 Corruption Perception Index.

83 Pierre-Guillaume Meon and Khalid Sekkat (2005). "Does Corruption Grease or Sand the Wheels of Growth?" *Public Choice* 122, 1–2.

84 Tina Søreide (2002). Corruption in Public Procurement, Causes, Consequences and Cures, Chr. Michelsen Institute, Bergen CMI Report R 2002:1 http://bora.cmi.no/dspace/bitstream/10202/185/1/R%20 2002-1.pdf.

- low-quality public goods and services delivered to citizens because of the low quality of goods and services bought from the best bribers or government officials' front/shell companies,
- state capture, whereby bribing firms and front companies of political elites determine the government policymaking processes,
- mistrust in government as political leaders prefer to award contracts to their friends, family members, or their front companies, and
- depressed private sector development and growth by providing special protections and privileges to the ruling party's and political leaders' owned or preferred companies that monopolize the market.

All these effects have been true for Ethiopia over the past three decades. Moreover, the risk of corruption increased with the increase in the level of expenditure and complexity of the technology involved, the urgency to procure the goods, and the level of discretionary authority given to public officials. Procurement rules are violated in several ways, including (a) limiting the call for bids, (b) designing tenders specific to the best-bribing vendors, and (c) providing confidential information to favor the bribing companies or ruling party officials' shell companies.

Corruption occurs through violations of procurement rules and deviations from standard procedures. There are legitimate reasons for bending the rules, such as speed during emergencies. Still, these reasons can be misused to benefit the most bribing vendors and must be avoided. Anticipation, early planning, acquisition, and prepositioning can address emergency needs more cost-effectively (see Annex 2.3).

Open, simplified, well-planned, and competitive procurement procedures reduce corruption. The government must establish a blue-ribbon commission (BRC) to eliminate corruption. The BRC would review and assess past contracts and determine the appropriateness of these contract awards and the quality of the work and product the awardees delivered. It would determine who authorized the procurement, where the goods and services were bought, and the quality of goods and commodities purchased. Findings of the BRC would be published and used to weed out the offenders on both sides of the transaction.

As noted above, developing and implementing an optimal tax regime must go hand-in-hand with the nation's objective of transforming the economy to catapult Ethiopia into a middle-income country. Citizens must improve their skills and educate themselves. Indigenous manufacturing capacity must be expanded and modernized to reduce dependence on imports. The agricultural sector must be transformed to be more productive and resilient to feed the country and export to the outside world at competitive prices. The livestock sector on which pastoralists depend also needs modernization. While private sector investment is critical, government strategic spending on infrastructure will drive modernization. Consequently, the required tax revenue to support government spending would require a robust tax system based on the whole of society's conversation and understanding and the steps outlined in Table 2.1.

The 2015 Addis Ababa Conference participants urged developing countries to rely on domestic resources for economic and social development programs.[85] The primary domestic resource is tax revenue collected from citizens, residents, and businesses. Thus, domestic resource mobilization (DRM), among other things, requires growing a country's tax capacity, widening the tax base, and increasing tax compliance. Indeed, as noted in Chapter 1, in 2019, tax revenue and service fees covered 73% of the GOE's expenditures for the fiscal year. Foreign aid covered only 1%, and the balance of government expenditures was funded through external borrowing. And according to the World Bank, Ethiopia has reached its debt limit. Thus, further external borrowing would be detrimental. Yet, as discussed above, the structural and transformational changes to be

---

85 Raul Felix Junquera-Varela, Marijn Verhoeven, Gangadhar P. Shukla, Bernard Haven, Rajul Awasthi, and Blanca Moreno-Dodson (2017). Strengthening Domestic Resource Mobilization: Moving From Theory to Practice in Low- and Middle-Income Countries. The World Bank Group, Directions in Development Public Sector Governance.

implemented to achieve the goal of ascending to a middle-income country status would require investing much more than at current levels. The question is, where will the government find the extra resources?

In my view, to implement and manage an optimal tax policy fairly, equitably, effectively, and efficiently, the government must first prioritize its development and investment programs. Second, it must scale back or eliminate tax incentives. It must also manage and control transfer pricing schemes through international tax agreements, intelligence sharing, and implementing transfer pricing audits. Control of investment tax incentives and transfer pricing would substantially increase tax revenue.

Third, the government must grow the tax culture and manage the informal sector strategically. The shadow market thrives because most commercial transactions are in cash. The government must deter and eliminate tax avoidance and illicit trade using good intelligence and decisive penalties. As much as possible, the government should encourage citizens and businesses to use traceable noncash instruments, such as bank checks, credit cards, e-payments, and bank transfers. The government must conduct tax education and provide tax compliance support to bring microenterprises and small businesses into the tax net. Tax compliance campaigns can be conducted quarterly using mobile tax units. Simplifying and expanding e-tax declarations and e-tax payments would also reduce tax compliance costs and encourage taxpayers to comply with the tax law.

Fourth, restructuring and reducing the current profit and income tax rates would generate more tax revenue while attracting foreign direct investment. The existing payroll tax structure and a 35% maximum tax rate on salaries and wages are too high for most civil servants and private-sector employees. Consequently, many capable civil servants leave the public sector to enter the private sector, searching for better income opportunities.

Fifth, significant tax revenue waste occurs due to system inefficiencies and corruption. Governments must strengthen staff capabilities in project planning, budgeting, implementation, management, supervision, inspection, monitoring, and evaluation to ensure that *projects are completed on time and within budget and to set quality and safety standards.*

Governments must initiate collaboration and resource sharing among budget holders for win-win outcomes by identifying and exploiting the strategic locus points for joint actions and resource sharing. Eliminating functional redundancies and redesigning, integrating, and streamlining internal processes would save resources. At the same time, this allows the government to deliver better and more services to citizens and achieve its development objectives. Cost-sharing, expanding the resource envelope, and strengthening citizens' participation in their community's economic and social development can be achieved through public-private, government, and community partnerships.

Sixth, build citizens' trust in government by measuring and communicating government organizations' service delivery performance. In this regard, measuring public-sector service delivery aspects that directly and indirectly affect citizens, residents, and businesses is essential. Measuring public-sector performance is complicated and needs a well-thought-out and streamlined measurement system. The performance measurement system must capture citizens', residents', and businesses' perceptions, experiences, satisfaction, and employees' motivations and performance. The allocated budget and the value, quality, and volume of the outputs and services generated and delivered during the budget year must be communicated to citizens, residents, businesses, and civil servants.

Table 2.1: An Optimal Tax Policy Framework

Steps	Actions	Approaches
1	Establish a high-level select committee representing all critical stakeholders to oversee technical committees that conduct analytic research and develop an empirical baseline including the country's worldwide standing concerning human resources development, citizens' living conditions, governance, ease of doing business ranking, infrastructure development, etc. Baselines are established for each socioeconomic sector.	Technical committees will use a combination of methods to collect information, such as administrative data, random sample surveys, focus group discussions, and key informant interviews.
2	Initiate a national conversation on the country's development goals and funding strategies focused on taxation, using a "national tax policy convention" platform. The objective is to develop and articulate the desired development results and outcomes consensually reflecting on the current 10-year homegrown development plan.	The convention organizers would develop an agenda that systematically and constructively guides the conversation. The agenda would incorporate a series of roundtable discussions to gather the collective views of the participants and revise the 10-year homegrown development plan collaboratively with the participants.
3	Consensually determine the programs and projects that would generate the desired development results, outcomes, and the required funding levels.	As in Step 2, this would require a series of roundtable discussions to allow the convention participants to suggest the programs, projects, and activities that must be implemented to achieve the desired results and outcomes.

Steps	Actions	Approaches
4	Let the convention participants suggest how much tax revenue can be collected based on the current tax policy, tax base, and tax compliance rate. Discuss if additional tax revenue would be needed.	After presenting the baseline information on the amount of tax revenue collected, tax effort, and tax compliance, solicit feedback from convention participants through a series of roundtable discussions.
5	Participants are organized into roundtable discussion groups and asked to develop a forward-looking tax policy that is simple to comply with, fair, and equitable to administer.	Drafting an optimal tax policy would require expanding the tax base and stemming corruption and tax evasion. A series of roundtable discussions would be necessary to gather the input of convention participants concerning an optimal tax policy commensurate with the country's ambitious development plan.
6	Through roundtable discussion, the convention participants identify current tax administration weaknesses and how to fix those weaknesses.	The information gathered from the convention would diagnose and improve tax administration weaknesses.
7	Ask and get input from the convention participants on the critical performance evidentiary information they would like the government to collect, publish and communicate to citizens, residents, and businesses every quarter.	Government transparency is critical for success. Thus, transparent budget and performance management systems are established. The performance information is published and communicated to all stakeholders quarterly.

Steps	Actions	Approaches
8	On an annual basis and systematically, obtain citizens', residents', and businesses' feedback about their satisfaction with the government's services and how they think the country is moving forward. They should also note any problems or anomalies they observe that would impede the country's socioeconomic progress.	Using longitudinal random sample surveys, focus group discussions, and key informant interviews, obtain stakeholders' feedback. The feedback is incorporated into the annual performance report with action items to correct failures and reinforce successes.
9	Examine the evidence with stakeholders and adjust programs and projects collaboratively with citizens, residents, and businesses for a better outcome.	Improving would require communities, state actors, and businesses to collaborate. The objective of the government is to sustain these collaborative mechanisms.
10	Repeat Steps 1 to 9 every 5 years.	The national convention is conducted following the installation of the newly elected parliamentarians at all levels of government.

2.5 MEASURING PUBLIC SECTOR PERFORMANCE

As noted above, public-sector performance is a critical issue that affects the quality and quantity of public services delivered and the effective and efficient use of scarce tax resources. When designing a public-sector performance measurement system, the first question would be, what result or outcome are we measuring?[86] Progress toward addressing citizens' needs and the overall goal of improving citizens' living conditions and attaining a middle-income country status by 2030 has to be translated into

---

86   Samuel Taddesse (2017). *Monitoring, Evaluating, and Improving: An Evidence-Based Approach to Achieving Development Results that Matter!* Lulu Publishing: Raleigh, North Carolina. www.samtaddesse.com.

measurable outputs, results, and outcomes. The performance measurement system must force alignment of the government organizations' vision, mission, objectives, and activities to improve citizens' living conditions and attain a middle-income-country status as laid out by the Homegrown Economic Growth Plan.

The second critical task is identifying key performance indicators. In other words, what performance indicators measure progress toward achieving the stated outputs, results, and outcomes? The third task is collecting data against those selected performance indicators. A standardized data collection format and different data collection methods are used, including administrative data, focus group discussions, random sample surveys, and field observations. The data are then compiled and analyzed collaboratively with stakeholders, and the findings are summarized. These findings must enable policy-makers and organizational managers to improve, modify, or continue their activities to achieve their objectives, mission, and vision. The selected performance indicators must produce evidence on resource-saving areas to take allocative and operational efficiency-enhancing measures.

Execution of a performance measurement system must incorporate collaborative review, interpretations of the findings, and adaptive learning with citizens, residents, businesses, and other relevant government organizations. It must facilitate the collective identification of issues addressed by employees and managers to provide effective and quality services to citizens, residents, and businesses. The problems identified could be related to the changing citizens' and businesses' needs and expectations, employee motivations, and the political environment. These problems must be addressed quickly, efficiently, and effectively. The process should also improve communication, collaborative problem-solving, and collective action among citizens, residents, businesses, national and subnational governments, and other actors.

We must establish a performance measurement system that monitors and measures progress toward achieving each organization's mission and vision. It must facilitate the continuous adjustment of strategies, plans, and activities in response to ongoing changes to citizen and employee needs, technological changes, and external shocks. The goal is to develop a performance measurement matrix to guide each organization's decisions and activities to achieve society's overall economic and social development goals.

We need to review, adjust and strengthen the current performance measurement systems. Over a decade ago, the FDRE introduced results-oriented planning, budgeting, and expenditure-tracking system using the balanced scorecard (BSC) approach.[87] All government organizations were required to articulate their strategic objectives and intermediate results, identify and set key performance indicators (KPIs), collect data, and measure their performance against set targets.[88] The selected KPIs were to show the relationship between costs incurred by the organization and the quality and quantity of services delivered to citizens.

Every year, government organizations at the federal and sub-national levels use a process called *gimgemma* (or ግምገማ) to review their performance. For example, each department within a ministry discusses what it has accomplished during the budget year. Then the ministers also discuss their accomplishments at the ministerial level. It is unclear if the process is meaningful in improving service delivery to citizens and stemming corruption and waste. It is also unclear if the BSC results are the basis for these discussions. Anecdotal evidence suggests that these *gimgemma*

---

87 Belete Jember Bobe, Dessalegn Getie Mihret, and Degefe Duressa Obo (2017). "Public-Sector Reforms and Balanced Scorecard Adoption: An Ethiopian Case Study," *Accounting, Auditing & Accountability Journal*, Vol. 30 No. 6, pp. 1230–1256. Emerald Publishing Limited. https://doi.org/10.1108/AAAJ-03-2016-2484.

88 The BSC was introduced by R. S. Kaplan and D. P. Norton. It was discussed in their Harvard Business Review article. See "The Balanced Scorecard: Measures that Drive Performance," *Harvard Business Review* Jan.–Feb. 1992, pp. 71–80.

meetings have blamed certain officials and managers and removed them from their offices for political reasons but not for performance reasons. Politics played a significant role.[89]

The BSC methodology is not sufficiently understood, and decision-makers do not use the BSC results. There are no follow-ups or support to reinforce the practical use of the BSC. The organization's many performance indicators also impede the BSC's practical use.

The BSC is a robust performance measurement tool that incorporates citizens, employees, and other stakeholders' feedback when appropriately used. Drs. Robert S. Kaplan and David P. Norton describe the BSC as a critical foundation in a holistic strategy execution process that, besides helping organizations articulate their strategies in actionable terms, provides a road map for strategy execution for mobilizing and aligning executives and employees and making strategy a continual process.[90] According to Paul Niven,[91] the BSC is a carefully selected set of quantifiable measures derived from an organization's strategic plan. The BSC represents a tool for leaders to communicate the performance of their organization's mission and strategic objectives to employees and citizens. The BSC is designed to measure an organization's performance in four areas:

1. **Financial Perspective:** The financial perspective uses traditional accounting measures to evaluate the organization's effective and efficient use of its budget to achieve stated results and outcomes.

---

89   Indeed, as the former prime minister of Ethiopia Meles Zenawi uttered many years ago, "the government places a great deal of weight on loyalty than on competence."

90   Robert S. Kaplan and David P. Norton (1992). "The Balanced Scorecard: Measures hat Drive Performance," *Harvard Business Review,* Jan.–Feb. pp. 71–80.

91   Paul R. Niven (2006). *Balanced Scorecard Step-By-Step: Maximizing Performance and Maintaining Results,* Second Edition, John Wiley & Sons, Inc.: Hoboken, New Jersey.

2. **Citizen Perspective:** The citizen perspective measures citizens' satisfaction with the organization's public goods or public sector services.

3. **Internal Business Processes:** This measures the performance of the realigned business processes and the additional changes needed to enhance organizational performance.

4. **Innovation and Learning:** This relates to the organization's ability to learn, adapt, and mobilize its employees to innovate means for achieving results and outcomes stated in its strategic plan.

By clarifying the organization's strategy and facilitating its communication, the BSC serves as a "pull rope" to efficiently align the organization with the defined strategic goals and actions. A meticulously designed BSC has a limited number of critical performance indicators, reduces information overload, and leads managers to prioritize and take steps on actionable issues more quickly. Finally, long-term planning, regular review and adjustment, and inclusion of future-oriented measures are urged. The top management team must be heavily involved in making the BSC work. After setting the strategy and creating a scorecard, the BSC's four perspectives must be carefully examined and understood. The evaluation findings and recommendations must guide top management decisions.

To some extent, the BSC has served as a valuable tool for sorting out organizations' business purposes and expected outcomes. However, critics of the BSC have indicated that the BSC has severe deficiencies in the knowledge-networked innovation economy of the twenty-first century.[92] The Ethiopian experiment shows that there is much confusion about performance measurement. Lip service is paid to the BSC development and its use. Still, decisions continue to be made by the managers' experience, gut feeling, and the need for self-preservation by refusing to admit failure.

---

92 Sven C. Voelpel, Marius Leibold, Robert A. Eckoff, and Thomas H. Davenport (2005). The Tyranny of the Balanced Scorecard in the Innovation Economy. 4th International Critical Management Studies Conference, Intellectual Capital Stream, Cambridge University, United Kingdom, July 4-6, 2005.

Indeed, there are numerous reasons for managers not to seek to base their policies and decisions on evidentiary information. They include the following:

- **Lack of understanding of what makes for evidence:** Decision-makers often do not have a clear idea of what comprises "evidence." Moreover, when making a decision, it is difficult to find relevant, comprehensive, accurate, credible, robust, timely, and useable evidence for implementation.[93] It is also tricky for a decision-maker to comprehend and connect the dots to make a concrete, evidence-based decision.
- **Competing influences and resistance to change:** The political environment, cultural and social environment, decision-makers' opinions and experiences, available resources, time constraints, and technical capacity all play roles in resisting evidence for making decisions.[94] There is also a cultural resistance to change, and decisions are based on a historical perspective. Often there is a lack of confidence in making changes based on research evidence.
- **Inadequate interaction between researchers and decision-makers:** There is a gulf between research institutions and decision-makers, leading to researchers' generation of evidence that does not meet the latter's needs.[95] Local, contextual research evidence and decent quality, reliable data are seldom available for decision-makers. Many high-level decision-makers perceive

---

93   Iqbal Dhaliwal and Caitlin Tulloch (2012). "From Research to Policy: Using Evidence from Impact Evaluations to Inform Development Policy," *Journal of Development Effectiveness*, Volume 4 (4).

94   Sophie Sutcliffe and Julius Court (2005). Evidence Based Policymaking. What Is It? How Does It Work? What Relevance for Developing Countries? Overseas Development Institute, November 2005

95   Sarah Bowen, Tannis Erickson, Patricia J. Martens, and Susan Crockett (2009). "More Than 'Using Research': The Real Challenges in Promoting Evidence-Informed Decision-Making," *Healthcare Policy*, Volume 4 (3).

research evidence produced by academicians as lacking practical application, leading to the underutilization of the evidence.[96]

- **Deficiencies in evidence dissemination strategy:** For evidence to be understood by decision-makers, it must be in the local language; have abstracts, summaries, and graphics; and clearly articulate the main findings and methodology.[97] Stakeholders must review and interpret the research/study findings where possible collaboratively. Lack of timely availability in layman's language for all to understand the evidence and its implications and poor dissemination leads to the evidence not reaching the target audiences, including decision-makers.

- **The scarcity of infrastructure and skilled human resources:** Poor infrastructure and institutional facilities, such as a lack of computers, internet, reliable electricity, research libraries, and formal organizational requirements to assess evidence, keep decision-makers from utilizing the available evidence. There is a shortage of technical staff in most local government offices to package the evidence in a usable format. For those present, researching for evidence is not a part of their job and is too time-consuming.[98] Most importantly, policy-makers and intermediaries lack the knowledge and skill to identify, synthesize, analyze, and utilize evidence for informed decision-making.

The FDRE introduced the BSC and the concepts of managing for results using performance indicators and monitoring and collecting data and evaluation. It failed, however, to change public-sector performance.

---

96 UNCTAD Virtual Institute (2006). Research-Based Policy Making: Bridging the Gap Between Researchers and Policy Makers: Recommendations for Researchers and Policy Makers Arising From the Joint UNCTAD-WTO-ITC Workshop on Trade Policy Analysis. Geneva, September 11–15, 2006.

97 UNICEF (2004). Bridging the Gap: The Role of Monitoring and Evaluation in Evidence-Based Policy Making.

98 Zahiruddin Quazi Syed, Abhay M. Gaidhane, and Sanjay Zodpey (2010). "Linking Research Evidence to Health Policy and Practice," *Journal of Public Administration and Policy Research* Vol. 2 (5).

The performance measurement data gathered by most organizations at both the federal and subnational levels are poorly organized and do not facilitate assessment and understanding or enable continuous learning in which evaluation findings are used to make ongoing improvements to programs and activities toward the achievement of the organization's mission and vision.

Also, the BSC used by government organizations did not gather data for assessing financial health, citizen satisfaction, quality of services delivered, or efforts to learn and improve. Consequently, the public sector failed to improve the quality and quantity of services delivered to citizens, residents, and businesses. Furthermore, the performance measurement system neglected to address the effects on employee morale, job satisfaction, and motivation and opened the government system to fraud and corruption.

As noted above, an effective performance management system requires a well-articulated results and outcomes framework and measurable key performance indicators. It also requires continuous monitoring, data collection, collaborative evaluation, learning, and timely feedback to decision-makers and stakeholders.

Basing management and policy decisions on the performance measurement system's findings and recommendations would ensure the possibility of achieving the stated results and outcomes. A robust performance management system would require strong information technology that pulls together and compiles data from different sources. The performance measurement system should also systematically incorporate employees' and citizens'/customers' feedback. It also requires a dedicated office that manages the data collection and collaboratively analyzes and interprets the data with key stakeholders to identify the key findings and recommendations.

An effective performance management system is built on a results chain cascading from an organization's vision to its strategies and activities. The planning and performance measurement framework must break down the organization into logical and interrelated business process chains. The logical framework, in general, follows the logic laid out below.

- Achieving an organization's vision is a function of achieving its mission.
- Achieving the organization's mission is a function of achieving the organization's objectives.
- Achieving the organization's objectives is a function of the strategy for achieving the stated goals and outcomes.
- Achieving the stated goals and outcomes is a function of attaining the outputs of the initiatives and actions implemented.

Performance measurement and tracking systems for management decision-making are, in general, objective, straightforward, quantifiable, outputs/results-oriented, and include easily understood qualitative and quantitative information.[99] The time and effort expended on the balanced scorecard approach for building a performance measurement system and culture was a waste for many reasons, including the following:

- The data collected and reported by directorates and divisions do not facilitate informed management decision-making. The data collected have little practical information on how well the organization performs, the status of employee morale or customer concerns, or service delivery quality. The data gathered does not assess the status of initiatives implemented to achieve the organization's objectives, mission, and vision.
- The data and information generated are not balanced to provide an accurate picture of the organization's overall finances and budget, service delivery quality and quantity, customer satisfaction, employee motivation, and progress on the organization's initiatives.

---

99 Samuel Taddesse (2017). *Monitoring, Evaluating, and Improving: An Evidence-Based Approach to Achieving Development Results that Matter!* Lulu Publishing: Raleigh, North Carolina. www.samtaddesse.com.

- Performance indicators are too numerous to provide meaningful information for senior management decision-making. Most of the performance measures are activity-focused. There are very few organizational-level performance measures to guide management decision-making.
- The performance data generated is not timely to provide a solid picture of the organization's progress toward achieving its outputs, intermediate results, and objectives.

The performance systems must generate timely and credible information for building shared beliefs, values, attitudes, and behaviors. It should provide sufficient information to decision-makers to catapult Ethiopia to middle-income country status by 2030 and eliminate abject poverty. They must support the organizational transformation processes to achieve the organization's mission and vision effectively and efficiently. Organizations must be agile and adaptive to changing conditions with better service delivery and performance in mind. Robust performance measures would provide organizations with the ability to

- use streamlined multi-dimensional sources of information to make decisions on improving, modifying, or continuing initiatives or services,
- facilitate efficiency and eliminate duplication of effort,
- proactively identify issues and propose solutions to ensure effective service delivery to citizens and customers,
- improve communication and collaboration among the main stakeholders and citizens,
- capture taxpayers' and citizens' satisfaction with services received, and
- increase levels of employee effectiveness and job satisfaction.

2.6 OTHER FUNDING SOURCES

There are limits on tax revenue and service fee generation for funding and achieving society's prosperity goals. While local communities have been willing to contribute to local economic development activities, there are limits to how much they are ready to fork out. The community contributions are often in addition to the taxes they pay under the tax law and can be regarded as double taxation.

One revenue source for funding development activities would be for the government to sell interest-bearing notes and bonds to citizens, backed by the government's good name and credit. These notes and bonds with different maturity dates would serve as investment and saving instruments for citizens, residents, and businesses. In the United States, at the start of World War I, the government sold treasury notes and bonds to citizens to fund the war effort. Since then, these Treasury notes and bonds have been used as low-risk saving instruments.

The GOE has effectively raised funds for the construction of the Renaissance Dam by selling interesting-bearing bonds to citizens and business enterprises. "It is my dam bond" is a clever slogan for raising funds for the dam's construction. It links citizens' patriotism and citizenship responsibilities to the dam's construction.

2.7 CONCLUSIONS

Taxes pay for the public goods and services a country's people need. Taxes enable a government to deliver on its primary responsibility of improving the quality of life of its citizens. Tax policies must be developed collaboratively with citizens, residents, businesses, and other stakeholders. They must address the development objectives of the country. Through a national prosperity convention, the government must collaboratively develop and articulate the country's economic development path with citizens, residents, businesses, academia, and other stakeholders. It should set strategies, programs, and objectives that must be implemented to generate prosperity for all. Tax policy and reform must be based on this consensus and not through technical assistance provisioned by multilateral and bilateral donors. Many researchers have noted that homemade tax systems generate more revenue and a high level of voluntary tax compliance.[100] [101]

All government organizations must do more with less to optimize tax revenue use. To this end, we must redesign government management systems. At the same time, we must change the existing "doing business" policies and guidelines.

The government can address critical issues to achieve its overall objectives, mission, and vision by breaking down organizational silos and collaboratively developing and implementing plans, budgets, and activities. This would optimize tax revenue use, eliminate corruption, and reduce waste. Infrastructure contracting, inspection, and approval must be transformed to eliminate favoritism and corruption, substandard materials, and absolute construction methods.

All other things equal, all governmental institutions must be transformed and reorientated to fulfill the 10-year homegrown development goal of catapulting Ethiopia into a middle-income country. We must produce and use quality homegrown products instead of wasting resources on imports of ordinary commodities. This would require reorganizing, streamlining, and changing how organizations function and deliver services. It would also require changing the mindsets of citizens, business leaders, political leaders, and government officials. The transformation aims to provide high-quality services, enhance and strengthen the enabling conditions for a better quality of life, and build trust and collaborative actions among the government, the business community, and civil society.

---

100 Victor Lido, Aaron Schneider, and Mick Moore (2004). Governance, Taxes and Tax Reform in Latin America, IDS Working Paper 221, March 2004.

101 Miranda Stewart (2002). Global Trajectories of Tax Reform: Mapping Tax Reform in Developing and Transition Countries. Available atSSRN: https://ssrn.com/abstract=319200 or http://dx.doi.org/10.2139/ssrn.319200.

A robust performance measurement system must be established to generate comprehensive information and evidence on how government programs are progressing and how tax revenues are utilized. The performance measurement system must provide evidence-based information to eliminate ineffective and wasteful programs/activities and strengthen and expand promising ones.

Furthermore, the government must provide citizens and communities with guidance and assistance in improving their productivity and applying their creative ideas to generate income opportunities for themselves and others. One approach is to institute the Prosperity Corps program. Another is establishing R&I hubs strategically placed in different towns and cities accessible to most citizens.

Citizens must take the lead and be responsible for the development of their communities. Community members must be involved in government decision-making and service provisioning processes. There is also a need to inject new and innovative ideas and approaches for catalyzing and enhancing citizens' productivity and incomes. This would be the role of the Prosperity Corps program.

Finally, it is suggested that the government look to nontax revenue sources, having exhausted all avenues for efficient and effective collection and use of tax revenues. Nontax revenue sources include issuing treasury notes and bonds that citizens can buy and use as income-saving instruments. These notes and bonds would provide more competitive interest income than interest-earning instruments offered by banks or the non–interest-bearing savings such as *Iqubb*.[102]

---

102 *Iqubb* is an Ethiopia term used to describe a special saving and borrowing system. Citizens and businesses form small groups whereby each weekend, each member contributes a specified amount. The money gathered from the group is given to a member selected by a lottery system. The process continues until all the members have received a collection. The individual recipients use the money received for building a house, opening a business, or expanding a business.

CHAPTER 3
WHO HAS THE MANDATE FOR TAX AND FISCAL POLICIES?

Natural-resource–poor nations rely heavily on tax revenues to fund their social and economic development programs. Other sources of government revenue include service fees collected from citizens, residents, and businesses; government facilities' rental and land lease fees; surpluses of state-owned enterprises (SOEs); and domestic borrowing. However, government borrowing from domestic financial intermediaries can crowd out the private sector and retard private investment and business expansion. In Ethiopia, the amount of service and other fees collected from citizens, businesses, and residents and surpluses of SOEs are insignificant relative to the needs of the government. Also, most SOEs are operated inefficiently and thus run up too much cost and have little profit to turnover to the government. For these reasons, the government depends on tax revenues collected from citizens, residents, and businesses.[1]

---

1   Wilson Prichard (2010). Taxation and State Building: Towards a Governance Focused Tax Reform Agenda. IDS Working Paper 341, Institute of Development Studies, Brighton, UK.

3.1 TAXATION IS CONSTITUTIONAL

A country's constitution typically identifies who shall draft the tax policy and implement the tax law. The tax law outlines what incomes and property are taxed and not taxed. It also outlines the tax collection procedures.

In Ethiopia, the federal government and the regional states' taxation powers are enshrined in the Federal Democratic Republic of Ethiopia Constitution, Proclamation No. 1/1995.[2] Article 51.10 of the Constitution states that the federal government *"shall levy taxes and collect duties on revenue sources reserved to the Federal Government."* Likewise, Article 52.2e says that the regional states have the power *"to levy and collect taxes and duties on revenue sources reserved to the States."* Article 55.11 states that the House of People's Representatives (HOPR) *"shall levy taxes and duties on revenue sources reserved to the Federal Government."*

The taxation powers of the federal government and the regional states, as enshrined in Articles 96 and 97 of the Constitution, are summarized in Boxes 3.1 and 3.2 below. Article 98 relates to the federal government and the regional states' concurrent taxation powers. Finally, Article 99 throws light on the undesignated power of taxation. It states, *"The House of the Federation (HOF) and the House of Peoples' Representatives shall, in a joint session, determine by a two-thirds majority vote on the exercise of powers of taxation which have not been specifically provided for in the Constitution."*

Box 3.1: Taxation Power of the Federal Government—Article 96

1. The Federal Government shall levy and collect custom duties, taxes, and other charges on imports and exports.
2. It shall levy and collect income tax on employees of the Federal Government and international organizations.

---

2   Proclamation No. 1/1995: A Proclamation to pronounce the coming into effect of the Constitution of the Federal Democratic Republic of Ethiopia, August 21, 1995.

3. It shall levy and collect income, profit, sales, and excise taxes on enterprises owned by the Federal Government.
4. It shall tax the income and winnings of national lotteries and other games of chance.
5. It shall levy and collect taxes on the income of air, rail, and sea transport services
6. It shall levy and collect taxes on income of houses and properties owned by the Federal Government; it shall fix rents
7. It shall determine and collect fees and charges relating to licenses issued and services rendered by organs of the Federal Government.
8. It shall levy and collect taxes on monopolies.
9. It shall levy and collect Federal stamp duties.

Box 3.2: Taxation Powers of Regional States—Article 97

1. States shall levy and collect income taxes on employees of the State and of private enterprises.
2. States shall determine and collect fees for land usufructuary rights.
3. States shall levy and collect taxes on the incomes of private farmers and farmers incorporated in cooperative associations.
4. States shall levy and collect profit and sales taxes on individual traders conducting a business within their territory.
5. States shall levy and collect taxes on income from transport services rendered on waters within their territory.
6. They shall levy and collect taxes on income derived from private houses and other properties within the State. They shall collect rent on houses and other properties they own.
7. States shall levy and collect profit, sales, excise, and personal income taxes on the income of enterprises owned by the States.
8. Consistent with the provisions sub-Article 3 of Article 98, States shall levy and collect taxes on income derived from mining operations and royalties and land rentals on such operations.
9. They shall determine and collect fees and charges relating to licenses issued and services rendered by State organs.
10. They shall fix and collect royalty for use of forest resources.

Regarding the apportionment of tax revenues between the federal government and the regional states, Article 62.7 states that the House of Federation *"shall determine the division of revenues derived from joint Federal and State tax sources and the subsidies that the Federal Government may provide to the States."* Box 3.3 summarizes how the Federal House of Federation determines the subsidies and grants to the regional states.

Box 3.3: Allocation of Subsidies to the Regional States by the HOF

The regional states receive block grants (Article 94) from the federal government based on their **relative fiscal capacity** to fulfill their constitutional responsibilities. For this purpose, the Federal House of Federation has developed an allocation formula that considers the regional states' relative revenue-raising potential and expenditure needs. The following revenue sources determine the relative revenue-raising potential of a regional state:

- Taxes from wages and salaries of both civil servants and employees of private organizations
- Agricultural income tax based on the estimate of landholding size and crop and livestock yield
- Land lease fees
- Rural land use fee
- Business profit tax
- Turnover tax
- Value-added tax (VAT)
- Service fees, including medical supplies (drugs and other medical supplies) and medical diagnosis and treatment fees
- Trade licensing fees

These sources cover about 80% or more of regional revenues, with some variations across regions. A regional state's **expenditure needs** are estimated as expenditures on the following:

- General administration and general expenditures (i.e., wages and salaries of regional administrative organs, public order, and security and justice)
- Primary and secondary education, including technical and vocational education and training (TVET)
- Public health

- Agriculture and natural resources development and management
- Clean water supply
- Rural road construction and maintenance
- Micro and small-scale enterprise development
- Work and urban development

The difference between the **expenditure needs** and the **revenue potential** determines the **fiscal gap** on which the federal grant allocation formula is based. The revenue potential of a regional state is its ability to raise revenue within its jurisdiction to pay for a standardized basket of public goods and services.

Expenditure needs for administration and general expenditures are adjusted for population size; the number of students, teachers, nurses, health extension works, and all other civil servants within the regional state; extreme weather conditions; remoteness that necessitates refrigeration, ventilation, etc.; and hardship allowances. The formula is also adjusted for

- expenditure needs for nationality zones and regional-level federation of nations and nationalities to address ethnic diversities in SNNP, Amhara, and Gambella, and
- expenditure needs for security and defense for regions that have international borders such as Tigray, Somali, and Afar

Source: FDRE House of Federation (2017). The Federal General-Purpose Grant Distribution Formula 2017/18–2019/20, Addis Ababa, Ethiopia, June 2017.

3.2 WHO IS MANDATED TO FORMULATE AND UPDATE THE TAX POLICY?

The Ethiopian Ministry of Finance and Economic Cooperation (MOFEC) is responsible for drafting the federal tax policy at the national level. MOFEC then presents the draft tax policy for discussion and feedback to the Council of Ministers (COM), chaired by the prime minister. The COM discusses the draft tax policy and provides comments, changes, and feedback to MOFEC. Based on input from the COM, MOFEC redrafts the tax policy. Once satisfied with the draft tax policy, the COM, through the prime minister's office (PMO), submits the draft tax policy to Parliament for discussion, correction, and ratification.[3] Once Parliament passes the tax policy, it is published in the Negarite Gazeta and becomes law.

Each regional state's Economic and Development Bureau follows similar processes to draft the regional state's tax policy. The draft tax policy is presented to the regional state's Parliament for ratification. Upon ratification by Parliament, the tax policy is published and becomes law.

At the federal level, the Ministry of Revenue (MOR) and the Ethiopian Customs Commission (ECC) enforce the tax laws and collect taxes and duties from citizens, residents, and businesses. Similarly, the regional state revenue bureau (RSRB) enforces the law at the regional state level. It collects the taxes due to the sub-national government. In some instances, it also collects taxes due to the federal government. Tax revenues and fees collected by sub-national governments may include the following:

- Payroll taxes
- Land lease/land use fees
- Turnover tax and VAT from businesses registered with the regional government
- Service fees, including fees for medical treatment and medical supplies, and drugs collected from citizens
- Waste disposal fees
- Trade licensing fees
- Sports fees
- Housing rental fees on houses owned by the government

---

3   In the United States, before a tax policy is ratified, Congress invites comments and inputs from scholars, civil society, the business community, and citizens. Scholars discuss the economic and social implications of the tax code. Business leaders and special interest groups argue to lower the tax burden on them. Civil society groups argue to preserve tax expenditures for social protection and healthcare. Ethiopia has a rubber stamp Parliament, and most of the delegates have low-level education and lack tax awareness.

- Housing rental taxes on homes rented by private individuals to businesses and individuals
- Business premises and warehouse rental income taxes
- Agricultural income tax

3.3 THE TAX POLICY DEVELOPMENT PROCESS

As indicated in Chapter 2, drafting a sound tax policy involves several steps. First, the nation's economic and social development plans and strategies are clearly articulated based on a series of constructive dialogues with citizens, residents, and businesses. Second, the programs and activities to be implemented are identified and appraised to determine their cost for budgeting purposes. Third, several analytical studies are conducted on the impact of taxation on the government's primary development objectives and citizens' standard of living. Fourth, the final draft tax policy must incorporate the recommendations from the analytic studies of MOFEC and the National Tax Convention Forum discussed in Chapter 2.

Tax policy directorates (TPDs) or tax policy units (TPUs) across different countries play a critical role in quantitatively analyzing and conducting an open debate on proposed tax policy changes. TPDs/TPUs (hereafter referred to as TPDs) ensure that all stakeholders in the round-table discussion have access to the best available data, facts, and independent-evidence–based analysis, including the impact of tax reforms on revenue levels, income distribution, and the nation's economic and social development goals.[4] In other words, TPDs are responsible for developing and proposing tax policies and reviewing and analyzing existing tax policy effects.[5] In many countries, TPDs provide oversight

---

4   IMF How to Notes No. 7 (2017). Fiscal Policy: How to Establish a Tax Policy Unit, Fiscal Affairs Department, International Monetary Fund, October 2017.
5   David Phillips (2018). Tax Policy Costings: Refining Approaches and Incorporating Behaviors. Institute of Fiscal Studies, London, March 23, 2018.

over the tax system's integrity. They also play a critical role in informing stakeholders along the path toward a coherent, manageable, fair, and efficient tax policy design.[6] As noted by the IMF, the responsibilities of TPDs may include

- initiating and formulating tax policies in close collaboration with the macroeconomic directorate, fiscal policy directorate (FPD), and the National Planning Commission to achieve the government's economic and social policy goals and objectives,
- evaluating the tax policy's impact on taxpayers' ability to pay and tax compliance, and the overall economic development of the country and inform and advise decision-makers,
- making annual and medium-term recurrent revenue forecasts and revenue performance analyses and communicating the results and their implications to decision-makers,
- gathering data and assessing the evidence, and making recommendations on new ways of widening the tax base rather than raising tax rates,
- working with the MOR's legal departments to simplify the language and application of the tax legislation to avoid misunderstandings and confusion among tax administrators and taxpayers alike, and
- handling negotiations of double taxation agreements, investment incentives, and transfer pricing issues.

Following the implementation of the tax policy, a technical working group chaired by the State Minister of Fiscal Policy and Public Finance meets regularly to review tax-related issues and concerns that need addressing. These issues are referred to the TPD for further analysis and recommendation. The TPD reports to the State Minister of Fiscal Policy and Public Finance. The TPD is responsible for drafting tax policies, conducting tax impact studies, and analyzing tax expenditures.

---

6   IMF How to Notes No. 7 (2017). Fiscal Policy: How to Establish a Tax Policy Unit, Fiscal Affairs Department, International Monetary Fund, October 2017.

3.4 ORGANIZATIONAL STRUCTURE OF TPDS

TPDs commission various studies, including background papers, policy memoranda, and analytical reports on the existing tax laws' economic and social effects, and develop additional studies on required domestic and international tax policy changes. TPDs also conduct tax expenditure analysis to determine the level of tax revenue foregone. This would include tax revenue allocated for social protection, notable exclusions from taxable incomes, tax exemptions, deductions from gross income or notable tax credits, preferential tax rates, tax holidays, deferral of tax liability, and other tax incentives.[7] These provisions reduce the government's tax revenue intake.

TPDs maintain and regularly use sizeable statistical data sets to analyze alternative tax proposals' economic, distributional, and revenue effects.[8] As noted in Chapter 2, TPDs must work with the technical committees appointed by the National Tax Policy Convention organizers and facilitate the process. The constructive dialogue and conversation among taxpayers, policymakers, civil society, and other relevant stakeholders lead to a sound tax policy formulation while raising tax culture and voluntary tax compliance.

TPDs conduct sample opinion surveys of citizens, taxpayers, and other stakeholders. They must also run a series of round-table discussions with citizens, taxpayers, and other stakeholders on specific tax-policy issues. The information gathered through sample opinion surveys and round-table discussions is analyzed to filter out the perceptions and recommendations of survey respondents and round-table discussants. In this regard, TPDs have many responsibilities to ensure that the most relevant pieces of evidence and recommendations are captured.

---

7   Christopher Heady and Mario Mansoiur (2019). Tax Expenditure Reporting and Its Use in Fiscal Management: A Guide for Developing Economies, How to Note 19/01. Fiscal Affairs Department, the International Monetary Fund.

8   US Department of The Treasury, Office of Tax Analysis.

To fulfill their responsibilities effectively and efficiently, TPDs must be organized logically, with different divisions that work in unison. Figure 3.1 illustrates a typical organizational structure for a well-functioning and mature TPD.

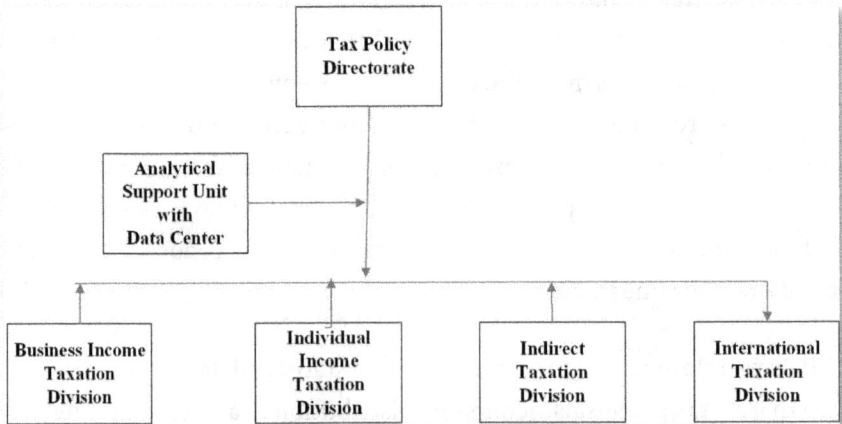

Figure 3.1: Organizational Structure of a Well-Functioning TPD

For example, the **Business Income Taxation Division** would analyze and propose tax legislation that enables increased investment and business expansion while increasing voluntary tax compliance. The division also conducts economic analyses and research on tax provisions affecting corporations, partnerships, other unincorporated enterprises, and financial institutions. It also analyzes the impact of taxes on products, energy, income, consumption, environmental pollution, capital income, and business excise taxes.[9] The specific tasks performed by the division include

- drafting legislation in the areas of corporate taxes,
- preparing and disseminating responses, instructions, opinions, and answers to written inquiries about the practical implementation of the corporate tax legislation and related tax holidays and investment tax incentives,
- analyzing and proposing tax measures and instruments to combat corporate tax evasion, tax avoidance, and corruption,

---

9   Ibid.

- coordinating and participating in the development of standard forms of corporate tax registration, tax declarations, and other documents to be used by corporate taxpayers, and
- participating in the alignment of drafts of international agreements on corporate income tax issues, including transfer pricing between related companies and contraband and illicit trade.

The **Individual Income Taxation Division** is responsible for analyzing the impact of existing and proposed individual income tax provisions on individual taxpayers' economic well-being and the tax burden distribution. Policy analytics would include studying the structure of tax rates, savings incentives, the tax treatment of pensions and health insurance, education incentives, and income tax compliance. This division is also responsible for assessing and developing payroll tax policies and tying them to the cost of living.

The **Indirect Taxes Division** is responsible for

- preparing draft tax legislation on sales taxes, VAT, excise duties, dividend income, insurance premium tax,
- preparing instructions, opinions, and answers to written inquiries about the practical implementation of the sales tax, VAT, excise duties, dividend income, and insurance premium tax legislation,
- gathering, consolidating, and analyzing the findings, opinions, and concerns of other directorates within the MOFEC, other line ministries, and agencies on the draft sales tax, VAT, and excise duties legislative acts,[10]
- analyzing and proposing tax remedies and other tools to combat sales tax, VAT and excise duty fraud, and evasion, and
- examining excise tax effects on the production, sale, and consumption of harmful products and services.

---

10 Republic of Bulgaria, Ministry of Finance https://www.minfin.bg/en/611

The **International Taxation Division** is responsible for developing analyses on international taxation issues. The division investigates and researches the taxation of income earned outside the country by citizens, residents, domestic corporations, foreign corporations, and non-residents. It also examines transfer pricing issues and their effect on tax compliance and revenue. The division also engages in international tax treaty negotiations with the legal directorate.

Some TPDs also have an **Analytical Support Unit** responsible for collecting data and producing analytical products supporting the work of the different divisions within the TPD. The analytical work of the unit may include

- revenue forecasts by establishing a baseline and tracking tax receipts over a given budget cycle,
- tax expenditure analysis to estimate the revenue forgone due to specific tax code provisions such as exclusions, deductions, tax credits, deferrals, tax holidays, and preferential tax rates,
- distributional analysis and determining the implications for income distribution among households, individuals, and businesses and the tax burden among groups of taxpayers and business sectors,
- economic impact analysis and evaluating the macroeconomic impact of tax-policy changes on the labor market, investment, aggregate inflation, and economic growth,
- execution of sample opinion surveys on specific topics, analyzing and reporting the findings to the appropriate divisions and decision-makers, and
- estimates of effective tax rates by sector and taxpayer categories to shed light on the distribution of the tax burden and tax fairness.

Properly structured and staffed TPD plays critical roles within the tax realm. It supports MOFEC in attaining its strategic goal of improving tax legislation and effectively analyzing and forecasting tax revenues. In all their analytical work, TPDs are expected to observe the principles of legality, transparency, objectivity, and replicability. TPDs require a diverse, competent, well-trained, and motivated professional workforce to execute their mandate and responsibilities. Among other professionals, they need a cadre of

- macroeconomists with econometrics and modeling expertise,
- microeconomists with expertise in value chain and supply chain analysis,
- statisticians capable of designing quantitative and qualitative surveys and research,
- experienced tax accountants,
- business income tax experts,
- individual income tax experts,
- international trade taxation experts, and
- consumption tax experts.

3.5 THE FISCAL POLICY DIRECTORATE (FPD)

TPDs work closely with their FPD counterparts during tax policy development. The FPD's primary task, in collaboration with line ministries and other government agencies, is to develop the **government's budget and spending plan.** As noted in Chapter 2, the government's business is *"laying the foundations for improved citizens' quality of life."* Governments influence economic growth and people's living conditions by changing the extent and composition of public spending and the degree of public debt and form of borrowing. To this end, FPDs make budgeting and spending recommendations that stimulate economic growth and create and strengthen the enabling environment to improve citizens' living conditions. FPDs, in close collaboration with the National Planning Commission, study and identify the areas of government investment and the amount to be invested within the government's technical, absorption, and resource capacity.

As noted above, government spending on physical and technological infrastructures can boost private-sector investment, create jobs and income opportunities, and reduce poverty. As those employed spend money on food, healthcare, clothing, housing, and other items, existing businesses thrive, and new business enterprises are created. The economy grows with the circular flow of money, and communities thrive and prosper.

The Keynesian fundamental equation of national income accounting measures a country's output and wealth. The **gross domestic product** (GDP) illustrates that the government's strategic investment and spending can increase wealth directly and indirectly. And as we learned in Macroeconomics 101, government spending and investments profoundly affect GDP or the wealth of a nation. The following equation illustrates how government spending and investments increase the wealth of a country.

$$GDP = C + I + G + NX,$$

where:

C = total private consumption
I   = total private investment
G = purchases of goods and services and investments
      of the government
NX = net exports, i.e., exports minus imports

All other things equal, the equation shows that increases in government spending and investment (G) increase GDP directly. Holding C, I, and NX constant, as G goes up, so does GDP. Government spending and investment indirectly increase C and I through employment creation and government procurement of goods and services from the private sector. It also facilitates business expansions by investing in critical infrastructures such as road networks, large-scale water irrigation schemes, electric power generation and distribution, telecommunication and information technology infrastructure, and research and development (R&D). All other things equal, as G goes up, I goes up, and the private sector creates new jobs.

Increased employment resulting from government investment or private-sector expansion means increased household income and consumption. As people get employed, they consume more goods and services; consequently, C increases. Salaries and wages are spent on food, clothing, shelter, education, healthcare, and other consumer goods and services, injecting monetary resources into the economy and directly influencing business investment, expansion, and GDP growth.

Increased government investment may necessitate purchasing goods and services from local businesses. Such spending would increase private companies' incomes. If government spending and investment continue sustainably, it will lead to a sustained increase in private-sector investment. The result would be a growing GDP year-over-year as prosperity holds on.

The fiscal policy of a country guides government spending and investment. In Ethiopia, fiscal policy development is vested with the MOFEC FPD.

As noted above, the FPD's functions include developing the government's overall budget. The FPD also develops budgets for these activities in collaboration with the responsible ministries and agencies. The budget classifies expected expenditures for the budget year. The budget is broken down by service and activity types, including spending on delivering essential public goods and services like public safety; road networks; primary, secondary, and tertiary education; public health; and social protection. The government may also engage in major agricultural and industrial activities.

The FPD maintains and updates the government budget by sector (i.e., education, health, agriculture, water/sanitation, justice, security and safety, defense, and so on) and tracks and maintains government expenditure by sector and project. The FPD also tracks the budget allocated to SOEs.

A related function of the FPD is identifying the funding sources for government programs—tax revenue, internal and external borrowing, and foreign aid—and advising the government on the risks of rising external debt and falling foreign assistance. The FPD estimates and advises the government on the funding gaps or surpluses. All other things being equal, the FPD's advice to the government may increase tax rates to raise more tax revenue. Or it may lead the government to borrow more internally or externally or scale back its spending and investment plans.

Another critical function of the FPD is monitoring and evaluating budget holders' performance and providing guidance. It examines the rate of budget drawdown and the progress made on the activities funded. The result informs whether budget holders are cost-efficiently achieving their stated objectives and goals.

One of the questions examined is, "Are the budget holders spending well in terms of effectiveness and efficiency, or is there budget waste?" The budget review is usually conducted biannually, and the budget holders are advised on the findings, conclusions, and recommendations. It is also possible that some budget holders have surpluses while others have budget deficits. In these cases, the FPD recommends that decision-makers shift the surplus resources from one budget holder to another to ensure that the government achieves its goals.

Suppose an FPD suspects resource wastages and inefficiencies due to lack of capacity, corruption, or other reasons. In that case, they may ask the Office of the Federal Auditor General (OFAG) to audit targeted budget holders. The FDP's Public Finance Management Division ensures that budget holders utilize appropriate procurement procedures and follow and maintains proper books of accounts and cash management systems. Officially approved receipts and vouchers must support all purchases and cash disbursements.

A well-functioning FPD can play a critical role in facilitating cooperation among stakeholders by providing essential budget data and objective analysis of potential outcomes of different fiscal policy options.[1] In addition, FPDs perform various beneficial tasks, including the following:[2]

- *Fostering budget discipline:* The FPD adds discipline to the budget process by its very existence. The ability to present preliminary information on the implications of current receipts and spending experience during the budget discussions imposes discipline on the entire process. The FPD's data and analysis are essential to fiscal policy planning.
- *Facilitate an informed policy dialogue:* The FPD pulls together information from budgeting, tax-policy–making, and tax revenue collection systems and analyzes how the budget systems function.
- *Ongoing monitoring and evaluation of government programs:* The FPD can flag problems early by continuously monitoring tax collections and expenditure flows. The constant tracking of events may provide policymakers with vital information on turning points in the economy, altered private consumption patterns, inadequacies of the tax system, or administrative delays in recording tax revenue collections.
- *Developing benchmarks for assessing policy and subsequent events:* Detailed forecasts and other information produced by the FPD provide standard measurement rules for controlling government spending. Significant deviations from the totals provided by the FPD become red flags indicating the possible need for remedial actions.

---

1   Jorge Martinez-Vazquez and Eunice Heredia-Ortz (2009). Designing and Establishing Fiscal Policy Analysis Units: A Practical Guide. Paper produced for USID under the Fiscal Reform and Economic Governance Task Order GEG-I-00-04-00001-00 Task Order No. 06, USAID.

2   Howard Nester (1992). Training in Fiscal Policy Analysis and Fiscal Models. Technical Memorandum No. 24. Guatemala Fiscal Administration Project. Atlanta: Georgia State University, College of Business Administration, Policy Research Center, Washington, D.C.: KPMG Peat Marwick Policy Economics Group.

- *Fostering appropriate data capture and reporting:* In many ways, meeting the FPD data requirements will improve the quality and consistency of financial data reported by line ministries and other government agencies. Improving the data collection, recording methods, and reporting systems from subnational governments to the federal government is critically important.

Also, the FPD's monitoring of federal and subnational governments' public finance management practices reveals problems associated with

- a flawed tax structure and tax administration or tax evasion,
- weak control over local governments' finances,
- the wastefulness of SOEs, or
- the rising costs in healthcare, education, and other essential services resulting from mismanagement, corruption, and waste.

Another function of FPDs is analyzing and determining whether government borrowing and spending crowd out the private sector. FDPs also ascertain how much domestic borrowing constrains the growth and expansion of the private sector and whether government spending exacerbates inflation and raises the cost of living.

As indicated above, government investment and spending stimulate economic growth. However, governments have different choices in targeting economic stimuli. For example, they may decide to target the stimulus on

(a) the poor, who are likely to spend the stimulus on goods and services entirely, resulting in a robust economic recovery,

(b) capital investments that create jobs and help bolster longer-term economic growth, and

(c) tax cuts that encourage businesses to take on more workers or invest in new capital equipment, further expanding the economy.

According to Horton and El-Ganainy (2020), during economic downturns, policymakers aim to calibrate the size of government spending and investment to the estimated downturn of the economy.[3] The stimulus effects of government investment and expenditure tend to be more significant when interest rates do not rise, and the country's budgetary position after the stimulus remains sustainable. The stimulus effects would be higher for spending measures than tax cuts or transfers.

As for timing, it often takes a while to implement spending measures (program or project design, procurement, execution). Once in place, the measures may be in effect longer than needed. However, if an economic downturn is expected to be prolonged, concerns over lags may be less pressing.[4] Some governments stress implementing "shovel-ready" projects that are already vetted and ready to go. For all these reasons and to gain the most positive effect, stimulus measures should be timely, targeted, and temporary—quickly reversed once economic conditions improve. Fiscal policy management improves as government institutions at the subnational and national levels enhance their project and program planning, project design, appraisal and budgeting, implementation, and expenditure management capabilities.

In Ethiopia, subnational governments have a weak technical capacity in project planning, assessment, budgeting, implementation and management, and expenditure management. Currently, the capabilities of the TPDs and FPDs of the MOFEC of Ethiopia are weak. They are understaffed and not appropriately structured. Both directorates have been unable to recruit and fill the open positions with capable persons because of the low civil service salary scale, given the country's high cost of living.

Moreover, there is a shortage in the supply of competent university graduates. Universities and training institutions have not produced sufficiently capable and skilled graduates. Ethiopia currently relies heavily

---

3   Mark Horton and Asmaa El-Ganainy (2020). Fiscal Policy: Taking and Giving Away, Finance & Development, the International Monetary Fund, February 24, 2020.

4   Ibid.

on external technical assistance provided through the World Bank, IMF, and other bilateral donors to develop its tax and fiscal policies.

3.6 CONCLUSIONS

Taxation is constitutional. Paying taxes is a legal obligation of citizens, residents, and businesses. In Ethiopia, it is mandated by the country's Constitution. Tax-policy–making is relegated to MOFEC. Two director-ates within the ministry influence tax policies and government spending. One is the TPD responsible for tax policy drafting. The second is the FPD, which is accountable for developing and tracking the government's budget and expenditures.

Tax is collected both at the national and subnational government levels. The MOR and the ECC enforce the law and collect taxes from citizens, residents, and businesses at the federal government level. The RSRB enforces the regional tax laws at the subnational level and collects taxes from citizens, residents, and companies doing business or earning income and profits within their geographic jurisdictions. The RSRB also collects taxes on behalf of the federal government.

Tax policy– and fiscal-policy–making require sound technical capabili-ties. Hiring staff with the right technical skills, expertise, and continuous on-the-job training would address the changing economic environment and emerging risks.

Ethiopia's TPD and FPD have a long way to go toward maturity. Both the TPD and the FPD are understaffed. They cannot conduct many critical analytical studies for a sound tax policy and fiscal policy without external assistance. Moreover, the country's academic institutions have not trained and produced competent graduates that the MOFEC could hire and retain. To attract, employ and retain the best tax professionals, the government would need to shift to merit- and performance-based hiring and promotion. It must also adjust the civil service salary structure in line with the rising cost of living. Finally, the government must design and embed a high-powered analytical unit within MOFEC to produce analytical studies to support the government's tax and fiscal policies.

CHAPTER 4
TYPES OF TAXES LEVIED

Taxes are necessary for society to supply the public goods and services citizens, residents, and businesses need. There are several taxes citizens, residents, and businesses may be asked to pay. Let us review some of the common tax types by category.

4.1 BUSINESS VERSUS PERSONAL TAXES

Taxes are paid by income-earning citizens, businesses, and residents. Taxes paid by businesses are referred to as business taxes. Businesses pay taxes on the profits they make. Profit tax is calculated as a percentage of what's left from business revenue after paying suppliers and workers and deducting overhead costs and accounting expenses such as property and asset depreciation. In other words, business tax is a percentage of the revenue left over after deducting all business expenses. It is not a tax on the gross revenue of the business. However, while suppliers and workers are paid with pre-tax income, profits are taxed before they are distributed to shareholders or owners of the company. In many countries, business profits are taxed at a flat rate. In Ethiopia, they are taxed at a flat rate of 30%.

On the other hand, personal taxes are levied on an individual's gross income. In countries with a federal system of government, income taxes on individuals are imposed at the federal and state levels. In many developed and developing countries, including Ethiopia, personal income taxes are imposed progressively on the earnings of individuals, with higher rates applying to higher-income earners.[1] Individual taxpayers are also taxed on their share of any partnership or trust profits they receive during the tax year.

4.2 INCOME VERSUS CONSUMPTION TAX

Income Tax

Taxes are classified into income and consumption taxes. Income tax is a tax on the earnings of individuals and businesses. For individuals, the income can come from labor income such as wages, salaries, bonuses, tips, or interest earned on financial investment, dividends received from investing in the shares or stocks of corporations, and capital gains on the sale of tangible assets and stocks or company shares. However, capital gains are taxed at a different rate than ordinary income.

Personal income taxes are paid on gross income after deducting specific expenses allowed by the tax law, including tax credits. For example, in the United States, standard tax deductions include interest paid on home mortgages (to encourage homeownership) and charity donations to promote philanthropy. In the United States, a tax deduction means that those amounts are not subject to federal income tax. Some taxpayers are also allowed to take tax credits. Tax credits are subtracted directly from a person's tax liability. Excluding specific types of income from taxation and tax credits reduces tax liabilities and the tax revenue collected by the government. However, tax credits result in lower tax payments to the government. To illustrate this difference, consider a person with an income tax rate of 20%. A $1 tax deduction means that the person's taxable income decreases by $1 or that the person's tax liability decreases by 20

---

1   Taxation in Australia, https://en.wikipedia.org/wiki/Taxation_in_Australia#Corporate_taxes.

cents. On the other hand, a $1 tax credit means that the person's tax liability drops by $1 instead of 20 cents.

Consumption Tax

Consumption taxes apply when an individual or a business buys supplies and services from vendors. The most common consumption tax is the sales tax levied on the purchase price of items bought. Specific consumer items are also tax-exempt. Some standard exceptions to the sales tax are food items and clothing.

In the United States, state and local governments levy sales taxes, which means that the sales tax rate may differ from one jurisdiction to another. Some states and local governments even have a sales tax of 0%. In the 1980s, when I lived in New Jersey, USA, sales tax on grocery items was 0%. Also, all types of clothing I bought in New York but shipped to my home in New Jersey were tax-exempt.

Value-added tax (VAT) has replaced sales tax in Europe and other countries. The main difference between sales tax and VAT is that VAT is passed through to the ultimate consumer. However, it is charged on sales of raw materials and semi- and finished goods. Still, the final incidence of the tax is on the final purchaser of the finished product. To illustrate, let us assume that Manufacturer A purchases raw materials to process and produce a semi-finished product. The semi-finished product is then sold to Manufacturer B, who makes a finished product using the semi-finished product it bought from A. The finished product is then sold to a wholesaler— the wholesaler sells it to a retailer, and the retailer sells it to a consumer.

Manufacturer A pays VAT to purchase the raw materials for producing the semi-finished product. When Manufacturer A sells the semi-finished product to Manufacturer B, it charges VAT on the value of the semi-finished product. The VAT is paid by Manufacturer B. However, since the VAT has to be remitted to the government, Manufacturer A remits the difference between the VAT charged to Manufacturer B and the VAT Manufacturer

A paid on the raw materials. In effect, Manufacturer A is compensated for the VAT it paid on the raw materials. When Manufacturer B sells the finished product to a wholesaler, it charges VAT on the value of the finished product, which the wholesaler pays. Again, Manufacturer B deducts the VAT paid on the semi-finished product before remitting the VAT collected from the wholesaler to the tax authority. The wholesaler does the same thing when it sells the finished product to retailers. Retailers also do the same thing when they sell the product to consumers. However, consumers cannot pass on the VAT; they must bear the VAT burden.

Consumption taxes include **excise** or **luxury taxes**, applied on specific items at rates that differ from the overall VAT or sales tax rate. Excise taxes are imposed to discourage the consumption of harmful products such as tobacco (resulting in lung cancer) and alcohol (contributing to liver cancer). On the other hand, luxury taxes are imposed to discourage the importation of unproductive assets and encourage the domestic production of indigenous goods.

4.3 REGRESSIVE, PROPORTIONAL, AND PROGRESSIVE TAXES

Over a couple of centuries, there have been disagreements among economists, politicians, and philosophers on what form of taxation would be fair and equitable. That is because the impact of income tax can be regressive, proportional, or progressive, as defined below:

- A **regressive tax** is when lower-income groups pay a higher fraction of their income than higher-income groups. Under a regressive tax system, the marginal tax rate is less than the average tax rate, meaning the tax on the additional income unit gets taxed at a lower rate. The more you earn, the less tax you pay.[2]

---

2   Steven Peters (2012). Could America Exist Without an Income Tax? Fort Lauderdaily, March 25, 2012, https://projectunity.wordpress.com/2012/03/25/could-america-exist-without-an-income-tax/.

- A **proportional tax** relates to a tax system where everyone pays the same fraction of income in taxes regardless of the magnitude of their earnings. Under the proportional tax system, the marginal and average tax rates are equal. In other words, the proportion of income you pay in tax remains the same as your earnings go up.

- A **progressive tax** is where lower-income groups pay a lower fraction of their income in tax than higher-income groups. Under a progressive tax system, the additional income earned gets taxed at a higher rate. You pay more tax on the additional income you earn.

- A **lump-sum tax** is where everyone pays the same amount of tax, regardless of income level. Therefore, a lump-sum tax is a regressive tax since a fixed amount of money will be a higher fraction of income for lower-income groups and a lower fraction for higher-income groups. For example, if I have to pay $100 when earning $1,000 and suddenly move to a job that pays me $10,000, I am only responsible for paying the levied $100. I pay only the fixed sum of $100 regardless of my income level. Lump-sum taxation is regressive.

Most countries have adopted progressive income-tax systems since it is fair for higher-income groups to contribute a higher fraction of their income to society. The rationale is that higher-income groups spend a much lower fraction of their incomes on basic necessities than lower-income groups. Progressive income tax systems also partially balance out other types of taxes that are likely to be regressive. For example, since lower-income households spend a more significant fraction of their income on purchases of vehicles, an excise tax on cars would be regressive. Also, lower-income families' sales taxes on items (food and clothing) purchased are regressive. These purchases constitute a significant fraction of their incomes. For this reason, in many countries, unprepared foods and groceries are typically exempted from sales tax or VAT.

4.4 REVENUE VERSUS SIN TAX

For various reasons, several types of taxes are levied on citizens, residents, and businesses. On the one hand, they are imposed to generate revenue to fund government operations to deliver public goods and services, infrastructure, and social protection. These taxes are referred to as "revenue taxes." Their primary purpose is to generate revenue for government spending. Revenue taxes do not change people's work or consumption behavior very much; instead, they are compulsory contributions to fund government programs.

On the other hand, other taxes are imposed to correct negative externalities or "bad" behaviors. The production and consumption of specific types of goods and services impact society negatively. For these reasons, taxes on such items are often called "sin taxes." They are also called "Pigouvian taxes," named after Arthur Pigou.[3] A Pigouvian tax is assessed against individuals or businesses for engaging in activities that create adverse side effects for society. Negative side effects include air, water, environmental pollution, and fire hazards. Some products, such as tobacco and alcohol, also harm human health and strain the public health system. These activities harm citizens' productivity and property. A sin tax that significantly affects producers and consumers is desired even if it doesn't raise much government revenue. The expected and desired behavioral change from society is "not producing, using, or consuming harmful products broadly speaking."

4.5 DIRECT AND INDIRECT TAXES

Taxes are also classified as direct and indirect taxes. **Direct taxes** relate to taxes borne by the businesses and individuals on whom the taxes are imposed. There is no expectation that the tax burden could be shifted to

---

3   Dennis W. Carlton and Glenn C. Loury (1980). "The Limitations of Pigouvian Taxes as a Long-Run Remedy for Externalities". *Quarterly Journal of Economics* 95(3), 559–566.

other companies or persons. In other words, the impact and incidence of direct taxes are on the same taxpayer. By contrast, **indirect taxes** are imposed upon businesses or persons who are likely to shift the tax burden to other companies or individuals. The impact and incidence of an indirect tax will be on different taxpayers.

According to J. S. Mill, "a direct tax is one which is demanded from the very person who, it is intended or desired, should pay it. Indirect taxes are those which are demanded from one person in the expectation and intention that he shall indemnify himself at the expense of another."[4] Thus, in the case of direct taxes, the taxpayer and tax-bearer are the same. Again, according to Mill's definition, indirect taxes occur when the taxpayer is not permanently the tax-bearer. Dalton also made a distinction between direct taxes and indirect taxes. According to Dalton, "direct taxes are paid by the person on whom it is legally imposed, while an indirect tax is imposed on one person, but paid partly or wholly by another, owing to a consequential change in terms of some contract or bargain between them."[5] As shown in Tables 4.1 and 4.2, direct and indirect taxes have advantages and disadvantages.

---

4   John Stuart Mill (2004). *Principles of Political Economy: With Some of Their Applications to Social Philosophy.* Abridged Edition with Introduction by Stephen Nathanson. Hackett Publishing Company, Inc.: Indianapolis / Cambridge (Chapter 3, p.223).

5   Hugh Dalton (September 1920). "The Measurement of the Inequality of Income." *Economic Journal,* September 1920, pp 348–361.

Table 4.1: Advantages and Disadvantages of Direct Taxes[6]

Advantages	Disadvantages
• **Equity:** Direct taxes imposed according to a person's ability to bear the tax burden are considered equitable. • **Certainty:** Taxpayers know what is taxed and when and where the tax must be declared and paid. At the same time, the tax authorities can estimate how much tax revenue they will collect more accurately. • **Economy:** The mode of tax collection is simple. Tax is collected at the source, for example, payroll tax, and thus the cost of tax collection is low. • **Elasticity:** Direct taxes are elastic. Thus, a slight increase in the tax rate would raise significant tax revenue for the government. • **Social Impact:** Since taxpayers are directly contributing to the coffers of the government, they are very keen to know how the government is using their tax money. Thus, direct tax helps to increase civic consciousness. • **Distributive Justice:** Since direct taxes can be progressive, they can effectively reduce income inequalities in society.	• **Unpopular:** Since direct taxes cannot be shifted, many taxpayers, especially higher-income groups, resist such taxes. • **Possibility of Evasion:** Direct tax is a tax on honesty. Direct taxes can be circumvented through creative accounting practices, profit shifting, and the use of dubious tax shelters unless the taxpayers are honest and the tax administrator staff are incorruptible. • **Costly:** Compliance and administrative costs of direct taxes are significant. From time to time, tax authorities assess and audit taxpayers to determine if taxpayers are filing and paying the correct amount of tax. Taxpayers employ and pay for the services of tax accountants and external auditors to prepare their tax returns. • **Arbitrary:** Determining a taxpayer's tax liability objectively and accurately depends on the clarity of the tax law, as direct taxes are imposed on various income sources. Also, arbitrariness may creep in when evaluating assets or conducting audits. • **Narrow Base:** In most countries, direct taxes touch only a section of the community. They do not have broad coverage.

---

6   See also Metha Moheeth (2019). Classifications of Taxes: 4 Types, https://www.accountingnotes.net/financial-management/public-revenue/classification-of-taxes-4-types/10059.

Table 4.2: Advantages and Disadvantages of Indirect Taxes[7]

Advantages	Disadvantages
• **Convenience:** Indirect taxes are not felt to the same degree as direct taxes. The tax is paid at the purchase of a commodity or a service. The tax is included in the price of the commodity or service. • **Elasticity:** Indirect taxes are elastic. In a time of prosperity, indirect tax revenues can go up, and the tax rates can be increased with less resistance from taxpayers. • **Broad Coverage:** Indirect taxes fall on consumable goods and services. All citizens and residents contribute to the tax revenue when purchasing an item. Exempting essential items consumed by most low-income citizens will address the equity issue. • **More Popular than Direct Taxes:** All who purchase a product or service feel the incidence of indirect taxes. • **Productivity:** By imposing a few taxes, such as VAT, the government can increase its revenue yield. • **Can Promote Social Welfare:** By taxing harmful goods and services at higher rates, the government can restricted the availability and consumption of such goods and services.	• Regressive in Nature: Indirect taxes on consumer goods affect low-income groups more than high-income groups. Low-income groups spend a sizable proportion of their income on consumables. • **Uneconomical:** Indirect taxes are difficult to administer. The cost of the collection of indirect taxes is relatively high. The tax authority must examine and understand how the different points of sale operate. Consumers must demand, and the merchants must provide legitimate sales receipts with the appropriate sales tax or VAT to remit to the government. • Extremely Uncertain: Tax revenue from indirect taxes is unpredictable. The tax authority cannot accurately estimate the total yield from the different indirect taxes. Tax revenue generated would depend on the demand and supply conditions for each good and service and the integrity and honesty of the sellers and buyers. • **Social Significance:** Indirect taxes do not promote civic consciousness. They are collected in small amounts through intermediaries and traders. Hence, people take little, if any, interest in how the government uses the tax collected.

---

7   Ibid.

Advantages	Disadvantages
• **Can Be Progressive:** Indirect taxes can also be made progressive by imposing higher tax rates on luxury goods and lower rates on essential goods.	• **Inflationary in Nature:** Indirect taxes generate inflation in the economy. For example, an increase in sales tax can lead to a sharp rise in product and service prices.

Taxation and government spending decisions have specific objectives. The primary goal is to raise sufficient revenue to fund the delivery of essential public goods and services to all citizens. Other goals include stabilizing economic fluctuations, narrowing the income inequality between the wealthy and low-income groups, and regulating and suppressing the production and sale of harmful goods and services. Governments can meet their need for increased tax revenue for funding service delivery by a combination of direct and indirect taxes.

Regarding the correction of income inequality in a society, direct taxes possess a specific built-in mechanism to achieve the redistribution of income in favor of low-income groups. Direct taxes can be structured progressively to achieve a society's desired income equality or fairness objectives. Also, by heavily taxing articles consumed by the wealthy and exempting from taxation items more frequently consumed by the low-income groups—such as bread, milk, and other food items—the tax structure can be made more equitable.

Direct taxes can function as automatic stabilizers during periods of economic fluctuation. Direct taxes can be increased in an inflationary period to reduce aggregate consumption. And during a recessionary period, they can be decreased to stimulate consumption and investment. Thus, direct taxes have built-in flexibility.

Indirect taxes do not have much flexibility because consumption tends to rise or fall disproportionately with the decrease in income. However, indirect taxes are more appropriate for regulating and curtailing conspicuous consumption and the production and consumption of harmful goods and services.

4.6 TYPES OF TAXES LEVIED IN ETHIOPIA

The Ethiopian Federal Income Tax Proclamation No. 979/2016 imposes numerous direct and indirect taxes on citizens, residents, and businesses (see Table 4.3). These direct and indirect taxes have specific proclamations, regulations, and implementation directives. Proclamations are developed by the Ministry of Finance and Economic Cooperation (MOFEC) and the Council of Ministers (COM) and ratified by Parliament. Regulations are prepared and issued by the COM. Directives, by contrast, are developed and administered by tax administrators, for example, the Ministry of Revenue (MOR), the Customs Commission, and the regional state revenue bureaus (RSRB).

Table 4.3: Types of Taxes in Ethiopia

Direct Taxes Federal Income Tax Proclamation No. 979/2016	Indirect Taxes Various Proclamations
1. **Personal Income Tax:** This tax includes income from employment, which is progressive and ranges from 10% to 35% (see Article 11).	1. **VAT:** Currently, the VAT rate is 15% on all articles bought and sold (see Value Added Tax Proclamation No. 285/2002; Value Added Tax [Amendment] Proclamation No. 609/2008; Value Added Tax [Amendment] Proclamation No. 1157/2019).

Monthly Employment Income	Tax Rate	Deductible from Tax Amount
0–600	0%	0.00
601–1,650	10%	60.00
1,651–3,200	15%	142.50
3,201–5,250	20%	302.50
5,251–7,800	25%	565.00
7,801–10,900	30%	955.00
Over 10,900	35%	1,500.00

2. **Excise Tax:** The rate varies by type of goods (see Excise Tax Proclamation No. 307/2002; Excise Tax [Amendment] Proclamation No. 610/2008; update the list of goods and the applicable excise tax rate published January 2020).

2. **Rental Income Tax:** This tax is progressive and ranges from 10% to 35% for individuals and a 30% flat rate for companies earning rental income (see Article 14).

3. **Turnover Tax (TOT):** The TOT rate is 2% on products sold locally; for services, 2% on grain mills, tractors, and combine harvesters, and 10% on others (see Turnover Tax Proclamation No. 308/2002).

Taxable Rental Income (per year)	Rental Income Tax Rate
0–7,200	0%
7,201–19,800	10%
19,8001–38,400	15%
38,401–63,000	20%
63,001–93,600	25%
93,601–130,000	30%
Over 130,000	35%

4. **Customs Duties & Taxes:** These are applied to imported goods, and the rates vary (see Customs Proclamation No. 859/2014; Customs 2017 Tariff Book).

Direct Taxes Federal Income Tax Proclamation No. 979/2016	Indirect Taxes Various Proclamations
3. **Business Profit Tax:** This tax rate is progressive for un-incorporated businesses (i.e., sole-proprietorship), ranging from 10% to 35%, and a 30% flat rate on incorporated companies (e.g., PLCs and Share Companies) (see Articles 19–27).	5. **Stamp Duties:** These are applied to memorandum and articles of association of any business organization, cooperative, or any other form of association; award; bonds; warehouse bonds; contractor agreements and memoranda thereof; security deeds; collective agreements; contracts of employment; leases, including sub-leases and transfers of similar rights; natural acts; power of attorney; documents (see Stamp Duty Proclamation No. 110/1998; Stamp Duty [Amendment] Proclamation No. 612/2008).

Individual's Taxable Business Income (per year)	Applicable Tax Rate
0–7,200	0%
7,201–19,800	10%
19,801–38,400	15%
38,401–63,000	20%
63,001–93,600	25%
93,601–130,800	30%
Over 130,800	35%

4. **Withholding tax:** This tax is levied on imported goods at 3% of the sum of cost, insurance, and freight (CIF). It is imposed on payments made to taxpayers at 2% on the value of goods involving a transaction of more than Birr 10,000 in any one purchase, contract, and service requiring payment of more than Birr 3,000 in a single transaction.

6. **Withholding taxes:** These are imposed on employment income, dividends, interest, and royalties (see Federal Income Tax Administration Proclamation No. 983/2016).

7. **Surtax:** This tax is levied and collected on imported goods. The current rate is 10% (see Import Sur-Tax Council of Ministers Regulation No. 133/2007).

Direct Taxes Federal Income Tax Proclamation No. 979/2016	Indirect Taxes Various Proclamations
5. Other Taxes: (i.e., taxes on income from royalties, rendering technical service, games of chance, dividends, rental property, or interest; see Articles 54–64).	

Other Income	Applicable Tax Rates
Royalties	5%
Dividends	10%
Interest	5% on savings; 10% in other cases
Income from games of chance	15% for winnings above 1,000 birrs
Income from the casual rental of assets	15%
Gains on the disposal of assets	15% for Class 'A' assets—immovable assets; 30% for Class 'B' assets—bonds and shares
Windfall profit	30%
Undistributed profit	10%
Repatriated profit	10%
Other income	15%

4.7 TYPES OF INCOME TAXED

As noted in Table 4.3, there are various sources of income, and they are taxed differently. For taxation purposes, the United States recognizes three distinct sources of income as follows:

1. **Earned income:** Earned income includes money earned from a job—salaries, wages, bonuses, and tips. It also includes self-employment income derived from work done as an independent contractor, consultancy, and income from business activities. Earned income includes alimony received and certain forms of retirement income like pensions, social security, 401(k)s, and traditional IRA distributions.[8]

2. **Investment income:** Investment income includes the income derived from investments, mainly interest income, capital gains, and dividends. Different tax rules apply to each of these categories of income. For example, **interest income** is taxed as ordinary income. It includes interest from checking and savings accounts, certificates of deposits, loans made to other people, and interest income from bonds. In the United States, interest income from municipal bonds is exempt from federal income tax.

Capital gains arise when selling an asset for more than the asset holder paid. The difference between the price you paid for the asset and the sales value of the asset when you sell it is a capital gain if positive or capital loss if negative. If you have held the asset for a year or less, the capital gain is considered short-term and taxed as earned income. However, long-term capital gains result from selling assets owned for at least a year and a day or more and are taxed at preferential rates.

---

8   Mathew Frankel, CPA (2018). The 3 Types of Income and How They're Taxed. The Motly Fool, https://www.fool.com/taxes/2018/09/21/the-3-types-of-income-and-how-theyre-taxed.aspx.

Dividends are taxed at preferential rates, just like long-term capital gains. However, investors must hold the stock/share for a minimum period to take advantage of the preferential tax rates. In the United States, the qualified dividend criteria have two exceptions: dividends from real estate investment trusts (REITs) and limited partnerships. These dividends are treated as ordinary income.

3. **Passive income:** Income from real estate investments and dividends received from REITs fall into the passive income category. Income from limited partnerships also falls into the passive income category. Passive income is taxed as ordinary income. Table 4.4 lists taxable and nontaxable passive income sources in the United States.

Table 4.4: Taxable and Nontaxable Income in the United States[9]

Taxable Income	Nontaxable Income
• **Alimony income:** Alimony income arises when couples separate through a divorce. It is the money paid to the spouse by a court order. Usually, the amount and period of payment are determined by a court and are taxable. • **Barter income:** Goods or services received in exchange for other goods or services are taxed based on reasonable market prices. For example, say you build a deck for your dentist, and he fixes your teeth. You must pay tax on the fair market value of your dental services.	• **Child support:** Money designated as child support is not taxable. • **Combat pays:** Combat pay is income earned while stationed in a designated combat zone in service to the U.S. military. In the United States, combat pay is not taxed. • **Disability benefits:** If an employee pays the premiums, the benefits are not taxable. Categories of disability benefits that are nontaxable include the following: – Any benefits received from supplemental disability insurance purchased through an employer with after-tax dollars

9   Internal Revenue Service, Tax Cuts & Jobs Act; see also https://www.taxact.com/tax-information/tax-topics/20-types-of-taxable-and-nontaxable-income; and Amy Fontinelle (2020). 12 Top Sources of Nontaxable Income, Investopedia, December 31, 2020, https://www.investopedia.com/taxes/sources-nontaxable-income/.

Taxable Income	Nontaxable Income
• **Bonus from an employer:** Bonuses are taxable. However, noncash employee achievement awards are excludable from income if the employer's cost is not more than US$1,600 and the award meets other specific rules. • **Cash income:** Income from odd jobs and "under the table" payments are taxable. • **Court awards and damages:** Income received for lost pay, punitive damages, business damages, etc., excluding compensation for physical injury, sickness, or emotional distress, is taxable. • **Disability benefits:** An employee pays tax on disability benefits if their employer pays the disability insurance premiums connected to government service. • **Gambling income:** Gambling income minus gambling losses incurred for the tax year are taxable. • **Hobby income:** Hobby income is taxable after deducting costs associated with the hobby. However, the deduction cannot be more than the income derived from the hobby. • **Interest and dividends:** Interest and dividend income are taxable. However, interest in certain government obligations, such as municipal bonds, is not taxable by the federal government. Dividends are not taxable when they are a return of capital. In other words, you don't pay tax when you receive back part of your investment because it is not a share of profits.	– Any benefits received from a private disability insurance plan that is bought with after-tax dollars – Workers' Compensation payments – Compensatory (but not punitive) damages for physical injury or physical sickness, compensation for the permanent loss of a part or function of one's body, or payment for permanent disfigurement – Disability benefits from a public welfare fund – Disability benefits under a no-fault car insurance policy for loss of income or earning capacity due to injuries • **Gain from the sale of a home:** If you sell your home at a profit, you may not have to pay tax on the first $250,000 of gain ($500,000 if filing jointly) if you owned and lived in the home for 2 of the last 5 years. You must not have taken this exclusion in the 2 years before the sale of the house. If you don't meet the qualifications to exclude any gain from the sale of your home, you may owe capital gains tax. • **Gifts received:** Gifts received from family members and friends are not taxable.

Taxable Income	Nontaxable Income
• **Jury duties pay:** All citizens must serve on a jury in the United States. Jury duty pay is taxable as miscellaneous income. Suppose an employee turns over their jury duty pay to their employer in exchange for continuing to receive salary payments. In that case, the employee can deduct the amount of money they turn over to their employer. • **Social security benefits:** Social security benefits may not be taxable if you have little other income. When your earned income gets above a specific limit, up to 85% of your social security benefits may be included in your taxable income. • **Required IRA withdrawals:** Withdrawals from traditional IRAs and other retirement accounts are taxable. • **Unemployment benefits:** Income from unemployment benefits is taxable.	• **Roth IRA or Roth 401(k) plan withdrawals:** Qualified withdrawals from a Roth IRA or Roth 401(k) plan are not taxable. • **Inheritance received:** Your inheritance is not taxable. The person's estate pays estate and inheritance taxes before paying any heirs.

In Ethiopia, for taxation purposes, the Federal Income Tax Proclamation No. 979/2016 (Article 8) classifies the sources of taxable income into the following schedules:

1. Schedule 'A': Income from employment
2. Schedule 'B': Income from the rental of buildings
3. Schedule 'C': Income from business
4. Schedule 'D': Other Income
5. Schedule 'E': Tax-exempt income

1. **Schedule 'A': Income from employment:** Schedule A relates to an individual's earned income from being an employee of a private, government, or international organization operating in Ethiopia. The individuals receive a monthly salary determined by the condition of their employment. As outlined in Table 4.3, employment income is taxed separately and progressively, and the tax rate increases with an increase in income. However, Article 65 of the Proclamation excludes certain types of income from taxable employment income, including

   - employment income not exceeding 5 years paid to expatriate professionals recruited for transfer of knowledge by investors engaged in export business,
   - income from employment received by an unskilled employee working for the same employer, whether continuously or intermittently for not more than 30 days within any 12 months, and
   - an amount paid by an employer to cover the cost of medical treatment of an employee. These may include medical insurance premium payments made by an employer on behalf of an employee under employees' "medical insurance schemes."

2. **Schedule 'B': Income from the rental of buildings:** Schedule B relates to income from the rental of facilities. According to Article 15 of Proclamation No. 979/2016, the taxable rental income is the gross income derived from renting a building for the tax year, less the allowed deductions, including

   - the annual lease payment of the land on which the building is situated,
   - epairs and maintenance expenses,
   - epreciation of the building, furniture, and equipment,
   - interest and insurance premiums related to the building, and
   - fees, but no tax, levied by a state or city administration regarding the land or the building.

Lessee details (Form 1202) and balance sheet (Form 1303) must be filed concurrently with rental income declaration.

3. **Schedule 'C': Income from business:** Schedule C relates to income from commercial activities. According to Proclamation No. 979/2016, Article 20, *"the taxable business income of a taxpayer for a tax year shall be the total business income of the taxpayer for the year reduced by the total deductions allowed to the taxpayer for the year."* Sub-article 2 indicates that *"the taxable business income of the taxpayer shall be determined in accordance with the profit and loss, or income statement."* Article 21 provides a detailed explanation of business income. And Articles 22 through 26 provide the allowable deductions from business income. Article 27 lists nondeductible expenditures and losses.

Article 19 of the income tax proclamation states that business income earned by unincorporated businesses is taxed at a progressive tax rate. The maximum business income tax rate paid is 35% for income above ETB 130,000 for the tax year. A business owned and operated by a single person is classified as a sole proprietorship. The business income tax rate levied on microenterprises is the same as the sole proprietor's tax rate.

Corporations generate income from the sales of goods and services. In general, the enterprise's total income equals gross revenue for the tax year plus gross proceeds from the disposal of trading stock and the gross fee for the provision of services plus the gain from the sale of business assets. A business enterprise can also realize

- **dividend income** from holding shares of other companies;
- **rental income** from renting out tools, equipment, and vehicles;
- **interest income** from holding bonds and interest-bearing bank savings; and

- **windfall gains** from external shocks such as a fluctuation in foreign exchange rates or sudden changes in government policies. Windfall gains affect most businesspersons and companies engaged in mining, petroleum, and financial services.

4. **Schedule 'D': Other income:** Schedule D relates to income described in Proclamation No. 979/2016 Article 51 through 58. It includes the income derived from

   a. a dividend paid to the businessperson or enterprise by a resident body,
   b. rental income from the lease of immovable property located in Ethiopia or movable property situated in Ethiopia,
   c. a gain arising from the disposal of an immovable property situated in Ethiopia,
   d. an insurance premium relating to the insurance of risk in Ethiopia,
   e. income from a performance or sporting event taking place in Ethiopia,
   f. winnings from a game of chance held in Ethiopia, and
   g. interest, a royalty, management fee, technical fee, or other income subject to tax under the Proclamation.

A businessperson or a business entity must keep and maintain income, expense, and other business records for two critical reasons. First, business owners want to ensure that their businesses are profitable and will continue generating the desired revenue and profit. Second, business taxpayers must calculate and estimate their tax liabilities and pay the taxes due to the tax authority. From time to time, the tax authority may want to review the tax liability calculation methodology to ascertain the accuracy of the tax liabilities. The tax authorities may ask for all the supporting documentation at that time.

5. **Schedule 'E': Exempt income** includes child support, combat pay, disability benefits, gifts, and inheritance.

4.8 VALUE-ADDED TAX (VAT)

Purchasers of goods and services pay VAT. In Ethiopia, VAT is applied to all purchases of goods and services. VAT is a significant source of tax revenue for the government. VAT currently contributes between 25% and 30% to the total tax revenue collected by the government.[10] The law requires that all businesses and traders register for VAT and issue VAT receipts to purchasers of their goods and services.

Article 18 of Proclamation No. 285/2002 (as amended in 2008 and 2019) and Article 8 of VAT Regulation No. 79/2002 govern the VAT registration. A VAT certificate request is made using a VAT registration form issued by the MOR. When a person conducting taxable transactions applies for a VAT certificate, the authority must register the person in the VAT register and issue a registration certificate within 30 days of the application. The VAT registration certificate contains the following details:

- Full name, address, and other relevant information of the registered person/entity
- Date of issuance of the VAT certificate
- Effective date of the registration
- Registered person's/entity's taxpayer identification number (TIN)

Depending on which date comes first, registration can occur on one of the following dates. In obligatory registration, the registration date can be on the first day of the accounting period following the month when the obligation to apply for registration arose. In a voluntary registration, the registration date can be on the first day of the accounting period following the month when the person/entity applied for registration. Otherwise, it shall be on the date the registered person/entity selects on their VAT registration application form.

---

10   Desalegn Mosissa Jalata (January–March 2014). "The Role of Value Added Tax on Economic Growth of Ethiopia." *STAR Journal* 3(1), 156–161.

The Proclamation also indicates that if a person/entity is required to register for VAT and has not done so, the authority may register the person on its own initiative and send the certificate to the registered person/entity. VAT-registered persons/entities must use their TINs on all VAT invoices, tax returns, and official communications with the tax authority. The tax authority may decline an application for VAT registration if the person/entity has no fixed place of business premises or there are reasonable grounds to believe that the applicant will not keep proper records or submit regular and reliable tax returns as required under the Proclamation.

According to Article 19 of the VAT Proclamation, a registered person/entity could apply to cancel the VAT registration within 30 days after ceasing to make taxable transactions. The VAT cancellation must be in writing, stating the date the person/entity ceased to make taxable transactions. The person/entity must report whether or not it intends to make taxable transactions within 12 months from that date. A registered person/entity may apply to have their VAT registration canceled at any time after 3 years of the date of their most recent registration for VAT, provided the estimated total taxable transactions for the 12 months beginning from the date of application for cancelation is not more than 500,000 Birr.

The cancellation of the VAT registration takes effect when the registered person/entity ceases to make a taxable transaction. It may also be canceled at the end of the accounting period when the person/entity stops making taxable transactions. Suppose a person's or an entity's VAT registration is canceled. In that case, the tax authority removes the person's or entity's name and all other details from the VAT register. It collects the VAT certificate from the person/entity.

Article 22 of the VAT Proclamation says that a person or entity registered for VAT and conducting a taxable transaction must issue a VAT invoice to customers. The VAT invoices/receipts are given to the customers upon delivery of the goods and services purchased but not later than 5 days after the transaction. A VAT invoice is a document executed in the form stipulated by the MOR and must contain the following information:

- Full name of the registered person/entity and the purchaser, and the registered person's trade name, if different from the legal name
- TIN of the registered person and the purchaser
- Number and date of the VAT registration certificate
- Name of the goods shipped or services rendered
- Amount of the taxable transaction
- Amount of the excise on excisable goods
- Sum of the VAT due on the given taxable sale
- Issue date of the VAT invoice
- Serial number of the VAT invoice

Suppose a VAT-registered customer has not received the VAT receipt from the seller. In that case, the customer must request in writing the VAT receipt within 60 days after the sales transaction date. The VAT-registered supplier must provide a VAT invoice regarding the taxable transaction within 14 days of receiving the written request. Where a VAT-registered recipient claims to have lost the original VAT invoice for a taxable transaction, the VAT-registered supplier may provide a copy marked "copy."

In the case of a VAT-registered person selling goods or rendering services to non-VAT-registered purchasers, the MOR may issue a directive allowing the seller to use a simplified VAT invoice instead of the regular VAT invoice. Furthermore, suppose the total amount for the entire sales transaction does not exceed 10 Birr. In that case, the MOR may waive a registered person's obligation to issue a VAT receipt or invoice for cash sales.

The VAT payment collected from customers is the tax authority's revenue. It must be declared and remitted regularly to the government. Article 26 of the VAT Proclamation and Article 14 of VAT Regulation No. 14 requires every VAT-registered person or entity to file a VAT return. According to the VAT (Amendment) Proclamation, No. 1157/2019, VAT-registered persons or entities with an annual revenue turnover of 70 million ETB or more must file a VAT return at the end of each calendar month. In contrast, persons or entities that generate an annual revenue turnover of less than 70 million ETB per tax year must file VAT returns quarterly. The VAT return is prepared and submitted using the MOR forms. The VAT must provide the information needed for calculating the tax payable for the accounting period regarding Article 20 of the Proclamation.

The VAT legislation requires that a VAT-registered person, or any other tax-liable person under the Proclamation, maintain VAT records in Ethiopia for 10 years. Records to be maintained include accounting records, a book of accounts, computer-stored information, or any other document, such as

- original VAT invoices received by the person/entity,
- a copy of all VAT invoices issued by the person/entity,
- customs documentation relating to imports and exports by the person/entity, and
- any other record as may be prescribed by the MOR.

Article 38 of the Proclamation requires VAT-registered persons/entities to notify, in writing, the tax authority of any change to the business within 21 days of the change occurring, including changes in the

- name, address, place of business, constitution, or nature of the principal taxable activity or activities of the person, and
- address from which the registered person conducts taxable activities.

Article 8 of the VAT Proclamation and chapter 2, articles 19 through 23 of the Council of Ministers VAT Regulation list commercial transactions exempt from VAT. For example, a limited number of food items, including bread and injera, are VAT-exempt. See Box 4.1 for a complete list of VAT-exempt items and services.

Box 4.1: VAT-Exempt Items in Ethiopia

1. Sale or rental of a dwelling house that has been used for at least 2 years
2. Financial service
3. Local or foreign currencies, warranty distribution, and importation except for cents and medals research services
4. Import of gold for the presentation to the National Bank of Ethiopia
5. Religious or spiritual-related services given by religious institutions
6. Educational services offered by educational institutions and childcare provided by kindergartens
7. Electricity, kerosene, and water supplies (do not include water processed by factories)
8. Except for different services or commission fees, goods or services presented by postal service institutions as per the authority given by its establishment proclamation
9. Transportation services
10. Permit and license payments
11. If 60% of the employees are disabled, the goods and services supplied by the institution employing these disabled individuals
12. Books
13. Selected food items
14. Goods like sealing plastic bags, sewing materials, and fertilizers for making insecticide-treated bed nets for the prevention of malaria
15. Transactions of pickled, wet blues and crust made by leather processing factories
16. Import of chemically processed clothes used for the sewing of insecticide-treated bed nets for the prevention of malaria
17. Government-imported wheat
18. Palm oils used for food
19. Sale of milk and bread
20. Drugs, medical supplies, and equipment
21. Agricultural fertilizers, pesticide chemicals, and select seeds
22. Pension fee services
23. Sale of airplane tickets by travel agencies
24. Publication and printing of books
25. Sale of processed leather by leather shoe factories or leather-processing factories
26. Manufacturing of stoves

The tax law also exempts the following from VAT assessment:

- An import of goods by a diplomatic or consular mission of a foreign country or a diplomat or consular official of a foreign country to the extent that the mission, diplomat, or consular official is exempt from VAT under the Diplomatic Relations Proclamation
- An import of goods by an international organization to the extent that the organization is exempt from VAT under a Proclamation or an Agreement
- An import of goods by a foreign government to the extent that the foreign government is exempt from VAT under an agreement between the Government of Ethiopia (GOE) and the foreign government to provide financial, technical, humanitarian, or administrative assistance to the government
- An import of accompanying baggage by a passenger to the extent it is exempt from duty under the customs legislation
- An import of seeds, fertilizer, pesticides, herbicides, or fungicides for use exclusively in agricultural activities
- An import of gold to be transferred to the National Bank of Ethiopia

4.9 INTERNATIONAL TRADE TAXES

International trade tax relates to the import and export of goods and commodities. Customs duties and taxes are assessed on all imports and exports. Only exempted imported or exported items and importers or exporters with a written duty-free privilege from the appropriate government authority are exempt from customs taxes. Several domestic statutes and international bilateral treaties govern Ethiopia's customs duties, tariffs, and taxes. The following documents contain the applicable international trade laws and regulations.

- Federal Tax Administration Proclamation No. 983/2016 and Council of Ministers Regulation No. 407/2017 on Federal Tax Administration
- The Tariff Book (ERCA, 2017)
- Customs Proclamation No. 859/2014
- Export Trade Duty Incentive Schemes Proclamation No. 768/2012
- Investment Proclamation No. 769/2012 (as amended in 2014) and Regulation No. 270
- The various tax proclamations (income, VAT, surtax, and excise tax)
- The Customs Tariff Regulations Amendment Council of Ministers Regulation No. 80/2002
- Customs Tariffs Council of Ministers Regulation No. 122/1993

The law requires importers of goods and commodities to collect and keep all purchase receipts, insurance documents, shipping receipts, and other relevant documents for the Ethiopian Customs Commission (ECC). These documents will be required if the importer contests the Customs Commission's tax and duties assessment.

Article 111 of the Customs Proclamation No. 859/2014 states

> Unless otherwise provided by law, the duties and taxes on import or export goods are assessed based on the law in force on the date of acceptance of the goods declaration or the date of correction under Article 93 of the Proclamation (deductive value method). Where it is impossible to determine the date of lodging or acceptance of the goods declaration, the duties and taxes are assessed based on the law in force on the date specified by the authority.

The Customs Tariff Regulation specifies the duty tax rate on all imported goods. Accordingly, there are six duty tax rates (0%, 5%, 10%, 20%, 30%, and 35%) applicable based on the type of imported items. The reason behind the variation of duty tax rates is the need to encourage the importation of some products by imposing a 0% tax rate and, simultaneously, to discourage the import of selected goods and commodities by setting a higher tax rate. The applicable duty and tax rate on imported items also depend on the type of material or goods. For example, raw materials, semi-finished products, and imported items for public use are taxed at a lower rate. Import tax on these materials is kept down or is at zero, keeping in mind that the imported goods enhance domestic production or are for public use, such as ambulances and medicines. Domestic manufacturers' rate for raw materials is zero; the tax rate for semi-processed goods could range from 10% to 20%. On the other hand, a higher tax rate applies to imports of finished goods, including those imported for sale to consumers, personal use, or nonproductive purposes. The tariff classification is used to determine the correct commodity code of duty and taxes payable on imports.

Like most countries, Ethiopia's tariff classification is based on the International Convention on the Harmonized Commodity Description and Coding System (HS). The national tariff book specifies the duties and taxes applicable to each imported good. The book is structured in two schedules (1st and 2nd). It also includes the tariff rate of the Common Market for Easter and Southern Africa (COMESA). The two schedules allow the importer to apply different customs duty rates for the same imported good, depending on the importation's intended purpose. The COMESA tariff rate applies to products originating in COMESA-member countries.[11]

---

11 The tariff book is structured as follows:
- **First schedule tariff:** import tariff at basic rates.
- **Second schedule tariff:** special privileges granted to business organizations involved in activities, such as producing goods and services. The second schedule consists of two parts, A and B.
- **Special customs tariff rates:** applicable to goods produced in and imported from member countries of COMESA (preferential rate).

The **customs duty** and tax rate on exports are set at 0%, except for select products, including hides and skins of animals. According to the Customs Commission publication, the applicable tariffs and taxes are outlined in the 2017 tariff book.

Table 4.5 illustrates the calculation of duty and tax on an imported item. The type and value of imported goods determine the tax and duty payable amount. A higher tariff and tax are paid on luxury items. In determining the cost of the item being imported or exported, Article 89 of the Customs Proclamation asserts that:

- the dutiable value for **imported goods** is the actual total cost of the goods up to the first entry point to the customs territory of Ethiopia, and
- the dutiable value for **export goods** is the exact total costs up to the final exit point from Ethiopia's customs territory.

The total dutiable cost of an imported or exported item is computed as the sum of

a. the price of the good at the place of origin (e.g., at the factory or dealership in City A),
b. insurance paid for the item while in transit, and
c. the transportation or freight and other charges, such as loading and unloading and storage charges.

Table 4.5: Calculation of Customs Duty & Taxes

Tax Type	Basis	Amount Customs Duty & Taxes Paid
	The total cost of imported goods = FOB cost + insurance + freight and other charges	
Customs duty	The total cost of imported goods × import customs duty	A
Excise tax	(Total cost of imported goods + A) × excise tax rate (if applicable)	B
VAT	(Total cost of imported goods + A + B) × VAT	C
Surtax	(Total cost of imported goods + A + B + C) × surtax	D
Withholding tax	The total cost of goods × withholding tax	E
Second schedule 1	The total cost of imported goods × second schedule 1	F
Total duty and taxes payable at the time of import		A+B+C+D+E+F

For example, for a vehicle with a free-on-board (FOB)[12] cost of US$15,000 and an additional amount of $3,000 for insurance, freight, and other charges, the total cost of the vehicle when it arrives at the customs border would be $18,000. Let us assume that the truck is brand new, is classified as "a vehicle exceeding 1,800cc but less than 3,000cc," and is not an exempt item. Also, let us assume the buyer does not have a duty-free

---

12 Free on board (FOB) and cost, insurance and freight (CIF) are international shipping agreements used in the transportation of goods between a buyer and a seller. They are among the most common international commerce terms established by the International Chamber of Commerce (ICC) in 1936. The specific definitions vary somewhat in every country, but, in general, both contracts specify country of origin and country of destination information that is used to determine where liability officially begins and ends, and outline the responsibilities of buyers to sellers, as well as sellers to buyers.

privilege. Thus, the amount of customs duty and taxes the buyer would pay to the ECC, using the calculations shown in Table 4.5, would be $44,916, as shown in Table 4.6. That is an increase of 250% in expenses to acquire the pickup truck. The government collects $27,000 in taxes— good for the government but bad for you.

Table 4.6: Customs Duty & Taxes Paid on a Pickup Truck with CIF Value of $18,000

	Tax Type	Applicable Tax Rate	Calculated Tax Liability
A	Customs duty	35%	6,300
B	Excise tax	100%	24,300
C	VAT	15%	7,290
D	Surtax	10%	5,589
E	Withholding tax	3%	540
F	Second schedule 1	5%	900
	Total tax liability = (A+B+C+D+E+F)		44,916

While the computation of customs taxes and duties looks straightforward, there are some issues regarding the truck's value. According to the current practice, the ECC does not accept receipts presented by importers for several reasons, one of them being a suspicion of under-invoicing. To verify the value of imported goods, Customs Proclamation No. 859/2014 provides six alternative methods of determining the imported item's value, as shown in Table 4.7. Depending on the valuation method, you may pay more taxes to the government.

Table 4.7: Alternative Customs Valuation Methods

Method	Proclamations	Exemptions
1	**Transaction value method** (Articles 90, 96, and 97): The transaction value of imported goods is the transaction value paid or payable for the goods when sold for export to Ethiopia.	Provided that a. there are no restrictions as to the disposal or use of the goods by the buyer other than restrictions imposed by law or by particular decisions issued based on such laws, a limit in the geographical area in which the goods may be resold, or limitations that may not affect the value of the goods, b. the sale or price of the goods is not subject to conditions or restrictions for which a value cannot be determined, c. no part of the proceeds of any subsequent resale, disposal, or use of the goods by the buyer may accrue directly or indirectly to the seller, d. the buyer and seller are related (e.g., legally recognized partners are linked by affinity or consanguinity). The transaction value is the basis for the duty valuation if the authority accepts it.
2	**Valuation of identical goods** (Article 91): Where the transaction value of the imported goods cannot be determined by method 1, it is determined by taking the transaction value of identical goods sold for export to Ethiopia at the same commercial level and in the same quantity at or about the same time as the goods being valued.	If this is not applicable, the value of the goods is determined based on the values of identical goods sold after making adjustments to account for differences attributable to the commercial grade and amount.

3	**Valuation of similar goods** (Article 92): Where the transaction value of imported goods cannot be determined by method 2, then the determination is based on the transaction value of similar goods sold for export to Ethiopia at the same commercial level and in the same quantity at or about the same time as the goods being valued.	
4	**Deductive value method** (Article 93): The deductive value method is applicable when the transaction value of imported goods cannot be determined as set forth in method 3. The deductive value method uses the unit price of the imported goods, identical or similar goods imported at or about the same time as the goods being valued and which are sold in Ethiopia in their original state in the greatest aggregate quantity to persons who are not related to the seller.	However, the price shall be reduced by a. the amount of commission usually payable or the profit and general expense equal to that usually reflected in sales within Ethiopia of such goods, b. the usual charges for the transportation, insurance, and other related costs to be incurred within Ethiopia for the goods, and c. import duties, taxes, and additional shares payable concerning the goods.
5	**Computed value method** (Article 94): Suppose the transaction value of an imported good cannot be determined based on the above methods. Then, the price of the imported item should be calculated based on the sum of a. the cost of manufacturing or processing the goods,	

	b.	an amount representing the general expenses and profit equal to that usually reflected in the sale of products of the same class or kind by producers in the country of export, and	
	c.	the transportation, loading, unloading, handling, and insurance costs associated with the transportation of the goods to the port of entry into the customs territory of Ethiopia.	
6	**Fallback method** (Article 95):		
	a.	Where the transaction value of imported goods cannot be determined under the provisions from Article 90 to Article 94 of this Proclamation, it shall be determined based on the data available in Ethiopia and using equitable methods consistent with the general principles embodied in the provisions of this Proclamation.	
	b.	When it so requests, the importer shall be informed, in writing, of the transaction value determined under the provisions of sub-article (I) of this Article and its method.	

The above valuation methods are also applicable to

- goods that have been released from customs control without paying duties and taxes but are required to undergo another customs procedure to pay duties and taxes,
- goods that may undergo a post-customs clearance audit,
- the valuation of noncommercial imports, and
- temporarily imported goods.

Customs valuation can be essential in preventing under-invoicing and other improper transactions between exporters and importers. Also, all valuations are different and often depend on individual customs officers' knowledge and professionalism. Some customs officers may accept the receipts and bill of lading (a detailed list of a shipment of goods in the form of a receipt given by the carrier to the person consigning the goods) presented without question. Other customs officers may want to validate the cost or price of the goods provided by the importer. Thus, depending on customs officers' integrity and professionalism, the dutiable value of similar imported items may differ for two different importers.

Automating the customs clearance process can reduce the human element of customs valuation. Once the importer enters their customs declaration into the system electronically, it automatically calculates the dutiable value and the applicable duties and taxes.

Articles 123–128 of the Customs Proclamation indicate that importers have the right to object to the customs assessment and request a refund for the following reasons:

- Overcharged duties and taxes
- Invalidated goods declaration
- Deteriorated, spoiled, damaged, or destroyed goods
- Short-landed goods

Overcharged duties and taxes are refunded if the overcharging results from incorrect commodity classification, tariff setting, valuation, or other calculation errors. If importers request a refund of duties and taxes, they must submit their request within one year after importing the goods in question. Customs duties and taxes are refunded for invalidated goods declarations. A goods declaration is canceled after duties and taxes have already been paid. Application for refund must be made within the prescribed period and include all the relevant documentation.

In addition to the assessed duty and taxes, there may be a service charge for customs services per Article 115 of the Proclamation. The service charges are related to the following:

- Warehouse licensing and renewal fee: according to the Customs Warehouse License Issuance Council of Ministers Regulations No. 24/1997, license and renewal fees for customs warehouses are ETB 1,250 (renewal ETB 500) licensing fee for general customs warehouses and private customs.
- Scanning fee: all goods subject to examination with a scanning machine are charged 0.07% of the dutiable value of the items scanned.

A review of the Customs Proclamation and its implementation suggests that revenue generation is Ethiopia's tariffs' primary purpose. In 2019, Ethiopian Customs ceased reducing or eliminating customs duties on imports of knocked-down and semi–knocked-down industrial inputs. This new revision has reclassified these products with basic tariff rates.

At the same time, Ethiopia aspires to be a leading manufacturing hub in Africa by 2025. Accordingly, the GOE prioritizes industrial park development and expansion. The GOE offers duty-free import incentives for investors in specific sectors, especially those located in the industrial zone and those planning to export goods and generate foreign currency.

Both VAT and excise taxes are imposed on imports. Registered persons' supply of goods and services is subject to a 15% VAT. Some products and services are exempt from VAT. In February 2020, Ethiopia reformed its excise tax policy. It increased excise taxes on specific products through a new excise tax proclamation.

4.10 CONCLUSION

Several types of taxes are levied on citizens, residents, and businesses. These taxes are classified as direct and indirect taxes. Direct taxes are also categorized as progressive, regressive, and proportional taxes. Some taxes are income taxes, and others are consumption and international trade taxes. Most countries have adopted progressive income taxation. Economists argue that all other things equal, progressive taxation can narrow society's income and wealth inequalities. However, the upper-income groups often resort to creative ways to evade the tax law or minimize their tax exposure through tax shelters and creative accounting.

Tax is levied on a person's gross income regarding personal earned income. By contrast, earned revenues of businesses are taxed after deducting business-related expenses. The tax law specifies deductible business expenses. They include both overhead and nonoverhead expenses. For example, the cost of goods sold, salaries, wages and benefits, communication and utility expenses, building rental and land lease, vehicle maintenance, fuel costs, interest paid, property taxes, and accounting depreciation of assets owned are tax deductible.

Individuals derive income from different sources. As laid out in the Ethiopian income tax proclamation, each type of income has its own tax rate. While employment income is taxed at a progressive rate, other forms of income are taxed at flat rates. For example, capital gains income realized after the sale of an asset is taxed differently from corporate income or personal income. For taxation purposes, dividend income is also treated differently from earned income, depending on the source of the dividend income.

Tax revenue from consumption tax makes up a significant proportion of the tax revenue collected by the government. However, the level of consumption tax collected is highly dependent on the honesty and willingness of merchants and traders to issue VAT receipts to their customers. Many merchants and traders are unwilling to give VAT receipts to customers to conceal their income and minimize their tax liability. In Ethiopia, VAT is regressive as low-income families pay a sizable proportion of their earned income on essential goods and services relative to wealthy households. A progressive VAT would generate more sales tax revenue and eliminate corruption and noncompliance by sellers and buyers alike.

International taxation or taxes on imported goods are also significant government revenue sources. Ethiopia imports a considerable amount of processed goods. Imported goods are taxed differently depending on whether they are essential or luxury goods, valuable to society, or dangerous. Luxury goods, as well as toxic and hazardous items, are taxed at higher rates.

CHAPTER 5
TAX ADMINISTRATION

Tax administration is about enforcing the tax law and collecting the correct amount of tax from citizens, residents, and businesses. Currently, the tax gap in Ethiopia is huge, i.e., the difference between the amount of tax collected and the taxes owed to the government. Simultaneously, the tax base is narrow, and tax evasion is high. In addition to tax collection, the other critical functions of tax administration are

(a) narrowing the tax gap,
(b) expanding the tax base, and
(c) controlling and eliminating tax fraud and tax evasion.

In Ethiopia, tax policy is administered by the Ministry of Revenue (MOR) and the Ethiopian Customs Commission (ECC) at the federal level and by regional revenue bureaus (RRB) at the sub-national level. Specific proclamations ratified by Parliament provide the tax administration mandates. Currently, the Federal Tax Administration Proclamation No. 983/2016 and Council of Ministers Tax Administration Regulation No.407/2017 govern tax administration at the federal level.

5.1 THE RESTRUCTURING OF THE TAX ADMINISTRATION

In 2008, Proclamation No. 587/2008 established the Ethiopian Revenues and Customs Authority (ERCA) by merging the MOR, the Ethiopian Customs Authority, and the Federal Inland Revenue Authority. The primary purpose of the restructuring was to improve service delivery to taxpayers, facilitate trade, enhance tax compliance, enforce tax and customs laws, and increase government tax revenue mobilization.

However, the restructuring of the revenue administration began in 1993. Debela and Hagos (2012) noted that, between 1993 and 1998, the government restructured the civil service organizations to fit the then-introduced Federal Political System of Administration. The focus was on realigning the civil service employees, organized under a unitary state, to the newly emerged ethnic federal states.[1] Nevertheless, according to Debela and Hagos, the restructuring of civil service organizations was not systematic.[2]

The second phase of restructuring was conducted between 2000 and 2011 when the government focused on enhancing the capacity of civil service employees by providing short-term training on different management topics.[3] A related objective was to improve the efficiency of public service delivery to citizens. The government sought to improve organizational performance by introducing results-based performance management (RBPM). To pave the way for the introduction of RBPM, the government started reorganizing civil service organizations in 2004, using Business Process Reengineering (BPR) as a strategic tool. However, the BPR did not achieve the expected organizational performance improvements.

---

1   Tesfaye Debela and Atakilt Hagos (June 2012). "Towards a Result-Based Performance Management: Practices and Challenges with Ethiopian Public Sector." *JBAS* 4(1), 79–127.

2   Ibid.

3   FDRE Ministry of Civil Service, Public Sector Capacity Building Program— Support Project, Implemented from November 2004 to June 2013.

In several regional state governments, resources for capital and operating expenses declined drastically soon after implementing BPR. The decline was very noticeable, particularly in the Amhara regional state, making it increasingly difficult to cover recurrent costs. A couple of reasons for this are the increase in the number of positions and business processes resulting from the BPR at the regional and woreda (district) levels and the assignment of additional staff by the regional bureaus without a concomitant increase in budgetary resources.[4] Key informants interviewed for the PSCAP final evaluation indicated that BPR had twin objectives. The first was to enhance public service delivery performance. But the second and sinister objective was replacing career professionals with political cadres loyal to the ruling party.

The ruling political party required civil servants at the federal and regional levels to affirm their loyalty and party membership after losing the 2005 election by a sizeable margin. The government laid off those civil servants that refused to sign the party membership and loyalty form. That ensured that all government bodies were operated and managed by party functionaries. The then-prime minister, Meles Zenawi, declared that he did not "care if the individuals appointed and running government affairs were technically incapable as long as they enforced the ruling party's mandate."

Consequently, the first phase of BPR and the subsequent personnel reshuffling failed to improve public service delivery performance.[5] There was also fear that the federal government may curtail public service delivery in geographic locations where it lost the national election. Following the 2005 election, the donor community initiated the social accountability program to protect essential public service delivery. The program was designed to protect and enhance public basic service delivery by engaging

---

4   World Bank (2010). Ethiopia Public Finance Review (PFR) (Draft Report No. 54952-ET), August 2010.

5   Samuel Taddesse, Country Director (2013). Public Sector Capacity Building Program—Support Project, Implementation Completion and Result Based Report (Draft Report), IPE Global, June 2013.

civil society organizations and communities to demand better and more services from the government.[6] The social accountability program was implemented at the local level as a pilot project in a limited number of woredas. Later it was expanded to 300 woredas, or 30% of the woredas across the country.

BPR is applied to an organization to improve its performance. It looks into the critical business processes and determines where inefficient organizational structures and unnecessarily complicated procedures lead to insufficient and low-quality service delivery. It also identifies areas that are susceptible to corruption. The BPR exercise uncovered corruption within civil service organizations. It also revealed severe problems in smuggling, money laundering, and tax evasion. The BPR study further defined the main tasks of the tax authority, including

- registering taxpayers and issuing taxpayer identification numbers (TINs), as well as detecting nonregistration and fake registration,
- receiving and processing tax returns submitted by taxpayers, tax withholding, excise tax and VAT remittances, and third-party information,
- conducting tax audits to uncover noncompliance with tax laws,
- processing and collecting unpaid tax debt,
- handling taxpayer appeals and complaints, and
- providing services and aid to taxpayers, including tax education.

In 2014, the Department for International Development (DFID funded and implemented the Tax, Audit, and Transparency (TAUT) Programme. The program determined that significant efficiency savings could be made based on improving the Standard Integrated Government Tax Administration System (SIGTAS) functionality. This would require reducing the manual processing of tax returns and increasing the integration and integrity of SIGTAS and other systems used within the

---

6   Samuel Taddesse, Biraj Swain, Merga Afeta, and Gadissa Bultosa (2010). Evaluation and Design of Social Accountability Component of the Protection of Basic Services Project, Ethiopia. New Delhi, India: IPE Global, 2010.

Ethiopian Revenue and Customs Authority (ERCA).[7] However, the Development Alternatives Inc (DAI) team's analysis found a consensus by senior management that ERCA's institutional effectiveness issues go much deeper than this. First, improvements in taxpayer registration and handling, tax audit strategy, and debt collection were areas of weaknesses identified by the Office of the Federal Auditor General (OFAG) at the request of the Government of Ethiopia (GOE) during the Growth and Transformation Plan I (GTP-I) period.

The decision to audit ERCA and the resulting analysis found a shared agreement among key GOE stakeholders on the need for broader reform. Second, new tax administration legislation was proposed to standardize procedures, penalties, and appeals across tax types, requiring new business processes. Melaku Fenta, a former head of ERCA, indicated that the biggest problem was the unwarranted interference of high-ranking officials in the ruling party and the government.[8] According to him, these officials functioned as a go-between between the business people and the tax authority. They bent the law in favor of those favored businesses.

Third, there was a widespread view, both inside and outside the government, that corruption issues continued to be widespread within ERCA. Several stakeholders voiced these perceptions, including those in high office in the government administration. It is also a widely held public perception. Subsequently, the Growth and Transformation Plan II (GTP-II) (2015/16–2019/20) identified fighting corruption in the revenue sector as a national priority.[9]

---

7   DAI (October 25, 2015). Tax, Audit and Transparency Programme (Draft), Inception Report.

8   Tamiru Tsige (2018). "From the Office to the Prison Cell: The Story of Melaku Fenta," *The Reporter,* July 28, 2018.

9   Federal Democratic Republic of Ethiopia (2016). Growth and Transformation Plan II (GTP-II), (2015/16–2019/20), Volume I: Main Text, National Planning Commission, May 2016, Addis Ababa, Ethiopia.

Other developed and developing countries' experiences suggest that radical personnel management reform and incentivization across tax administration departments can counteract deep-seated corruption. Program inputs in this respect would be contingent on the agreement of decision-makers inside and outside ERCA to attempt a comprehensive approach to staff recruitment, hiring, incentivization, monitoring, discipline, and dismissal or promotion, with a degree of autonomy of more comprehensive civil service reform processes and procedures.[10] ERCA recognized that employees' talent, skills, and motivation are crucial and endorsed the DAI Team's recommendations. However, the DAI-suggested reforms for professionalizing the staff and eradicating corruption were not implemented.

In 2018, after Prime Minister Abiy Ahmed took office, ERCA was renamed the Ministry of Revenue (MOR) by Proclamation No. 1097/2018, Article 31. At the same time, the ECC was split from the MOR and reorganized to manage international trade-related customs duties and taxes. The drivers of this decision were (a) the need to increase tax compliance and tax revenue and (b) getting rid of the ingrained corruption in the system.

5.2. CORE FUNCTIONS OF MOR AND ECC

The core functions of the MOR and the ECC are similar to those of ERCA. The MOR is responsible for enforcing domestic tax laws and collecting direct and indirect taxes from citizens, residents, and businesses. The ECC is responsible for international trade duties and taxes and controls illicit trade, contraband, and money laundering. A review of the Council of Ministers' (COM) regulations, as well as the MOR and ECC internal directives, indicates that these institutions are responsible for the following tasks:

---

10   DAI (October 25, 2015). Tax, Audit and Transparency Programme (Draft), Inception Report.

- Collecting and reviewing tax returns and ensuring citizens, residents, and businesses pay the correct amounts of taxes on time
- Auditing and assessing additional taxes if warranted and also preventing tax evasion and fraud
- Collecting workers' and private organizations' social security contributions
- Collecting delinquent taxes and clearing the tax debt on time
- Surveilling by Customs of goods imported and exported and appraising the value of the goods, and collecting the appropriate duties and taxes
- Examining and evaluating the quality and safety of imported items at customs borders to protect society against fake and dangerous products such as expired medicines and consumables, unauthorized importation of firearms and explosives, etc.

Concerning the MOR, Table 5.1 lists the core tax administration processes identified by Cowater in 2019 that needed redesigning and streamlining.[11]

Table 5.1: MOR Core Functions and Business Processes

Core Processes	Sub-Processes
Registration and Taxpayer Service Process	• Registration • Deregistration • Change notification • Customer support • Record management • Tax clearance • Complaint management • Tax agent registration • Tax agent follow-up and monitoring • Account management (Customer Relations Management)

---

11 Cowater International (2019). Tax System Transformation Programme (TSTP): Detailed Technical Diagnostic for Organizational Health, July 26, 2019.

Core Processes	Sub-Processes
Return Filing and Processing Process	• Manual filing returns • Electronic filing • Return processing • Data quality assurance • Non-filer—identification, notification, and follow-up (estimated assessment) • Assessment • Refund
Payment and Revenue Accounts Reconciliation Process	• Cashing • E-payment • Bank-to-bank payment • Bank reconciliation (CPO/Cash daily reconciliation) • Revenue reporting and consolidation • Revenue sharing • Payment reversing and adjusting
Debt Management Process	• Current debt management (below 60 days) • Old debt management (61 days and above) • Payment plan • Write off • Pre-seizure • Seizure • Offsetting (transfer in and transfer out) between tax accounts • Checking a taxpayer's account for clearance purposes
Risk and Tax Compliance Strategy Process	• Risk management • Risk analysis • Risk assessment • Risk trigger • Data matching • Case selection for audit (Risk engine) • Risk criteria—(Including Risk cycle loop) • Tax compliance strategy and plan • Risk monitoring and evaluation

Core Processes	Sub-Processes
Taxpayer Education Process	• Call center • Inbound service • Outbound service • Face-to-face service (HQ) • Information desk • Availing information on the website • Training material preparation and documentation • Taxpayer training provision-related processes (Selection, preparation, conducting, channel, evaluation, report)
Tax Audit Process	• Comprehensive audit (From notification to the taxpayer, planning, execution, completion to the issuance of audit assessment) • Service audit • Refund audit • Issue audit • Transfer pricing audit • Audit quality assurance
Intelligence and Tax Fraud Investigation Process	• Intelligence study • Intelligence operation • Evaluation of intelligence deterrent impact • Investigation audit (criminal) • Case selection for investigation audit • Jeopardy audit
Tax review in MOR Process	• Branch tax review • HQ tax review
Tax Appeal Process	• Appeal commission • Tax appeals to federal courts • Tax appeal case monitoring

Core Processes	Sub-Processes
Tax data management Process	• Issuance and focalization of cash register (CR) • CR usage monitoring • CR repair and maintenance • CR vendor management • Disposal of CRs • Inventory management • Invoice management • Taxpayer data management • Third-party data management • Fair market data management

The MOR's organizational functions outlined in Table 5.1 compare favorably with some of the requirements identified by the European Commission (2007). However, it has to continue reshaping the organization to develop the core elements for a robust, modern, and efficient tax administration, as illustrated in Table 5.2.[12]

Table 5.2: Core Processes for Robust Tax Administration

Core Process	Sub-Processes
Framework, Structure, and Basis	• Adequate autonomy with a clear mission, vision, and objective • Well-resourced and effective organizational structure • Stable legal framework • Responsible for own performance
Human and Behavioral Issues	• Developing and using ethical standards enterprise-wide • Objective, merit-based recruiting, hiring, and promotion • Effective internal management control and a robust internal audit system to prevent fraud and irregularities

---

12 European Commission (2007). Fiscal Blueprints: A Path to a Robust, Modern, and Efficient Tax Administration. Taxation and Customs Union.

Core Process	Sub-Processes
	• Clearly articulated and communicated fair and proportional sanctions for misconduct • Strong human resource management strategy, policies, and procedures with autonomous recruitment, retention, performance management and assessment; promotion; career progression; continuous training; and staff development policies, strategies, and practices that motivate and protect employees • Taxpayer awareness of their rights and obligations
Systems and Functions	• Establishing and using comprehensive and integrated revenue collection strategies, policies, and processes • Automated revenue receipts and accounting systems • Robust and effective debt collection system • Enforced debt collection based on risk assessment and performance • Effective risk-based refund procedure in place • Effective and efficient risk-based tax audits • Collaborative and cooperative relationships with third parties to counter tax evasion and tax avoidance • Robust and professional intelligence and investigation to stamp out tax fraud and avoidance and increase tax compliance
Taxpayer Service	• Defining and publicizing taxpayers' rights and obligations • Providing sufficient legal security to taxpayers • Respecting taxpayers' privacy and confidentiality of their information

Core Process	Sub-Processes
	• Ensuring taxpayers are represented or defended in any legal matters • Fair and balanced appeals procedures; comprehensive and accurate systems for recording details of the taxpayers and their tax returns • Clear and simple tax returns; promoting voluntary compliance actively, including taxpayers' education and accessible and understandable guidelines and instructions
Support	• Using cost-efficient, flexible, stable, and secure ICT to support the tax administrator's business operations • ICT enables taxpayers to access tax forms and instructions, file tax returns, and make online payments • Communicating by email, short mobile phone messages, and voice messages with taxpayers in a clear, precise, and prompt manner to help them comply with the tax law

With the ambition of fulfilling its responsibilities competently and efficiently with integrity and fairness, the MOR is in the process of redesigning and restructuring its business processes with technical assistance from Cowater International. To start, it has established an in-house training center to train its employees.[13] The MOR also participates in a policy formulation task force with the Ministry of Finance and Economic Cooperation. It shares its successes and challenges and provides suggestions to improve the tax legislation. The difficulties and challenges it faces in implementing the existing tax policy are analyzed, documented, and shared with all stakeholders to facilitate the tax policy reform debate.

---

13 Cowater International (2019). MOR Core Tax As Is Process Map, Bizagi Modeler, September 29, 2019.

The MOR is also involved in the COM's discussions in deciding how to execute the proposed tax provisions. Through this mechanism, the hope was that the tax law would be made clear to government officials, taxpayers, and tax officers and increase tax compliance and tax revenue collection. However, while the MOR's Tax Transformation Office (TTO) presentations to the task force are impressive, a careful review of the content and substance indicates they are shallow and repetitive. They do not lead to any meaningful institutional performance-enhancing changes.

With the Tax System Transformation Programme's (TSTP) technical assistance, the MOR is working to reduce the cost of tax compliance. At the same time, it is working to make its operations taxpayer friendly, efficient, and effective, directly affecting the cost of tax compliance. It has established taxpayer assistance desks and telephone lines in MOR's branch offices and headquarters. These desks are tasked with answering taxpayers' questions, providing the correct tax forms, and sometimes assisting taxpayers in completing tax declaration forms. However, the personnel assigned to these desks have insufficient understanding of their duties, and many are not customer centric. At the same time, MOR has introduced *e-tax*, *e-filing*, and *e-pay*. These are works in progress and will take time to run smoothly. They also depend on the country's electricity, telecommunication, and ICT infrastructure.

ERCA developed a draft customer charter in 2015.[14] The charter expressed the determination of the authority to show respect and courtesy when dealing with taxpayers and to deliver services based on the standards set in the charter. The charter set time limits for different services. It was designed to encourage investment, speed up development, expand economic activities, and collect the correct tax revenue. However, the standards outlined in the charter are not strictly followed because of personnel turnover and other reasons.

---

14 ERCA (2015). Customer Charter, Addis Ababa, April 2015 (translation from Amharic).

The current emphasis on raising revenue and using aggressive tactics by MOR to collect tax revenues is under discussion. We expect the MOR to rely more on efficient and effective taxpayer services and tax education, as well as respecting taxpayers' rights, as priorities to enhance tax compliance.

The customer charter is under revision. We hope the revised charter will enshrine, in writing, taxpayers' specific rights and obligations. The charter must also spell out the tax administrator's responsibilities to taxpayers. It is not sufficient to place posters highlighting the institution's vision, mission, and objectives, or the time to complete a task.

MOR must use all avenues to explain and demonstrate to taxpayers MOR's obligations for quality taxpayer services. It must also communicate taxpayers' rights and responsibilities, using drama, radio/TV talk shows, mobile radios, and group discussions in marketplaces around the country. Quarterly campaigns to enroll unregistered traders for taxpayer identification numbers (TINs) and assist micro and small enterprises complete and declaring their tax returns would expand the tax base and reduce informality.

MOR has established a tax day and has started recognizing good taxpayers by giving out certificates and medals. However, our criteria analysis using third-party data and data matching to choose the taxpayers for recognition is flawed. Our research shows that the most significant tax cheaters were wrongly recognized as tax-compliant taxpayers and awarded certificates and medals. The current selection criteria must be refined. It must use robust analytics to identify the most compliant taxpayers for recognition.

The MOR needs to develop and implement an employee code of ethics. All MOR personnel should have a written copy of the code, as well as a taxpayers' obligations and rights manual. In addition, all the employees must be given in-depth training on taxpayers' rights and obligations and the employees' code of ethics. Employees must know the consequences of violating taxpayers' rights or engaging in nefarious, improper, and corrupt acts. Tax administrators' employees must refrain from improper disclosure of taxpayers' information, keep it confidential, and use it only for intended tax administration purposes.[15] They should also refrain from soliciting or accepting bribes from taxpayers.

All MOR employees must have an overall understanding of the MOR's operations and responsibilities. Frontline tax officers, in particular, must be well-versed in the MOR's operation and requirements to solve taxpayers' problems without referring taxpayers to other officers and offices. The front-line officers must be technically proficient, professional, courteous, and respectful of taxpayers' rights. Tax officers must also be knowledgeable to respond to government bodies with supervisory responsibility and internal organizations responsible for reviewing and evaluating tax administration procedures, processes, and practices.

Key performance indicators (KPIs) must be used for appraising the performance of both the MOR and the ECC. The KPI matrix must include employees' and taxpayers' satisfaction with the MOR and ECC performances and the substance of the tax laws, regulations, and directives. The tax authorities' performance measures must also help employees decide how to fulfill their assigned responsibilities.[16] These performance measures must support the vision of the MOR and ECC for fair, consistent administration and enforcement of tax laws.

Not only should the MOR and ECC regularly collect feedback from the taxpaying public, importers and exporters, tax professionals, employees, and other stakeholders on the quality of their services and overall performance, but they also need to act on the feedback received in order to enhance their performance and service delivery. A willingness to ask for

---

15 Mathijs Alink and Victor van Kommer (2016), Handbook on Tax Administration, second edition, Chapter 2. Core Business of Tax Administration, IBED https://www.ibfd.org/sites/ibfd.org/files/content/pdf/15_090_Handbook_on_Tax.

16 Ibid.

and be responsive to feedback from stakeholders will improve the tax-paying public's confidence in the tax system. This confidence is crucial for expanding voluntary tax compliance.

Within MOR and ECC, integrating and streamlining similar functions would enhance both organizations' responsiveness and cost efficiency. The DFID-funded TSTP recommended BPR. The BPR was developed jointly with process owners to rapidly integrate and streamline processes to simplify the taxpayer journey, as shown in Figure 5.1.

The BPR method stems from the notion that operational processes often slice through the functional layers of an organization, this layering thus being an obstacle to optimal operations.[17] The advantages of a well-designed business process are that it eliminates gaps, duplications, and unnecessary bureaucracies.[18] The BPR removes bottlenecks and redundant functions within critical business processes. It also assigns process owners specific tasks. The redesigned processes and the total business operation are evaluated for effectiveness, efficiency, and additional process integration opportunities.

Until the BPR is implemented, the MOR and the ECC must continue to evaluate, learn, and strive to improve their existing business processes and procedures.[19] There are several aspects or areas to consider when applying BPR. Organizational efficiency, effectiveness, and performance are more than streamlined taxpayers' services and tax compliance enforcement. They require having access to adequate resources and integrating support services such as human resources management and staff training and development, planning capabilities, management control, and internal auditing.

---

17 Ibid.

18 Cowater International (2019). MOR Core Tax to Be Process Map, Bizagi Modeler, September 30, 2019.

19 In Ethiopia, the "as is" business processes of the MOR were assessed in 2019 and 2020 by Cowater International, and recommendations for the "to be" business processes were made to the Minister.

The current BPR would benefit from implementing a Delphi technique that involves all stakeholders discussing and identifying the performance gaps within the MOR and ECC. Such a methodology will help refine and redesign the organization to fit its purpose. See Annex 5.1 for a discussion of the Delphi methodology for organizational capacity building.

In the last BPR, the role of internal auditing was minimized. The World Bank (2012) report affirms that the qualification and experience requirements for procurement and internal audit staff tended to be lower than necessary to perform effectively.[20] According to the World Bank, possessing a diploma is usually an academic requirement for internal auditors. For accounting staff, a bachelor's degree is the primary educational requirement. As a result, an anomaly has arisen. Internal auditors tend to be less qualified and experienced than audited staff. The only internal audit-specific training received by many internal auditors in the woredas visited by the IPE assessment team consisted of a one-week course provided by the Ministry of Finance.[21] In effect, this situation compromised the internal auditors' effectiveness. It is difficult for internal auditors to command respect from their auditees and have a professional arms-length relationship. Also, the sharing of the same working space by both auditors and auditees compromises the effectiveness of the internal auditors.

And yet, internal auditing is a crucial function for

- reviewing, assessing, and communicating to management the reliability and integrity of the information generated by the organization,

---

20 World Bank, 2012. Ethiopia: Country Integrated Fiduciary Assessment, Fourth Draft Report, January 12, 2012; pp.171–172.

21 Samuel Taddesse, Berhanu Denu, Fanta Tesgera Jetu, Mammo Alemu, Tesfaye Gudeta, and Zegeye Dechassa (2013). Federal Regional States & City Administration PFM Assessment Synthesis Report, Federal and Regional Public Finance Management (PFM) Contract No.: Co/PBS-c-08/11, IPE Global, Ethiopia, July 2013.

- compliance of the organization and its employees with government policies and regulations,
- the proper functioning of internal procedures and processes,
- the safeguarding of the organization's assets, and
- the efficient and effective use of organizational resources.

Internal audits encompass financial activities and operations, taxpayer services, human resources management, and compliance with internal and external government regulations.

At least once a year, MOR and ECC must take stock of how they perform with taxpayers and their employees while meeting their revenue targets. Annex 5.2 lists some key performance indicators (KPI). The most critical measures of tax administration performance are customer service, user-friendliness, and employee satisfaction.

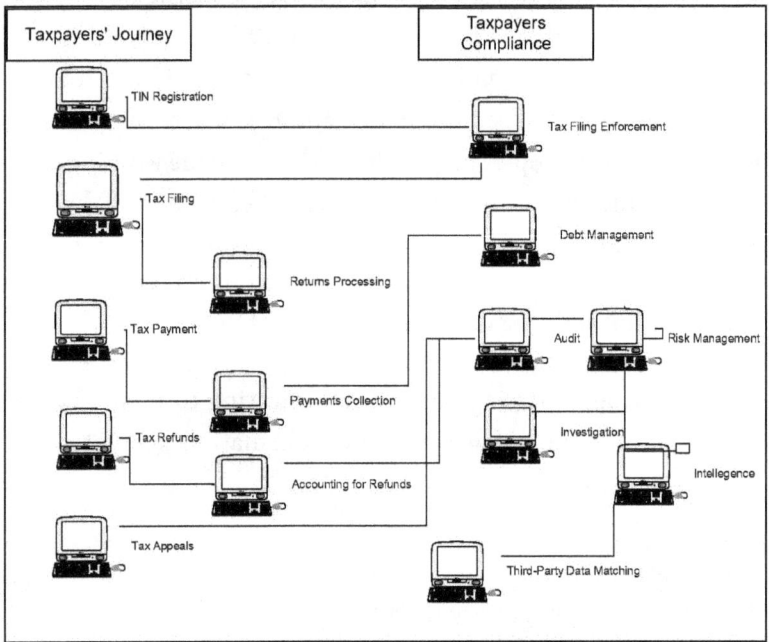

Figure 5.1: The Taxpayers' Journey and Tax Administration Function

5.3. INFORMATION MANAGEMENT

The information and communication technology infrastructure is crucial for supporting the optimal performance of tax administration. For example, taxpayers must file and remit to the tax authority VAT and withholding taxes collected from their customers. In addition, at the end of the tax year, they must file their income tax declarations. Importers have to declare the value of the goods and commodities imported and pay customs duties, taxes, and in some cases, VAT and excise taxes. The Customs Declaration indicates how much VAT, excise, and other taxes the importer has paid on the goods and commodities it cleared through the ECC.

The MOR has separate departments for VAT collection, excise and withholding tax collection, and income tax collection. While implementing TSTP, we found that these departments are not sharing taxpayers' data regularly because of incomplete information communication technology. However, the VAT and withholding tax data are vital for validating the completeness and correctness of the income tax declared and paid by a taxpayer. Because of these data- management and data-matching weaknesses, countless large- and medium-sized taxpayers have avoided paying their fair share of taxes.

As shown in Figure 5.2, tax officers must review different types of taxpayer information to determine each taxpayer's compliance with the tax law. Gathering and collating a complete set of taxpayer information using the taxpayer's TIN and business license ID is essential. It will enable the tax administrator to determine how much tax revenue is owed and paid and whether the taxpayers fully comply with the tax law.

There is currently a lack of a real-time taxpayer information digital system to collect, collate, and maintain the data in a central location. Such a system would have the taxpayer data readily available and accessible for tax officers to review for completeness. For example, the Tax Data Directorate (TDD) collects taxpayer data about how much sales they have conducted daily. Taxpayers submit the information online, in hard-copy, or on CDs.

Branch offices also receive from taxpayers VAT, income tax, and other types of tax declarations. However, the data maintained by the TDD does not match with data received and processed by the branch offices. The Ethiopian MOR needs a functioning Networked Enterprise Data Management System (NEDMS). A system architecture that breaks down the silo and integrates taxpayer data in a single place can significantly improve MOR's performance in enforcing and fostering tax compliance.

An NEDMS can enable the government to collect the correct taxes in real time. The NEDMS would allow tax officers to gather the taxpayer's information using the taxpayer's TIN or business license ID. It would also capture unified business registration, taxpayer records, and payments. The NEDMS architecture must complete the taxpayer's story by gathering data from third parties, including the Ministry of Trade and Industry (MTI), the Ministry of Finance, the ECC, other organizations, and regional states. The NEDMS must have a robust algorithm to automatically flag those businesses that have obtained business licenses but have failed to register for a TIN and those taxpayers with fake and duplicate TINs.

As mentioned above, a tax administration's core business is providing taxpayers with support and guidance. The design of the NEDMS must include a website where taxpayers can get up-to-date information on the tax law and administration and download the correct tax forms. Taxpayers should be able to get online tax services and information quickly. Taxpayers' questions and queries should also be addressed promptly through online chat followed by email.

The tax administrator will also benefit from getting accurate taxpayer data to forecast the tax revenue and compare it against the actual tax collected. The NEDMS can also incorporate the enterprise's performance information. It can analyze and summarize the KPI for tax collection, audit yield, and taxpayers' compliance rates. The result can be translated and posted as a dashboard for senior management to review and take appropriate action to improve tax administration performance. Furthermore, linking the tax administration's NEDMS to the Ministry of Finance's data system will provide more accurate government budget management information, tax expenditure, and tax gap analysis.

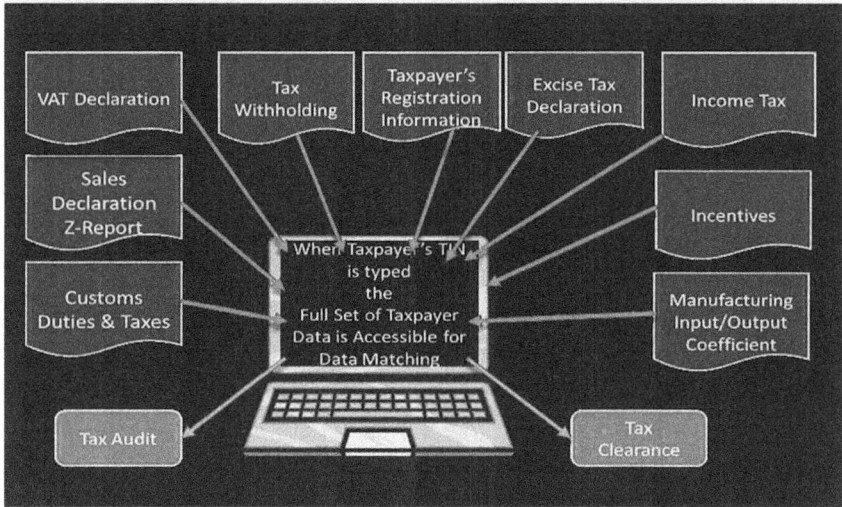

Figure 5.2: The Tax System Information Technology Architecture

Currently, MOR's SIGTAS data management system is broken. The government has been using SIGTAS for over 14 years. SIGTAS was to help the government

- track taxpayer TIN registration from one place,
- get an integrated view of taxpayer liability (through an integrated tax account),
- urge taxpayers to send remittance forms, assessment notices, and various taxpayer correspondence automatically,
- track tax liability, exemptions, refunds, and suspensions,
- identify taxpayer errors or omissions through tax declaration processing,

- automatically calculate the tax amount to be paid, as well as penalties and interest for overdue payments and incorrect tax declarations,
- automatically reconcile bank receipts,
- track late-filing and late-payment reminders,
- integrate collection case management,
- automatically carry forward deficits and tracking of depreciation, and
- cross-checking monthly payments against annual statements.

SIGTAS did not live up to its promises for one reason or another. First, the maintenance and operation of the system were heavily reliant on expatriate staff that rotated every two years without proper transfer of knowledge and expertise to their Ethiopian counterparts. Second, the directorate was poorly staffed and resourced. The personnel responsible for operating and maintaining the system did not receive adequate training. Third, the slow and unreliable telecommunication and internet infrastructure hampered the functionality of SIGTAS. Fourth, the slow manual data entry did not allow real-time data entry into the system. The system could not be relied on because of the vast data entry backlog. Finally, the maintenance of the system was dependent on fragmented donor assistance.

Self-assessment income tax declarations should directly flow into the data management system rather than be reentered manually by MOR staff. This will reduce data entry time and the potential for errors. Tax and other incentives provided by the MTI and the Ministry of Finance should also directly flow into the data management system. Currently, the MOR has introduced e-tax, e-filing, and e-payment. Because of the problem with the internet infrastructure nationwide, the frequent electricity outages in the country, and the low computer skills of many taxpayers, the uptake has been slow and costly.

Furthermore, there is no interface with third-party systems that may contain vital taxpayer information. That said, third-party data are still

Excel-based and not readily available. And yet, third-party data is critical for estimating the amount of tax owed to the government and detecting tax avoidance or tax fraud. A government-wide interconnected and secure information management system is required to facilitate real-time taxpayers' information exchange. Such an information exchange system can promote taxpayer education and enhance tax compliance.

5.4. CONCLUSIONS

The MOR and the ECC administer the national tax policy in Ethiopia, while regional revenue bureaus (RRB) implement the sub-national tax laws. These tax administrators' core business is collecting tax revenue from citizens, residents, and businesses to fund government operations. They also promote voluntary tax compliance through tax education, investigation and enforcement, and targeted tax auditing.

To keep tax compliance and enforcement costs from rising, tax administrators require continuous process improvements. One approach for tax administrators is to continuously improve their business processes by applying BPR. BPR is a technology for realigning and streamlining the tax administrators' processes and functions for optimal, fair, and equitable service delivery to taxpayers.

However, BPR is heavily reliant on a tax administrator's personnel policies, including hiring and promotion. Merit-based hiring and performance-based promotion would significantly enhance the performance of any tax administrator. Strengthening internal controls and audits can also considerably improve the effectiveness of tax administrations. It can also bolster the integrity and professionalism of tax officers.

The effectiveness and efficiency of tax administration would also improve with the development and use of an NEDMS. All taxpayer information, including third-party information, must be readily available to a tax officer. This would enable tax officers to review, analyze, and audit the data to verify if the taxpayer is declaring and paying the correct amount of tax owed to the government.

Tax administration performance must be measured using indicators of taxpayers' satisfaction, tax administration employees' satisfaction and motivation, and the tax revenue yield.

CHAPTER 6
TAXPAYERS' OBLIGATIONS AND RIGHTS

Various legislation and regulations grant tax administrators powers to collect direct and indirect taxes from citizens, residents, and businesses. The tax laws and regulations also obligate the taxpayers to pay the levied taxes when due. At the same time, the law protects the privacy and confidentiality of taxpayers' information.

In a constitutional democracy, taxation is governed by constitutional laws. Constitutional laws identify who shall pay tax, on what, and how much. These questions are fundamentally political, both in the domestic and international context. The law clearly should lay out the taxation process and its enforcement.

The rule of law also requires clarity in the tax law and a strict interpretation of the tax law to provide legal certainty. Taxpayers' relationships with the government are governed by laws and regulations to limit arbitrary tax actions by the government on any individual or business taxpayer.[1]

---

1   Pushpender Pal (2018). Taxpayers' Rights and Obligations, Accounting Notes https://www.accountingnotes.net/international-taxation/taxpayers-rights-and-obligations/4520.

Also, no individual or organization is above the law or availed preferential treatment.

In a democratic society, a fundamental principle affecting tax law is that Parliament, representing the people's will, must ratify all tax policies and regulations. The law must also clearly identify what is taxed, the associated tax rates, and the persons or entities to be taxed. The law must indicate how to determine the tax base, the allowed tax exemptions, the audit process, and the penalties for tax law violations by either a taxpayer or a tax officer, or both.

In addition, taxation based on the rule of law requires that an independent judiciary body interpret the tax law, whose decisions must bind the government, its agencies, and the taxpayers. Thus, in democratic societies, taxpayers and tax administrators are bound by the judiciary's interpretation of the tax law. That will protect the tax system and the taxpayers, provided the judiciary is free from political influence and the executive branch of government. Also, for the clarity of the tax law, the court would deem the tax laws void if they are vague and subject to different interpretations. The rule of law requires that the government and its agencies act by laws, not decrees or internal directives, as is often the case in many developing countries, including Ethiopia.

Taxpayers must have legal certainty. They should be able to predict the tax consequences of their income-generating activities in advance with sufficient certainty. Table 6.1 summarizes the fundamental rights and obligations of taxpayers.

Table 6.1: Basic Rights and Obligations of Taxpayers[2] [3]

Rights	Obligations
1. **Right to be Informed, Assisted, and Heard:** Tax authorities must provide taxpayers with up-to-date information on the tax law and how their tax liabilities are assessed and determined. Also, the information provided must assist the taxpayers in better complying with the tax law. And where the tax law is complex, they can promptly request and get clarification and assistance from the tax authorities officers in easily understood language. 2. **Right of Appeal:** The right of appeal against any tax authorities' decision is granted by law to all taxpayers. All tax authorities' decisions regarding applying the law, administrative rulings, or tax audit findings are appealable.	1. **Obligation to be Honest:** Taxpayers' honesty is fundamental to the operation of any tax system. Taxpayers must exercise reasonable care and diligence to comply honestly with their tax obligations. 2. **Obligation to Be Cooperative:** Modern tax systems can only function effectively if there is a high degree of voluntary compliance, keeping enforcement activity to a minimum. The cooperative behavior of most taxpayers allows the government to run the taxation system at a low cost and minimizes unnecessary intrusion into taxpayer affairs. Hence, taxpayers must cooperate with the relevant tax authorities and comply with their tax obligations.

---

2   Adopted from the OECD (2003). *Taxpayers' Rights and Obligations-Practice* Note, General Administrative Principles, Center for Tax Policy and Administration Taxpayers' Rights and Obligations. https://www.oecd.org/tax/administration/Taxpayers'_Rights_and_Obligations-Practice_Note.pdf.

3   Pushpender Pal (2018). Taxpayers' Rights and Obligations, Accounting Notes https://www.accountingnotes.net/international-taxation/taxpayers-rights-and-obligations/4520.

Rights	Obligations
3. **Right to Pay No More than the Correct Amount of Tax:** Either because of ignorance of the tax law, wrong interpretation of the tax law, or some accounting and calculation error, taxpayers must not pay more tax than is appropriate. Taxpayers are also entitled to reasonable support from the tax authority to receive all the tax reliefs and deductions they are entitled to under the law. 4. **Right to Certainty:** The goal is that taxpayers anticipate the results of their ordinary personal and business affairs. Achieving this goal is often tricky because tax systems are complex. Thus, tax authorities are expected to clarify the tax consequences of these complex issues to taxpayers. 5. **Right to Privacy:** All taxpayers have the right to privacy. Taxpayers expect the tax authorities not to intrude unnecessarily on their privacy. This would include unreasonable searches of their homes and requests for information irrelevant to determining the correct amount of taxes due. Strict rules apply to entering a taxpayer's dwelling or business premises by a tax official in a tax investigation and obtaining information from third parties. Taxpayer's consent is required to visit a taxpayer.	3. **Obligation to Provide Accurate Information and Documents on Time:** All taxpayers must provide tax authorities with accurate and trustworthy information on their tax affairs, including their income sources. Tax authorities use taxpayer information to identify the taxpayer and account for taxes paid or payable. 4. **Obligation to Keep Records:** Taxpayers must verify the taxes payable and keep good contemporaneous records of their income and financial transactions as required by law. The tax authorities use these taxpayer records to confirm that the information provided by a taxpayer is accurate. Most tax authorities specify what records must be kept and for what length. 5. **Obligation to Pay Taxes on Time:** All taxpayers must pay their taxes on time as stipulated by the tax law. Taxpayers should be encouraged to discuss their circumstances with the tax authority, as it may be possible to allow additional time for payment in some cases.

Rights	Obligations
In most countries, a signed warrant from a court of law is necessary to enter a taxpayer's home who objects to a visit by the tax authority. Similarly, strict rules apply to obtaining information from third parties on a taxpayer's affairs. The taxpayer must sign a consent form authorizing the release of information to a third party.	
6. **Right to Confidentiality and Secrecy:** The information provided to or held by the tax authorities on a taxpayer's affairs is strictly confidential and must only be used for the purposes specified in the tax legislation. Tax legislation usually imposes hefty penalties on tax officials who misuse taxpayers' information.	

6.1. INDIVIDUAL TAXPAYER'S OBLIGATIONS AND RIGHTS

Tax laws obligate citizens, residents, and businesses to pay the levied taxes required by the law. The law also requires individual and business taxpayers to register with the tax authority and obtain a taxpayer identification number (TIN). In addition, taxpayers must assemble their income information, calculate their tax liabilities, and declare and pay the amount owed to the government on time. These are necessary legal obligations that every income earner must abide by. Let us review these obligations separately.

6.1.1 Registering as a Taxpayer

In Ethiopia, Article 9 of the Federal Income Tax Administration Proclamation No. 983/2016 requires that all taxpayers register for a TIN before declaring and paying their taxes. Article 14 requires all taxpayers to write down their TIN on tax declaration forms and other documents filed with the tax authority.

A TIN is a randomly generated, well-designed, and unique numeric code consisting of ten digits. All tax declarations must include the taxpayer's TIN. It is unlawful to share a TIN with other taxpayers or use another taxpayer's TIN for any purpose.

Applying for a TIN is done using the Ministry of Revenue's (MOR's) approved form. As the law specifies, the applicant must provide an updated personal identification card (ID), like Kebele ID, driver's license, or employer's ID, including a biometric identifier, to obtain a TIN. The current biometric identifier is a fingerprint of both hands of the applicant. First, take fingerprints of the little, ring, middle, and index fingers, and then the left and right hands' thumbs. The applicant must also provide a passport-sized color photo of their face. The TIN registration form gives the tax authority information about the applicant's identity.

The tax law requires that the MOR register and provide a TIN to the requesting person as mandated by the tax law provided the individual fulfills all requirements and meets the criteria. The MOR provides a unique TIN for the person requesting a TIN under sub-article (1) of Article 9 of Proclamation No. 983/2016 if satisfied that the person is liable for tax under the tax law. Suppose the Authority refuses to register a person who has applied for TIN registration. In that case, the tax authority shall serve the person with written notice of the refusal within 14 days from the TIN application date.

A taxpayer can apply for a TIN at the Mistry of Revenue or any one of the ten regional state revenue bureaus (RSRBs); in Addis Ababa administration sub-cities; at the Dire Dawa administration; and at MOR sites, including the

Addis Ababa main branch office, large taxpayers' office, Hawassa, Nazareth, Mekele, Bahirdar, Dire Dawa, and Jimma branch offices. Sometimes, the appropriate place for TIN registration is the locality where the individual is employed or is conducting business. But enterprises that register with the federal government, such as private limited companies and share companies, may obtain their TIN from the MOR and its branch offices.

6.1.2 Tax Filing

All taxpayers must file their income taxes annually with the appropriate tax office. As outlined in Chapter 4, one source of personal income is **employment income**. Article 12 of the Federal Income Tax Proclamation No. 979/2016 defines employment income as "salary, wages, an allowance, bonus, commission, gratuity or other remuneration received by an employee in respect of past, current or future employment" and includes "the value of fringe benefits received by an employee in respect to past, current or future employment," plus "an amount received by an employee to termination of employment, whether paid voluntarily, under an agreement or as a result of legal proceedings, including any compensation for redundancy or loss of employment or a golden handshake payment."

In Ethiopia, employers withhold the payroll tax and pension contribution and pay the tax and pension contribution directly to the responsible tax authority on behalf of their employees. Tax liability is assessed on the employee's total income, whether paid in cash or in-kind, as defined by the tax law. However, certain benefits and allowances are exempted from taxation and include

- transportation allowances up to ETB 800
- weather allowance for persons working in arid regions, and
- Per diem paid to employees when working further away than 25 km from their workplace. However, per diem must not exceed 4% of each employee's monthly salary. The maximum allowed per diem per month is ETB 1,000, provided it does not exceed 4% of the employee's monthly salary.

Transportation expenses incurred while an employee is traveling for work-related purposes should be based on documentary evidence (i.e., receipts for taxi service, buses, or fuel) and should be in line with (should not exceed) the prevailing land or air transportation fares. Also, transportation expenses incurred when an expatriate worker leaves the country, having terminated their employment contract, should be as per the agreement specified in their employment contract and should be in line with (should not exceed) the prevailing land or air transportation fares with their luggage not exceeding 300 kilograms.[4]

6.1.3 Paying Taxes

Individuals earning taxable income other than employment income must report their income and pay their taxes. Also, sole proprietors must record their daily income and expenses, calculate their net income and tax liability for the tax year, and pay their taxes. To determine net income for the tax year, they must record all income from business transactions and write down and deduct all the business expenditures incurred during the tax year. As much as possible, personal expenses are recorded separately from business expenditures. Box 6.1 describes the records taxpayers are expected to keep and maintain to support their tax liability computations.

According to Article 21 of Proclamation No. 979/2016, the individual's gross business income is the gross proceeds from the sale of goods and services for the tax year plus a gain from the sale of a business asset during the tax year. It may also include income from renting business premises or movable assets. And Article 22 highlights the expenses deducted from gross income, including the following:

- The cost of inventory sold to customers[5]

---

4   MultiLink, Personal Income Tax in Ethiopia, https://www.oecd.org/tax/administration/Taxpayers'_Rights_and_Obligations-Practice_Note.pdf - Bing.

5   Cost of goods sold is the direct cost incurred in the production or acquisition of the goods or services sold to customers. In the case of manufactured or processed goods, it includes material cost, direct labor cost, and direct factory overhead costs.

- Advertising costs
- Business facility rental
- Cost of land lease
- Employee salaries, wages, and benefits
- Depreciation of business assets
- Loss on sale of a business asset
- Interest expenses on bank loans
- Loss carried forward

Income tax declaration is made using the MOR forms. The taxpayer must also declare and remit value-added tax (VAT) and tax withholdings collected from customers on behalf of the tax authority. The taxpayer may also be owed a VAT refund on purchases made from other vendors or suppliers. Usually, when declaring and remitting VAT and tax withholding, the taxpayer deducts from the total VAT it paid to other businesses.

6.1.4 Obtaining a Tax Clearance Certificate

Once taxpayers have filed and paid taxes, they can request and obtain a tax clearance certificate. A tax clearance certificate is required to renew business licenses, participate in public tenders, and obtain vehicle inspection stickers from the road transport authority. To ensure that taxpayers file their tax returns on time in compliance with the law, the Federal Income Tax Administration Proclamation 983/2016 Article 61, sub-article (4), requires that

> "No Ministry, Municipality, Department or Office of the Federal or a State Government, or other Government body shall issue or renew any license to a taxpayer or allow the taxpayer to participate in a public tender unless the taxpayer produces a tax clearance certificate."

A taxpayer can apply for a tax clearance certificate using the approved form issued by the tax authority. The authority must give the taxpayer a tax clearance certificate within 14 days of applying for a tax clearance certificate under sub-article (1) of Article 61. The use of the tax clearance certificate also has a time limit and expires on a specific date. It is possible to extend the expiration date by writing to the tax authority.

Box 6.1: Recordkeeping

A businessperson must retain all tax-related documents (see Article 82 of the income tax proclamation), including

- A record of all business assets and liabilities, including a register of fixed assets showing the acquisition date, the cost of acquisition, and cost of improvement, and the current net book value
- A record of daily income and expenditures
- A record of all purchases and sales of trading stock (i.e., inventory), including the suppliers' invoices with the suppliers' names and TINs and copies of the receipts issued to buyers
- A record of trading stock (i.e., inventory) on hand at the end of the tax year including the type, quantity, and cost, including valuation method
- A record of employees' salaries, wages, and benefits register

The specific records a taxpayer must keep and maintain depend on the taxpayer's category: "A," "B," and "C." The Council of Ministers Federal Income Tax Regulation No. 410/2017 Article 59 specifies that category "C" taxpayers may keep a book of accounts that category "B" taxpayers must maintain. It also says that the tax liability of category "C" taxpayers that have books of account shall be assessed in accordance with such books of account as are acceptable to the tax authority.

The regulation also requires that category "C" taxpayers who employ workers must keep documents showing any amount of employment income paid to the employees and any amount withheld in tax from such income. Article 60 of the regulation also states that category "C" taxpayers shall pay income tax per turnover-based standard presumptive business tax or indicator-based presumptive business tax methods. Category "C" taxpayers engaged in the business of transportation services, on the other hand, shall pay the withholding tax from employment income together with their business income tax.

6.2. BUSINESS TAXPAYERS' OBLIGATIONS AND RIGHTS

The Ethiopian Commercial Code of 1960 and the Commercial Registration and Licensing Proclamation No. 980/2016 recognize several types of business formations, as listed in Table 6.2.

Table 6.2: Types of Business Formations[6]

Type of Business	Description
Partnership	Two or more persons form a partnership to conduct economic activities and participate in the profits and losses. According to the Commercial Code of Ethiopia, each person shall contribute money, debts, other property, or skill. Using one's property for the partnership may count as a contribution. Unless otherwise agreed, the partnership contributions shall be of equal value and of nature and extent required for conducting the partnership's purposes.
Joint venture	A joint venture is formed based on terms mutually agreed upon between partners. It is subject to the general principles of law relating to partnerships.
General partnership	A general partnership is formed by partners who are personally, jointly, and fully liable between themselves and the partnership firm's undertakings. Each partner assumes the consequences of the other partner's actions. All members also share the management of the business.

---

6   AddisBiz (2015). Types of Business Organizations in Ethiopia (Blog). Mar 19, 2015, https://www.oecd.org/tax/administration/Taxpayers'_Rights_ and_Obligations-Practice_Note.pdf.

Limited partnership	A limited partnership is a business where some members are general partners who control and manage the business and may be entitled to a more significant profit share. In contrast, other partners are limited and contribute only to the company's capital. Limited partners take no part in control or management and are only liable for debts to a specified extent. A legal document outlining specific requirements must be drawn up for a limited partnership.
Share company or private limited company	In this type of company, capital is fixed in advance and divided into shares. Liabilities are met only by its assets. The members shall be liable only to the extent of their shareholding. Formation of a share company shall be by a public memorandum—memorandum of association, which consists of – names, nationalities, and addresses of the members, the number of shares that they have subscribed to, provided that a member may not subscribe to less than one share, – name of the company, – head office and the branches, if any, – the business purpose of the company, – amount of capital subscribed and paid up, – par value, number, form, and classes of shares, – value of contributions in kind, the price at which they are accepted, the designation of the shareholder, and the number of shares allocated to them by way of exchange, – manner of distributing profits, and – the number of directors and their power.

Sole proprietorship	A sole proprietor is fully responsible for all debts and obligations related to their business. The sole proprietorship terminates by law upon the death of the sole proprietor, with very few exceptions. Estate planning documents for the sole proprietor may grant another person, such as a spouse, the right to continue the business as a sole proprietor.
Cooperatives	Cooperatives are formed by individuals associating voluntarily and pulling together their resources to promote their economic interests. People with financial constraints tend to form cooperatives to benefit from joint efforts, scale, and greater purchasing power.

6.2.1 Registering a Business

Any person or group of individuals interested in operating a business within Ethiopia must apply for a business license with the Ministry of Trade and Industry (MTI). It must also obtain a TIN certificate from the MOR. The MTI and the MOR require the applicant to submit a memorandum, articles of association, and trade names.[7] Founders or business organization members must sign the memorandum and articles of association at the federal or regional Document Authentication and Registration Agency (DARA).

---

7   The memorandum of association of a company is an essential corporate document. It is the document that regulates the company's external affairs and complements the articles of association, which cover the company's internal constitution. It contains the fundamental conditions under which the company is allowed to operate. It includes the "objects clause," which lets the shareholders, creditors, and those dealing with the company know its permitted range of operation broadly. It also shows the company's initial capital. The articles of association is a document that, along with the memorandum of association, forms the company's constitution and defines the responsibilities of the directors, the kind of business to be undertaken, and the means by which the shareholders exert control on the board of directors.

The primary laws and regulations governing business registration and licensing include the following:

- 1960 Commercial Code of Ethiopia
- Proclamation No. 980/2016 on Commercial Registration and Business Licensing
- Proclamation No. 1150/2019 on Commercial Registration and Business Licensing (Amendment)
- Regulation No. 461/2020 on Commercial Registration and Licensing (Amendment)

The MTI and trade bureaus of the respective regional states are the principal government organ to regulate and administer commercial registration, trade name registration, and business license per the Commercial Registration and Business Licensing Proclamation No. 480/2016 Article 4 and Article 21. The MTI is obligated by article 4 of Proclamation No. 980/2016 to establish and administer a central commercial register and trade name register with a nationwide application and make it open and accessible to the public.

Commercial and trade name registration is undertaken by the regional organs administering commercial activities and the Ethiopian Investment Commission (EIC) when delegated[8]. Similarly, the MTI registers and issues certificates to sectoral associations established at the federal level, such as the Ethiopian Chambers of Commerce, Ethiopian Leather Products Association, etc., while regional organs administering commercial activities register sectoral associations at regional state levels and issue certificates of legal personality. Some of the government organs with authority to grant a business license for specific sectors include the following:

---

8   2Merkato (2008). Regulation of Commercial Registration and Business Licensing in Ethiopia, https://www.2merkato.com/articles/starting-a-business/41-regulations-of-commercial-registration-and-business-licensing-in-ethiopia.

- The **Ethiopian Investment Commission (EIC).** The EIC issues business permits for foreign investors, investments jointly established by domestic and international investors, or domestic investors who want to benefit from the commission's incentives.
- The **Ministry of Mining and Petroleum** issues business licenses for prospecting and mining minerals.
- The **Ministry of Water, Irrigation, and Electricity** issues business licenses for various waterworks services, excluding waterworks construction services.
- The **National Bank of Ethiopia** issues business licenses for banking, insurance, and microfinance services.

As listed in Table 6.3, a businessperson has rights and obligations regarding obtaining and maintaining a business license.

Table 6.3: Businesspersons' Rights and Obligations[9]

Rights	Obligations
According to Proclamation No. 480/2016, Article 25, a businessperson issued a business license has the following rights: 1. to engage in a business activity within the scope of the business license, 2. to not be compelled to obtain an additional business license for branch offices opened for engaging in similar business activity, 3. to receive information on commercial registration and licensing services, 4. to alter or amend commercial registration, trade name, and business per this proclamation, and 5. to conduct other similar activities allowed by the proclamation and other laws.	According to Proclamation No. 480/2016, Article 26, a businessperson issued a business license has the following obligations: 1. to execute the various business activities for which business licenses have been issued in separate places or premises, where carrying on such activities at the exact location or premises endangers public health and safety or property, 2. to comply with the obligation that the nature of the business activity demands, to fulfill standards, and to render service, 3. to display a price list in a noticeable place in the business for the goods and services sold by the business or by affixing price tags on the goods and services provided by the business, 4. to display the business license in clearly recognizable areas within the business premises, or in the case of branch business offices, display copies of the business license affixed with the seal of the licensing authority,

---

9   Federal Democratic Republic of Ethiopia Proclamation No. 480/2016. See also, 2Merkato (2008). Regulation of Commercial Registration and Business Licensing in Ethiopia, https://www.2merkato.com/articles/starting-a-business/41-regulations-of-commercial-registration-and-business-licensing-in-ethiopia.

Rights	Obligations
	5. to not assign the business license to the benefit of any other person or business, pledge or lease out the license,
	6. to not make use of the business license, where an administrative or court decision is passed to dissolve the business organization or to ban a sole proprietor,
	7. to notify the registering office within one month in case of a change of business address,
	8. if it is a share company or private limited company, this shall cause an audit of the company's financial statements by an external auditor every fiscal year and the reports submitted to the licensing authority as well to the tax authority,
	9. to provide the information requested by interested offices concerning the activities of the business, and
	10. to comply with administrative measures taken by concerned authorities and other obligations in other laws.

Furthermore, according to Article 45 of Proclamation No. 480/2016, a businessperson's business premises could be inspected by relevant authorities to enforce the law. However, an inspector deployed by the competent authority must show their special identification cards related to their inspection duties. Furthermore, inspectors can only inspect business establishments during government working hours. Yet, inspectors may inspect business establishments after hours after obtaining an approval letter from the relevant authority for such a purpose.

Also, businesspersons must be aware that any violation of the proclamation's provisions is punishable by law. Per Article 49 of the proclamation, a businessperson who

1. prepares or uses false business license, certificate of commercial registration or special certificate of commercial representation shall, without prejudice to the confiscation of their merchandise, service provision, and manufacturing equipment, be punished with a fine ranging from ETB 150,000 to ETB 300,000 and with rigorous imprisonment ranging from 7 to 15 years,

2. engages in business activity without having a valid license or any businessperson involved in a business outside the scope of his business license shall, without prejudice to the confiscation of merchandise, service provision, and manufacturing equipment, be punished with a fine ranging from ETB 150,000 to ETB 300,000 and with rigorous imprisonment for 7 to 15 years,

3. undergoes or attempts to undergo commercial or trade name registration or obtains or tries to obtain a business license or special certificate of commercial representation upon presentation of false documents or uses or attempts to use such documentation for renewal of his business license or the special certificate of commercial representation shall, without prejudice to the confiscation of any benefits he may have earned, be punished with a fine ranging from ETB 60,000 to ETB 120,000 and with rigorous imprisonment from 7 to 12 years,

4. transfers business license to a third party by way of sale, lease, donation, or in a similar fashion is punished with a fine ranging from ETB 50,000 to ETB 100,000 and with rigorous imprisonment from 5 to 10 years. Suppose the business license has been transferred to a foreign national. In that case, the fine shall range from ETB 200,000 to ETB 300,000. The imprisonment shall be from 7 to 15 years,

5. fails to notify the change of business address to the registering office within the period specified in the regulations shall be punished with a fine ranging from ETB 5,000 to ETB 10,000 with simple imprisonment not exceeding 3 months,

6. fails to notify the registering office within 30 days of changes that warrant amendments in the commercial register under the Proclamation shall be punished with a fine ranging from ETB 5,000 to ETB 10,000 and imprisonment not exceeding 3 months,

7. refuses to provide information or attempts to obstruct the duties of workers or supervisors sent by the relevant authority as part of activities for the enforcement of Proclamation No. 480/2016, regulations, or directives issued hereunder shall be punished with a fine ranging from ETB 5,000 to ETB 10,000 and with simple imprisonment not exceeding 3 months, and

8. violates the other provisions of this proclamation and is punished with a fine ranging from ETB 10,000 to ETB 30,000 and simple imprisonment from 1 to 3 years.

However, Proclamation No. 480/2016, Article 47, provides that business-persons who feel aggrieved by the relevant authority's deliberation **can submit their grievances** to the head of the appropriate authority within 10 days. The head of the relevant authority to submit the petition must notify his decision within 5 business days. Notably, suppose the head of the relevant tax authority fails to notify the businessperson of such a decision within the specified time frame. In that case, the businessperson may lodge a petition to a court of law having jurisdiction over the matter.

Regardless of the type of business formation selected, the business must obtain a business license and TIN and register its trade name. The TIN application form will ask for the name and physical address of the busi-ness. The application for TIN, in most cases, is completed and submitted within 21 days of becoming liable to apply for registration or as required by the tax authority.

A businessperson who hires people to work for the business must ensure that all the employees are registered for TIN. Article 9 also obligates employers to apply for TIN registration on behalf of their employees unless they are already registered. Sub-article (3) of Article 9 shall not relieve the employees of the obligation to apply for TIN registration under sub-article (1) of this Article should the employer fail to make the application for the employee. Also, in the case of an application made by an employer for an employee under sub-article (3), the biometric identifier required under sub-article (5)(b) shall be provided by the employee.

The MOR can, by written notice, cancel the TIN of a taxpayer (Article 15) when satisfied that:

1. the taxpayer's registration has been revoked under Article 11 of the Proclamation,
2. a TIN has been issued to the taxpayer under an identity that is not the taxpayer's true identity, or
3. a TIN has been given to the taxpayer previously, and the TIN is still in force.

It may also, by written notice, cancel an existing TIN of a taxpayer and substitute it with a new TIN at any time. The employer also withholds and remits to the revenue authority employees' pension contributions.

6.2.2 Receipts for Commercial Transactions

Sole proprietors and corporations are obligated by law to issue legal receipts and invoices that accompany all commercial transactions to customers. A receipt is a document that sellers or suppliers provide to the buyers of their goods and services. The receipt shows the name of the item sold, the price paid, and the transaction's date. It includes the TIN and the buyer's name if the buyer has a TIN.

Receipts are legal documents. Receipts used by traders and service providers must conform to the MOR's requirements and be approved by a tax officer. Indeed, according to Tax Administration Proclamation No. 983/2016, Article 19, the business must register with the tax authority the types and quantities of receipts to be used before having such receipts printed. Any person operating a printing press engaged by a taxpayer to print receipts must ensure that the type and number of receipts are

registered with the MOR before printing the receipts. A business establishment may require various kinds of receipts, including the following:

- **Cash Sales Invoice:** This transaction confirmation document is issued by the seller to those who purchase a product or service.
- **Credit Sales Invoice:** This transaction confirmation document is issued by the seller to those who purchase a product or service with credit.
- **Cash Receipt Voucher:** This provides confirmation of any payment that is paid in the name of the taxpayer in cash, bank check, or bank transfer that is not related to the business and is a confirmation of payment for a good or service previously sold with credit to the buyer and does not include a receipt for the sale of goods or services.
- **Cash Payment Voucher:** This is a receipt confirming that the businessperson or body has purchased goods, commodities, or services from vendors by cash or bank check. For example, a daily laborer is paid in cash and must sign the cash payment voucher, affirming he has received payment.
- **Purchase Confirmation Receipt:** The buyer prepares this document to prove that a purchase has been made for transactions recognized by the tax authority.
- **Receipts for Withholding Tax on Payments:** This document indicates that the buyer has retained a 2% withholding tax to be remitted to the tax authority.

Customers of businesses and traders have the legal right to request and receive receipts for their commercial transactions. The receipt must contain the total value of the purchase and the sales tax or VAT charged. A business customer may also withhold 2% of the transaction value before VAT to remit to the tax authority. Sometimes, the receipt displays the 2% withholding at the bottom of the sales receipt.

Ethiopian tax law requires that sellers charge VAT and other taxes depending on the product sold or the service rendered. The seller may also charge excise and other types of taxes as applicable. The various taxes collected from customers belong to the government. They must be declared and remitted to the appropriate tax authority.

6.2.3 Use of a Cash Register Machine (CRM)

The government introduced CRMs in 2008, and the law requires all businesses and service providers to use such devices. These CRMs allow the MOR to trace business sales and obtain accurate direct and indirect tax information. Also, the latest programs and technology enable the tax authority to identify the machine's location. Attached to each CRM is a device that transmits daily sales transactions directly to a central database. These machines also have SIM cards and record all daily sales. The SIM card is renewed annually. Nationwide use of

CRMs were designed to help tax authorities in four ways:

1. Record cash sales
2. Enhance VAT compliance
   - Registration in the system
   - Timely filing
   - Timely payment of obligations
   - Timely provision of accurate information
3. Secure information for audit purposes
4. Reduce tax collection cost

The law requires that the CRM contain the merchant's full name, TIN and VAT number, and address of the business premises. The merchant or company must print out a receipt for each business transaction and provide the customer's receipt. The sales register machine receipt must contain the customer's name, TIN, item(s) bought with the sales price, the total before VAT, the VAT amount, and the total cost, including the VAT. Also, its total amount should include other taxes, such as excise tax, as appropriate. If the transaction amount exceeds 10,000 Birr, the buyer must calculate and withhold 2% of the transaction's value before VAT and remit it to the MOR. Also, the law requires all users of the CRMs to place a conspicuous notice containing the following information at the place where the machine is installed:[10]

1. Name of the user, trade name, trade location, TIN, accreditation, and permit numbers for the Sales Register Machine
2. Text stating that "In case of machine failure, sales personnel must issue manual receipts authorized by the Authority."
3. Text that reads, "DO NOT PAY IF A RECEIPT IS NOT ISSUED."

Merchants are required to print out a daily summary report called a Z-report. When declaring and filing VAT or tax withholding declarations, monthly, quarterly, and annual summary reports are printed and filed with the tax authority. All CRMs are inspected annually and repaired to ensure their functionality.

Despite all these requirements, it does not seem that the tax authorities have exploited the CRM's full potential. The central database for receiving daily sales transactions is not operational. Many businesses still have to submit hard copies of daily transactions instead of electronically transmitting the data. Also, many taxpayers do not understand the purpose and use of these CRMs. Entering into the system product codes and prices has been challenging.

Enforcing the strict use of CRMs by merchants has been difficult. Some merchants do not want to issue VAT receipts to customers to hide their business revenue from the tax authority. Customers also do not request a VAT receipt to avoid paying an additional 15% on purchased items.

6.2.4 Accounting and Bookkeeping

Corporations are also obligated to maintain a book of accounts. Bookkeeping is the recording of the financial transactions of a business. Bookkeeping involves collecting all documents related to the business's

---

10 Sales Register Machines Penalties and Offences, https://www.taxinethiopia. com/Sales%20Register%20Machines%20Penalties_offences.html.

transactions and operations. Business transactions include purchases of supplies, sales, salaries and wages, other remunerations to employees, rental payments, and other payments to individuals and corporations. Ethiopia has adopted double-entry accounting.

The objective of any business is to generate profit through exchanging goods and services. To determine if a business is making a profit, the businessperson must know how to manage the business's day-to-day operations. This includes managing goods purchased from suppliers and selling products and services to consumers. It also involves how to manage cash to pay for expenses and the cash and the checks collected from customers or paid to suppliers.

Cash withdrawals from a CRM or bank account must be recorded. The record must identify whether the cash withdrawal is for business expenses or personal use; otherwise, it is unclear how much money the business made or spent. The businessperson must also manage their investment assets, such as vehicles, buildings, and machinery, and keep maintenance records. It is essential to keep copies of receipts issued to customers and receipts and invoices received from suppliers.

Bookkeeping and accounting track the flow of investment, sales, debts, expenses, and revenues. All business transactions must be recorded.[11] For example, the money received from the sales of an item must be registered. For instance, the cash received must be recorded if a business sells 10 kilograms of coffee. Simultaneously, the amount of coffee sold must be noted and deducted from the business's coffee inventory. When a business deposits money into a bank, the entry will look like the following:

Transaction	Debit	Credit
Checking		1000
Revenue	1000	

---

11 Raes Associates, Accounting and Bookkeeping Services—Benefits of Accounting and Bookkeeping Services, https://www.taxinethiopia.com/Sales%20Register%20Machines%20Penalties_offences.html.

Every time a business sells something, revenue must be credited to recognize the cash or check payment received from the customer. In turn, when the business buys a product or service, they are spending money. The business checking account or cash holdings must be debited for the payment, and the inventory must be credited.

All accounting systems use a chart of accounts (COA) identification code. Further, the COA is broken down according to the different types of accounts as follows:

1. Assets: e.g., cash, inventory, building
2. Liabilities: e.g., utility bills, rent, loans, interest, taxes
3. Equity: e.g., Assets – Liabilities
4. Revenues: e.g., money from sales of goods, gains from the sale of assets
5. Expenses: e.g., cost of goods sold, payroll, rent paid, the utility paid

Assets are items one owns.

Liabilities are items that one owes to others.

Equity is the net worth of a business. Equity equals Assets minus Liabilities.

Revenues are money received by providing services or selling products and goods.

Expenses are money spent in the process of the pursuit of revenues. It may include expenses on the following:

- Facility rental
- Land lease
- Utilities (e.g., electricity, water)
- Communication (telephone, fax, internet)
- Transportation
- Office and business supplies

- Fuel
- Payroll
- Interest payment on loans
- Taxes owed

Assets are recorded at their netbook value. Netbook value represents the asset's value after deducting depreciation from its original price. In theory, the accumulated depreciation at the end of the asset's life represents money kept aside for replacing the asset. At the fiscal year-end, two financial statements are produced. The first is the balance sheet (see Table 6.4), which lists all the assets, liabilities, and equity.

The MOR has provided a balance sheet form with annexes for income and profit tax declaration. This form must be completed carefully by the taxpayer or its accountant.

Table 6.4: Balance Sheet

Assets	Liabilities and Equity

• Current assets
  – Cash
  – Receivables
  – Inventory
  – Prepayments
• Fixed assets
  – Plant
  – Structure/building
  – Machinery and equipment
  – Vehicles
  – Less depreciation
• Other assets
  – Patents
  – Goodwill
	• Current liabilities
	  – Accounts payable
	  – Interest payment
	  – Dividends payable
	  – Other
	
	• Shareholders' equity
	  – Shareholder's capital contribution
	  – Retained earnings

Total assets	Total liabilities and equity

The second financial statement is the **income** or **profit and loss statement**. The income statement immediately tells whether a business is profitable for the accounting period. It reflects the health of the enterprise for the accounting period. Records maintained concerning revenue/income and the expenses incurred during the accounting period determine the profitability of a business, as reflected in the profit and loss statement. As stated in the FDRE Income Tax Proclamation No. 979/2016, the profit and loss or income statement form the basis for a business's tax liability. For example, Article 20, sub-article (2) of the proclamation, states that

> *the taxable business income of a taxpayer for a tax year shall be determined in accordance with the profit and loss, or income statement, of the taxpayer for the year, prepared in accordance with the financial reporting standards ....*

Established by the Financial Reporting Proclamation No. 847/2014 and the Council of Ministers Regulation No. 332/2014, the Accounting and Auditing Board of Ethiopia (AABE) determines the taxpayers' and their accountants' financial reporting standards. Since 2019, Ethiopia has shifted from Generally Accepted Accounting Principles (GAAP) to International Financial Reporting Standards (IFRS). AABE has raised awareness of tax accountants on IFRS.[12] Also, the Ethiopian Federal Tax Administration Proclamation No. 983/2016, Article 17, requires taxpayers to maintain financial and related records. For example, sub-article (1) states that

> *A taxpayer shall, for the purposes of tax law, maintain such documents (including in electronic format) as may be required under the tax law, and the documents shall be maintained in (a) Amharic or English; (b)in Ethiopia; and (c) in a manner so as to enable the taxpayer's tax liability under the tax law to be readily ascertained.*

---

12   The Accounting and Auditing Board of Ethiopia (AABE), Gives an Awareness Creation on International Financial Reporting Standards http://www.aabe. gov.et/aabe-gives-awareness-creation-ifrs/.

Sub-article (2) also indicates that

> *subject to sub-article (3) of Article 17 or a tax law providing otherwise, a taxpayer shall retain the documents referred to in sub-article (1) for the longer of (a) the record-keeping period specified in the Commercial Code or (b) 5 (Five) years from the date that the tax declaration for the tax period to which they relate was filed with the Tax Authority.*

Furthermore, sub-article (3) states that

> *When at the end of the period referred to in sub-article (2) of this Article, a document is necessary for a proceeding under the Proclamation or any other law commenced before the end of the period, the taxpayer shall retain the document until the proceeding and any related proceedings have been completed.*

Article 102 of the Proclamation indicates that failure to maintain documents may result in a penalty. For example, sub-article (1) states that

> *Subject to sub-article (2) of this Article, a taxpayer who fails to maintain any document as required under a tax law shall be liable for a penalty of 20% of the tax payable by the taxpayer under the tax law for the tax period to which the failure relates.*

Also, sub-article (2) provides that

> *If no tax is payable by the taxpayer for the tax period to which the failure referred to in sub-article (1) of this Article relates, the penalty shall be (a) birr 20,000 (Twenty Thousand Birr) for each tax year that the taxpayer fails to maintain documents for the purposes of the income tax; or (b) birr 2,000 (Two Thousand Birr) for each tax period that the taxpayer fails to maintain documents for the purposes of any other tax.*

Also, sub-article (3) indicates that

> *Where the penalty to be imposed pursuant to sub-article (1)*
> *of Article 102 is less than the penalty to be imposed pursuant*
> *to sub-article (2) of this Article, the penalty in sub-article (2)*
> *of this Article shall apply.*

Furthermore, sub-articles (4), (5), and (6) indicate that failure to maintain documents for more than 2 years results in the cancelation of the taxpayer's business license (sub-article [4]). Specifically, sub-article (5) states that

> *a Category 'A' Taxpayer who fails to retain documents for*
> *the period specified in Article 17 (2) shall be liable for a*
> *penalty of birr 50,000 (Fifty Thousand Birr),*

and sub-article (6) indicates that

> *a Category 'B' taxpayer who fails to retain documents for*
> *the period specified in Article 33 (4) of the Federal Income*
> *Tax Proclamation shall be liable for a penalty of birr 20,000*
> *(Twenty Thousand Birr).*

In summary, the law requires category A taxpayers to keep books of account. The books of account must adhere to the financial accounting reporting standards. Category A taxpayers must also keep the following records:

1. A record of the business assets and liabilities of the taxpayer
2. A record of all daily income and expenditures related to the taxpayer's business
3. A record of all purchases and sales of trading stock and services provided and received
4. A record of trading stock on hand at the end of the taxpayer's tax year, including the type, quantity, cost, and method of valuation used

5. Any other document relevant to determining the tax liability of the taxpayer

Category B taxpayers must keep the following records:

1. A record of daily income and expenditure
2. A record of all purchases and sales of trading stock
3. A salary and wages register
4. Any other document relevant to determining the tax liability of the taxpayer

In addition, category A or B taxpayers liable for tax under Schedule B of this proclamation shall keep the following records:

1. A record of rental income received
2. A record of fees paid to a state or city administration concerning the building
3. A record of any expenditures incurred regarding the building (e.g., land lease fees), including building maintenance cost
4. A register of rental buildings showing the acquisition date, cost of acquisition, any costs of improvements to the building, and the current net book value of the building
5. A record of any sub-lease arrangements concerning the building

On the other hand, category C taxpayers may keep a gross income record and are only required to keep records specified in the regulation.

6.2.5 Declaring and Paying Taxes

All taxpayers must file their tax returns on time, and a tax declaration must be filed using the approved tax forms. Under certain circumstances, the tax authority is not bound by a taxpayer-provided, self-assessment tax liability. The tax authority may determine a taxpayer's tax liability based on other reliable and verifiable information sources.

When preparing a tax declaration, a certified public accountant must be used. However, the final financial statement, including the balance sheet and income statement, must be reviewed and verified by a tax auditor registered as a certified public auditor. Suppose the public auditor fails to comply with the tax law when reviewing and certifying a tax declaration. In that case, the tax authority shall notify the AABE or the Institute of Certified Public Accountants of Ethiopia of the failure of the public auditor and may request the board or the institute to withdraw the auditor's license.

Articles 21 through 24 of the Federal Income Tax Administration Proclamation No. 983/2016 provide instructions on how and when taxpayers must declare their taxable income and pay the taxes due. Subject to Article 22, sub-article (6), and Article 82, a taxpayer shall sign a tax declaration filed by him. The tax declaration shall contain a taxpayer's representation that the tax return is complete and accurate, including any attached documents. A taxpayer's tax representative or licensed tax agent shall sign the taxpayer's tax declaration and make the representation referred to in sub-article (5) of this Article when the taxpayer is

1. *not an individual,*
2. *an incapable individual, or*
3. *an individual who is otherwise unable to sign the declaration provided the taxpayer has authorized the representative or tax agent in writing to sign the tax declaration.*

Before the tax declaration is signed by the taxpayer's tax representative or licensed tax agent, the taxpayer must know and understand the contents of the tax declaration. The law treats the taxpayer as representing the tax declaration's completeness and accuracy referred to in sub-article (5) of Article 22 of the tax proclamation.

The law requires the taxpayer's tax representative or agent to be licensed. Tax agents must provide the taxpayers with certificates certifying that they have examined the taxpayer's documents. To the best of their knowledge, the declaration, together with any accompanying documentation, correctly reflects the data and transactions it relates. A licensed tax agent who refuses to provide a certificate referred to in sub-article (1) shall give the taxpayer a statement in writing the reasons for such refusal.

A licensed tax agent who prepares or assists in preparing a tax declaration shall provide the taxpayer a certificate under sub-article (1) of this Article or a statement under sub-article (2) of this Article. Under Article 17 (2) of the Proclamation, the licensed tax agent must keep a copy of certificates or statements provided to client taxpayers and produce the document to the authority when written notice requires.

Article 22 of the Proclamation obligates a taxpayer who stopped their income-generating activity to notify the tax authority, in writing, within 30 days from the date of the end of the income-generating activity. According to sub-article (1) of Article 22, within 60 days after the date that the taxpayer ceased to carry on the income-generating activity, the authority may notify the taxpayer to

    a. *file an advance tax declaration for the tax period in which the taxpayer ceased to carry on the activity and for any prior tax period for which the due date for filing has not arisen, and*
    b. *pay the tax due under the advance tax declaration when filing the statement.*

If a taxpayer is about to leave Ethiopia during a tax period and the taxpayer's absence is unlikely to be temporary, the taxpayer shall, before leaving

    a. *file an advance tax declaration for the tax period and for any prior tax period for which the due date for filing has not arisen by the time the taxpayer leaves, and*
    b. *pay the tax due under the advance tax declaration when filing the tax declaration or make an arrangement satisfactory to the tax authority to pay the tax due.*

Suppose, during a tax period, the authority has reason to believe that a taxpayer will not file a tax declaration for the period by the due date. In that case, the tax authority may, by notice in writing and at any time during the tax period, require

- *the taxpayer or the taxpayer's tax representative to file an advance tax declaration for the tax period by the date specified in the notice being a date that may be before the date that the tax declaration for the tax period would otherwise be due, and*
- *pay any tax payable under the advance tax declaration by the due date specified in the notice.*

The law also provides that if a taxpayer is subject to more than one tax return, this Article shall apply separately to each tax return. Also, a tax declaration filed on behalf of a taxpayer is treated as having been filed by the taxpayer or filed with the taxpayer's consent unless the contrary is proven.

6.3 AUDIT, INVESTIGATION, AND ENFORCEMENT

Individual and corporate taxpayers will be subject to an audit at some point. Auditees are selected based on risk or randomly using a computer algorithm for efficiency reasons. The choice of taxpayers for audit shall be reasonable and non-discriminatory. Here too, the law limits the tax administrators as follows:[13]

- There shall be specific statutory authorization for tax audits and investigations, specifying reasonable and proportional limits. Taxpayer audits by the tax administration should be free from interference by the executive or other branches of government.

---

13 Pushpender Pal (2018). Taxpayer's Rights & Obligations, Accounting Notes https://www.accountingnotes.net/international-taxation/taxpayers-rights-and-obligations/4520

Taxpayers must also be given prior notification of an audit and the opportunity to request postponement of the audit if they have good reasons.

- Clear guidelines should set out audit procedures, the rights and duties of the taxpayer during an audit, the settlement practices of the revenue authorities, and the avenues for objection and appeal against assessments arising out of the audit.

- Taxpayers must be advised of their right to have professional representation during the audit. Taxpayers should have the right to request the recording of all audit interviews. An audit should not interfere unreasonably with the proper running of a taxpayer's business or cause it to suffer commercial loss as a direct result of the audit activity.

- During the audit, the taxpayer should discuss matters arising in the audit with the tax auditor. There should be a discussion of the final issues arising from the audit that will affect the tax assessment.

- Negotiations should occur under proper, fair, and consistently applied settlement processes. There should be clear guidelines, procedures, and approvals for tax administrators to provide information or assistance under an information exchange or mutual assistance agreement.

- Powers of the tax administration to search premises and seize assets should be subject to strict limits and used as a last resort. A search of a private dwelling should require a warrant or similar document from a court, magistrate, or equivalent independent official.

- Except in exceptional circumstances, the taxpayer must be informed of the seizure of assets before the search or seizure occurs. Searches should occur during regular business hours or by appointment unless the circumstances are exceptional. Searches of premises should not typically extend to persons.

- Where assets are seized or information is taken, a receipt should be given to the taxpayer that includes the name and authority of the seizing officer. Where possible, originals should remain with the taxpayer, and information required by the tax administration should be copied and certified, if necessary.

- Taxpayers should have the right to claim privilege on confidential communications to which this right applies. The privilege can be extended to the taxpayer advisers who advise on the legal interpretation or application of tax rules.
- Tax collection and enforcement procedures must be documented and provided to the affected taxpayers. Taxpayers should be given appropriate notice and reasonable time to comply with demands for payment before enforcement measures are taken. These measures should be exercised in proportion to the tax payable.
- There must be clear guidelines governing extensions of time to pay with appropriate monitoring mechanisms to ensure fairness. There should be clear criteria and procedures for the decision to pursue criminal sanctions against a taxpayer.
- Revenue authorities should be empowered to negotiate the collection of tax and application of enforcement procedures where the taxpayer can show hardship. The onus of proving hardship in such cases must be reasonable.
- In tax matters, taxpayers should have the right to representation, be advised of that right, and be allowed to exercise it. There should be a clear basis for the imposition of penalties and interest. The mutual assistance agreement should set out procedures to ensure taxpayers are adequately protected.

As indicated above, taxpayers have the right to object to the audit findings and assessments and appeal to a court or administrative tribunal of an independent status within a reasonable time. The right of appeal shall apply to as wide a range of decisions and actions of the tax administrator as possible. Taxpayers shall be informed of their rights and applicable appeal time limits. The conduct of the appeal should be subject to due process and a fair hearing.

In a successful appeal, taxpayers should have the right to compensation for legal costs and expenses incurred. They should also have the right to compensation for personal or economic loss resulting from any unlawful actions taken by the tax authorities. Monetary compensation should be available for tax auditors' negligent and intentional or reckless actions.

6.4 CONCLUSIONS

Citizens, residents, and businesses are obligated by law to pay taxes to the government on earned income, the value of assets, and commercial transactions. Tax authorities are mandated to enforce the tax law and collect the levied taxes from all taxpayers. However, tax authorities are bound by the rule of law. They must follow specific ethical procedures in enforcing and collecting taxes from taxpayers.

Tax authorities must collect taxes fairly and equitably. They may not intrude on taxpayers' privacy and must keep taxpayers' data and information confidential. The tax authority must deal with all taxpayers transparently and, where necessary, provide taxpayer services, education, and explanations to facilitate tax compliance.

Regarding taxpayers, their obligation is honesty in recording and filing tax returns. Taxpayers must have all the supporting documents for their claims. Taxpayers can use tax accountants and external auditors to prepare and review their tax returns. In all cases, tax accounting must follow the standards set by the International Financial Reporting Board. The primary right of taxpayers is to be treated fairly and equitably under the law and have the option to lodge appeals for redress.

Business taxpayers are required by law to purchase and use tax-authority–approved CRMs and issue appropriate VAT receipts to customers. They must also maintain all financial and other relevant documents to support their tax filings and tax refund claims. When requested, these records and documents must be kept in an accessible format for the tax authority officers.

The Ethiopian tax law is detailed and explains the direct and indirect taxes that apply to individual and corporate taxpayers. The MOR and the ECC need to publish a crisp and clean taxpayers' charter defining taxpayer obligations and rights and then issue this charter to taxpayers as a user guide. They must also publish and distribute a binding code of conduct to stem corruption and provide taxpayer-centric services to all employees and officers. The taxpayer chart must cover taxpayers' rights and obligations, the tax administration's service standards, and avenues for redress.

CHAPTER 7
TAX AUDIT

Citizens' tax compliance is directly connected to taxpayers' patriotism and honesty in declaring all their incomes and paying the correct tax amounts, considering all allowed tax deductions and exemptions. Although all taxpayers, including citizens, residents, and businesses, are presumed to be honest and pay their fair share of taxes in full and on time, the tax authorities conduct tax audits of the returns of some taxpayers.

The tax audit may cover one or all tax categories—income tax, stamp tax, value-added tax (VAT) collections and remittances, excise tax collections and remittances, withholding tax collections and remittances, and other taxes. A tax audit seeks to verify if the taxpayer has fully reported all income earned during the tax year. It also seeks to determine if the taxpayer has reported and remitted all the VAT, excise tax, and tax withholdings collected from customers on behalf of the government. It also determines if the taxpayers have correctly estimated and paid their tax liability in full and on time as the tax law requires.

The audit process involves reviewing all the tax records, books of accounts, and other taxpayer information. The data is cross-checked against information collected from third parties to ascertain if the information the auditee provided is complete and correct. In general, tax auditing has four primary objectives as follows:

1. Recover unpaid taxes from non-compliant taxpayers. The probability that an audit will uncover non-compliant behavior and the associated penalty directly influences taxpayers' compliance with the tax law. The fear of being discovered as tax cheats by the tax authority makes many taxpayers compliant.

2. Give taxpayers advice and guidance on how to comply with the tax law. The audit process provides the tax administrator an excellent opportunity to educate taxpayers on their legal obligations. It also offers an opportunity for the tax authority to explain to taxpayers the fairness of the audit process as well as records and bookkeeping requirements, thereby improving future tax compliance. Any taxpayer's tax return correction due to a misunderstanding of the tax code or calculation error is explained to the taxpayer and must benefit the taxpayer.

3. Provide feedback to policymakers on the policy implications of audit findings. Suppose the tax audit concludes that most taxpayers make mistakes in estimating their tax liabilities because of the tax law's complicated nature. In that case, this feedback to tax policy decision-makers would simplify the tax legislation. It could also result in streamlining the tax administration business processes.

4. Foster the fair and equitable taxation principle by enforcing the tax law without exempting some taxpayers from rigorous audits. The tax audit process would treat all businesses and sole proprietors fairly with an equal chance of being selected for a tax audit regardless of their affiliation with the ruling party, high-level government officials, or familial relationship with some tax auditors.

7.1 AUDITEES SELECTION PROCESS[1]

As noted above, citizens, residents, and business taxpayers should expect to be audited by the tax authorities at some point. They are selected for tax audits using one of the following methods:

1. **Manual Selection:** In this case, tax authorities conduct a 100% audit of taxpayers or rely on the tax auditors' knowledge and expertise to select taxpayers that should be audited. In the latter case, tax auditors manually select the taxpayers to be audited based on their understanding of the taxpayers' behaviors. This method of taxpayer selection is widely used in developing countries, including Ethiopia. However, it has its risks, including the following:

    - It increases the risk of corruption. It opens a window of opportunity for corrupt taxpayers and rent-seeking tax auditors to negotiate to lower the taxpayer's tax liability for a price and deprive the government of tax revenue.
    - It increases arbitrariness and the political abuse of specific taxpayers. Historically, many businesses were forced to close shops because of political targeting. And others were targeted because of personal conflict with a political leader. Tax auditors are directed to find fault in the targeted taxpayers' tax returns and load up the tax liability with a hefty penalty to bankrupt the taxpayer. During the Provisional Military Administrative Council (PMAC) or the DERGE regime (1975–1990), specific taxpayers were targeted and audited with the intention of bankrupting them. During the Tigrayan Peoples Liberation Front (TPLF) era—1991 to 2018—taxpayers affiliated

---

1 Manawar Sultan Khwaja, Rajul Awasthi, and Jan Loeprick, editors (2011). Risk-Based Tax Audits: Approaches and Country Experiences, The International Bank for Construction and Development/The World Bank, Washington, DC.

with the ruling party or businesses indirectly owned by high-level government officials were exempted from paying their share of taxes.

- It increases the risk of missing some aspects of non-compliance. The manual process limits the tax authorities' ability to uncover non-compliance patterns hidden in specific industries, economic sectors, or as determined by other taxpayer characteristics.
- It limits the extent of external information gathering, data matching, and triangulation to uncover patterns and areas of tax non-compliance and fraud.

2. **Random selection:** Auditees are selected based on stratified or straightforward sampling by industry, sector, and taxpayer size. A random sample of taxpayers for tax audit offers several benefits, including the following:

- It is perceived as a fair selection strategy. All taxpayers in the same income level and industry or sector have an equal chance of being selected for the tax audit.
- It reduces the risks of corruption and arbitrary selection of taxpayers.
- It provides the tax administrator information about compliance and other aspects of taxpayers' behavior without audit selection bias.
- The tax system's effectiveness, efficiency, and areas of improvement in the tax policy and administration are assessed effectively with the built-in criteria of the random selection method.

3. **Risk-based selection:**[2] Auditees are selected based on tax risk criteria. The main objective is to identify those taxpayers most likely to be non-compliant, resulting in the highest likelihood

---

2   Ibid.

of yielding more significant amounts of audit adjustments and penalties. The approach requires developing and applying a risk-scoring technique. A score is generated for each taxpayer based on (a) specific attributes (size, industry, compliance history) and (b) knowledge acquired during previous audit campaigns (whatever the selection strategy). Implementing risk-based auditee selection requires technical capacity and a robust database containing sufficient information on all taxpayers. Taxpayers are segmented by size, sector, score, and other criteria using sound scoring criteria. However, the risk-based auditee selection is as good as the risk-scoring criteria developed and used. Ethiopia is in the early stage of implementing and using risk-based auditee selection.

Many tax administrators have begun adopting a risk-based selection rather than conducting a 100% tax audit. Computer algorithms are developed to identify non-compliance risks based on analysis of business trends and patterns of tax avoidance by industry and economic sectors. Taxpayer characteristics, in combination with profiles of economic sectors, are used in risk-scoring systems to identify and assess the risk of non-compliance.[3] The risk-based auditee selection process enhances the cost-effectiveness of the tax audit process since it enables resource allocation to high-risk groups and economic sectors.

Properly functioning automated information and communication infrastructure facilitates risk-based auditing by allowing:

1. the gathering of third-party data and matching it with taxpayer-reported data,
2. the undertaking of selective examination of tax returns based on risk analysis,

---

3   Eva Eberhartinger, Reyhanch Sufaei, Caren Sureth-Sloane, and Yuchen Wu (2020). Are Risk-Based Tax Audit Strategies Rewarded? An Analysis of Corporate Tax Avoidance, DIBT Research Seminar at WU Vienna.

3. the assurance that the law and the procedures are being applied uniformly across business sectors and taxpayers,

4. the provision of adequate, timely information to support management decision-making and tax policy formulation, and

5. the standardization of payment processes (through banks) and accounting requirements.

Auditees are informed in advance about their selection for a tax audit. If possible, auditees' wishes are considered when scheduling the tax audit. Sometimes, a tax audit is conducted without advance notice when there is a reasonable suspicion that the taxpayer will hide their assets or flee the country.

7.2 TAX AUDITORS' OBLIGATIONS

All tax audits must be conducted professionally, ethically, and without bias. Before commencing a tax audit, tax auditors must examine the auditee's tax data and information within the tax authority before asking for additional information from the auditee or third parties. Second, they must review and understand business and tax compliance trends in the auditees' economic sector. This will speed up the audit process and help the auditor(s) refine and focus on their audit questions. The evidence includes the auditees' sales data, CIT, VAT returns, payment control data, third-party data, and advance rulings from the tax authorities, if any. The tax auditors also examine the reports on previous tax audits of the same auditees and the taxation practice and case law relevant to the auditees' industries or business lines.

The tax authority must require that tax auditors be meticulous and impartial. The auditors' findings, proposals, and conclusions must be based solely on the facts. Tax auditors are responsible for their actions jointly with the tax office. The tax authority is liable for any damage or losses caused by its tax auditors to the auditees. The tax auditors must correctly document the relevant facts and findings in the tax audit reports.

The law requires that the tax auditors notify the auditees and discuss their findings point by point in person before making a final decision. The tax audit results must be resolved collaboratively with the auditees whenever possible. Auditors must enter into evidence any additional information offered by the auditees.

The tax audit process should start with an initial meeting with the auditees. At this meeting, the tax auditors explain the purpose of the audit, the procedures, and the methods to be used. Based on the initial meeting and additional information, the tax auditing team will build a comprehensive picture of the auditees' industry profile, business operations, accounting, and tax affairs management. The following issues are among those that are addressed at the initial meeting:

- Profile of the auditee's industry
- Type, extent, and unique characteristics of the business operations and the places of businesses[4]
- Affiliated companies and their locations
- Ownership and the owners' participation in business operations
- Owners' other business affiliations
- Number of employees disaggregated into full-time, temporary, or part-time employees
- Primary customers

At the end of the audit process, a closing or exit meeting is held with the auditee. At this meeting, the auditors inform the auditee of their findings. The audit findings are discussed in detail to allow the auditee to respond to the findings and provide explanations. Any errors and unpaid tax liability revealed in the tax audit are explained to the auditee as fully as possible. The auditee is also informed of further action that will follow. The auditee is notified of any tax debt, postponement, or relief measures in writing and how to appeal.

---

4   Vero Skatt (2017). Good Tax Auditing Practices, https://www.vero.fi/en/detailed-guidance/guidance/49204/good_tax_auditing_practic/.

The tax auditors' supervisors must approve the tax audit report. Approval means that the tax auditors' superiors verify that the tax audit process, method, and final tax audit findings meet the tax authority's audit standards. A tax auditor's supervisor ensures that the tax audit report compiled by the tax auditor is meticulous and that its findings, conclusions, and recommendations are legally justified.

7.2.1 The Tax Audit Methodology

A tax audit's objective is to determine any adjustments required to the auditee's tax returns and any additional tax liability owed to the government. However, the audit process and methodology used by the auditors must satisfy the following criteria:[5]

- *Accurate*: The audit is based on a correct interpretation of the tax law. It leads to a more precise tax liability assessment.
- *Fact-based*: All audit findings are based on verifiable evidence collected from the auditee and third parties.
- *Transparent*: Audit findings are fully documented and explained in writing. These findings are also thoroughly discussed with the auditee during the audit process.
- *Complete*: The auditors conduct a meticulous examination and analysis of the evidence following the law within a specified time frame. The auditee is informed of the start and end points and knows when the audit will be completed.
- *Defensible*: The audit findings are legally justifiable. They can withstand external scrutiny because different auditors can reach the same conclusions.
- *Consistent*: The determination of the additional tax liability must use a standard approach and methodology that other auditors can replicate to arrive at the same findings, given the evidence.

---

5   OECD (2006). Strengthening Tax Audit Capabilities: General Principles and Approaches. Forum on Tax Administration's Compliance Sub-Group, Center for Tax Policy and Administration, October 16, 2006.

The tax audit methodology must relate to tax audit objectives, which include

- administering and enforcing the tax law in full,
- recovering unpaid taxes,
- fostering accuracy in self-assessments of taxes by educating taxpayers on the tax laws and regulations and financial reporting standards, and
- promoting voluntary tax compliance of taxpayers through "visibility" of audit presence.

As shown in Figure 7.1, the audit process follows several steps. Careful planning and preparation will save time and cost for the tax authority and the auditee. As noted above, once an auditee is selected, the first task is understanding the auditee's tax-related data and information, including answering the following questions:

- In what economic sector is the auditee operating?
- What are the characteristics of the taxpayer's economic sector?
- What is known about the auditee's tax compliance history?
- What other questions and issues should be investigated?

The second task is gathering and compiling the data collected from various sources and outlining the analytical methodology to be applied. The analytical procedure may include recalculating the auditee's self-assessed tax return to determine (a) calculation errors, (b) omission of specific categories of income, and (c) if the tax return is completed following the tax law and the government's accounting financial reporting standards. Are there underreported income sources? In many cases, matching the taxpayer-reported data with the information gathered from a third party uncovers unreported taxable income.

The third task accurately documents the audit questions, the audit methodology, and the audit findings. The fourth task is meeting with the auditee and reviewing the audit plan, the issues to be investigated, and the audit timeline.

Also, before finalizing the audit report, the auditors must review their results and next steps with the auditee. If the auditee offers additional information, the auditors must accept and review it and determine if it would change their findings.

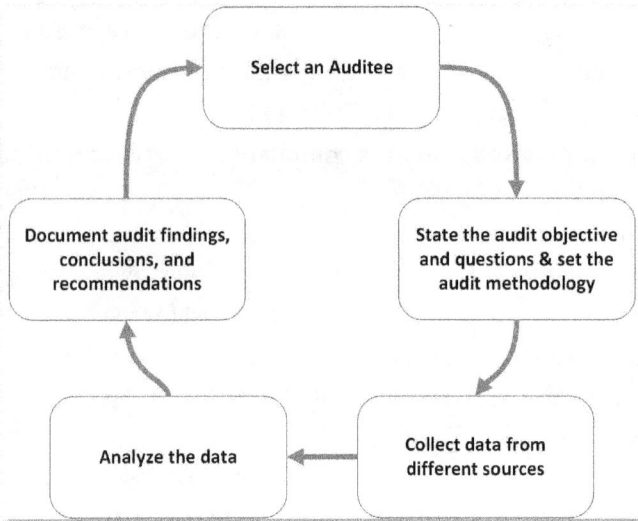

Figure 7.1: The Tax Audit Process

7.2.2 Auditees' Obligations and Rights

The taxpayers selected for a tax audit are obligated to provide all the information requested by tax auditors. The auditees must disclose all information in a timely and accessible manner to facilitate the tax audit. The auditees must disclose and make available for inspection their accounting records and all other materials and assets that might bear on taxation. An auditee must also disclose information stored in electronic format. All the relevant information must be provided for a tax audit, regardless of the confidentiality of the information.

Auditees must respond to tax auditors' requests and questions within a reasonable time. The audit process must allow auditees sufficient time to respond to auditors' questions or information requests.

Auditees are treated courteously and respectfully, and their requests are responded to promptly. Also, the auditees are given detailed information on the audit results to react and respond to the findings. The auditees are also informed of further action that will follow any tax debt, postponement, or available relief measures and how to appeal.

7.2.3 Third Parties' Obligations

The law obligates third parties to provide the information requested by the tax auditors. Data gathered from third parties are used to verify the correctness of the auditee's tax information. The tax authorities are entitled to such information, which must be given to the tax auditors upon request. The information requested can include bank records, tax incentives, and other investment incentives provided to the auditee. Information on the ownership of business premises, warehouses, and other properties used or operated by the auditee and the auditee's payment of payroll taxes and pension contributions of employees can be obtained from Woreda (district) and Kebele (village) administrations.

7.2.4 The Tax Review and Appeal Process

After completing the audit, any adjustments made to the auditee's tax declarations are explained to the auditee. The report should indicate if the auditee owes the tax authority an additional tax, including interest and penalties. Otherwise, if there are no audit findings, it should state that the auditee's tax return has no changes or that the auditee is owed a tax refund. The auditee is provided copies of all documents in possession of the tax auditors that led them to their conclusion. These may include the following:

- The auditee's tax returns
- Reports prepared by the tax auditor to support the assessment
- Working papers prepared by the auditor that are relevant to the issues under dispute
- Information obtained from third parties with whom the taxpayer is doing business, such as sales invoices, purchase orders, etc.

- Information obtained from the Ministry of Trade and Industry (MTI)
- Information obtained from the Ethiopian Customs Commission (ECC)
- Information obtained from the Ethiopian Investment Commission (EIC)
- Information obtained from commercial banks and the National Bank of Ethiopia
- The detailed calculations of the disallowed deductions or amended revenue figures used to arrive at the audit assessment, including penalties and interest

The auditee has two options:

- Option 1: Approve the audit findings.
- Option 2: Disagree with the results.

If the auditee approves the audit findings, it will settle the tax liability, including the additional tax penalties and interest. If the auditee owes more taxes than they can afford to pay in full, the auditee can request to pay through a payment plan.

Suppose the auditee disapproves or disagrees with the audit findings. In that case, the auditee has up to 30 days to lodge a complaint and request a review of the audit findings by the tax authority's tax audit review team. The review team will review the audit findings and the auditee's specific objections and resolve the matter. If the auditees are still unsatisfied with the audit review decisions, they can appeal to the Tax Appeals Commission.

The Tax Appeals Commission would usually request full details of the case, including the following:

- The auditee's tax returns
- Reports prepared by the tax auditors to support their assessment, including the decisions of the Tax Review Team

- Working papers prepared by the auditors that are relevant to the issues under dispute
- Records of discussions between the auditee and the tax auditors during the tax audit
- Information obtained from third parties with whom the auditee is doing business, such as sales invoices, purchase orders, bank records showing money transfers, etc.
- Detailed calculations of disallowed items or amended revenue figures to arrive at the assessed amount, including penalties and interest

7.3 CONCLUSIONS

Tax authorities have the right by law to audit taxpayers' tax affairs even though taxpayers are presumed to fulfill their tax obligations honestly and truthfully. The objectives of the tax authority for conducting tax audits are threefold:

- To determine if the government is owed additional tax revenue and collect the unpaid taxes
- To educate and inform auditees on the tax law for future tax compliance
- To gather the information that can inform the tax policy reform process

From efficiency, fairness, and equity points of view, the risk-based selection of auditees is preferred. First, risk-based tax audit strategies are practical tools to curb tax avoidance across firms of all sizes. Second, risk-based tax audits decrease tax enforcement costs and improve tax authorities' performance. Risk-based tax audit strategies also positively reduce taxpayers' tax avoidance behavior and enhance voluntary tax compliance.

Tax auditing must be fair, accurate, and conducted professionally; it should also protect the auditees from unnecessary search and seizure of property. A confidentiality clause also protects auditees' tax and business information provided to the tax authority. Auditees also have the right to appeal the tax authority's rulings and get redress.

The experiences of many taxpayers in Ethiopia indicate that the tax audit process is aggressive and, in some cases, incorrect, unfair, and lacks transparency. The professionalism, competencies, and integrity of some tax auditors are questionable. The Ethiopian tax authority has not yet implemented the risk-based auditee selection methodology. Some taxpayers allege that the tax authority has failed to educate auditees and their tax accountants and prepare them for future tax compliance. The tax authority is bent on maximizing tax collection by whatever means necessary, including error-prone audits. This approach introduces undue stress on taxpayers and may drive many to the informal sector.

CHAPTER 8

TAXPAYERS' BELIEFS IN TAX EQUITY AND FAIRNESS

All other things equal, a tax system viewed as fair and equitable would have a higher tax compliance rate. Most taxpayers in Ethiopia consider the tax system unfair. Tax compliance is also low for various reasons, including

- low taxpaying culture,
- high compliance cost,
- willful tax evasion,
- perception of lack of governance and transparency in expenditure management, and
- a belief that the tax system is unfair and corrupted.

Citizens often equate the lack of transparency in government expenditure management with corruption and fund embezzlement. Citizens' and business owners' beliefs and perceptions about the tax system's fairness were captured through a random sample opinion survey and focus group discussions.[1] In the presentation, we use fictitious names and characters.

In February 2020, the Tax Fairness Cooperation Project (TFCP) surveyed a sample of Merkato merchants. The survey revealed that only 21% believed the tax system was fair. By comparison, 46% indicated it was somewhat fair, and 33% reported that the system was not fair (see Table 8.1). This is a very alarming finding. It is one of the causes for business taxpayers to resort to tax avoidance strategies, including a preference for operating in the shadow market hidden from tax authorities.

Table 8.1: Tax System's Fairness Survey of Merkato Traders

Survey Question: As a result of the 9 rounds of tax training, do you believe the tax system is fair?	Number of Respondents	Percent of Respondents
☐ I don't believe it is.	79	33%
☐ I believe, to some extent, it is.	111	46%
☐ I believe very much it is.	52	21%
Total Number of Survey Respondents	242	

Source: Tax Fairness Cooperation Project (TFCP) Merkato Traders Tax Education Survey, February 2020.

Table 8.2 discusses tax equity and fairness issues that emerged during the group discussion with Iddir members in Sebeta and the Merkato traders and merchants covered by the TFCP project.

---

1   The Tax Fairness Cooperation Project (TFCP) collaboratively implemented in February 2019 by the Ministry of Revenues (MOR) and Addis Ababa Revenue Authority is a project whose primary purpose is educating, registering, and bringing into the tax net the shadow market traders. In January and February 2020, it held a series of consultative meetings with groups of Merkato traders. Also, focus group discussions were held in community meetings using as a vehicle the Ethiopian Social Accountability project, implemented by VNG International.

Table 8.2: Tax Systems Fairness and Equity Issues

No.	Issues	Explanation	Citizens/Taxpayers Response and Views
1	Horizontal Equity	The question discussed was, *"Am I being charged the same tax rate as the next person?"* Horizontal equity is associated with the idea that all individuals and businesses should be taxed at the same rate. According to Article 19 of Ethiopia's Federal Income Tax Proclamation No. 979/2016, incorporated companies pay a flat profit tax rate of 30%. In this regard, the corporate income tax is an excellent example of horizontal equity. For example, the eatable oil manufacturer and the rebar manufacturer will pay an income tax of 30% on their profits. Another example of horizontal equity is the value-added tax (VAT). The VAT rate, set at 15%, remains the same, regardless of (a) the amount and volume of goods purchased and (b) who makes the purchase. For example, the VAT rate remains the same whether you spend \$15,000 or \$100,000. Also, whether Person A or Person B or a rich or a poor person is making the purchase, the VAT rate does not change.	Many individuals at the Iddir meeting argued that the current VAT implementation is unfair. For example, some consumer goods are VAT-exempt, but furnishings and garments are not. Many discussants indicated that VAT exemption or a lower VAT rate, for example, 5% or 0% instead of the current 15% on items consumed by most households, would be fair.

No.	Issues	Explanation	Citizens/Taxpayers Response and Views
2	Vertical Equity	Vertical equity relates to the principle of the ability to pay. High-income earners would pay taxes at a higher rate compared to low-income earners. For example, a person earning $100,000 should pay tax at a higher rate than an individual earning $10,000. An example of vertical equity is the federal employment income tax legislation. The employment income tax rate published in the Federal Income Tax Proclamation No. 979/2016 – Article 11 is progressive because the tax rate is higher for high-income earners. The degree of progressivity of income taxation determines the tax system's equity and fairness.	While the individual income tax rate is progressive, many discussants in the Iddir discussion argued that the income bands are too narrow, given the rising cost of living. When considering the cost of living, the current employment income tax rate is too high, and low-income earners bear the tax burden disproportionately.

No.	Issues	Explanation	Citizens/Taxpayers Response and Views
3	The Subjectivity of Tax Assessments by Tax Authorities	For traders and merchants that do not maintain books of account and financial records for determining their tax liabilities, the tax authorities determine their tax liabilities. The tax authorities estimate how much income has been earned and calculate the tax liability owed to the government. Unfairness creeps in whenever the taxable income is determined by government fiat without clear guidelines and criteria. A tax assessment based on guesstimates without factual data is arbitrary; it hurts some and benefits other individuals and businesses. The corrupt behavior of some tax assessors also worsens the situation. In 2017 demonstrations and riots occurred throughout Ethiopia when the regional governments tried to assess the taxable incomes of small and microenterprises (category C taxpayers).	Many discussants suggested that the government commission a study to determine how much net revenue the vendors selling coffee or food at street corners are making. For example, how much revenue are they making over six weeks? Use the average as a benchmark to determine the taxable net income of these businesses. They also suggested the study factor in these businesses' locations and the inflation in the price of inputs. In addition, they suggested that the study be conducted for small enterprises by sector and location. Based on the analysis, a formula is developed to estimate the taxable revenue of category C businesses.

No.	Issues	Explanation	Citizens/Taxpayers Response and Views
4	Competition with Street Vendors and Hawkers	The Addis Ababa City Government Regulation No. 88/2017, which recognizes and regulates street vendors and hawkers, introduces an element of unfairness for taxpaying merchants and traders that operate from a fixed location. These street vendors and hawkers are registered with the local government. They have a taxpayer identification number and photo identification card (ID), which they must always display. They pay ETB 50, an annual fee for renewing their ID cards but are exempt from paying income tax. These street vendors and hawkers can stand on both sides of the designated roads and in front of legitimate tax-registered traders' premises and compete for customers without paying tax or rent. These street vendors sometimes sell similar items at a lower price.	Merchants operating out of rented business premises indicated that this action of the city administration is unfair. They may not pay their full share of taxes until these street vendors and hawkers are removed from their storefronts. They say they are losing customers to these hawkers and street vendors. Some of these street vendors and hawkers have resorted to mafia and gangster tactics and intimidated them. One of the discussants suggested that the city administration build a fixed marketplace for these hawkers and street vendors, remove them from storefronts and the streets, and settle them in a fixed location. He also suggested that these hawkers and street vendors gradually be pulled into the formal economy and made tax compliant.

No.	Issues	Explanation	Citizens/Taxpayers Response and Views
5	Political Favoritism and Corruption	Many businesses and individuals affiliated with the ruling party are exempt from paying their fair share of taxes because of their political connections, ethnicity, or ability to corrupt tax officers through family connections or unethical government officials. Furthermore, some discussants alleged that some individuals are charged lower rent because of their ethnicity and political association. These differential treatments of some businesses add to the unfairness and inequity of the tax system.	Some discussants suggested that the local government not be in the housing or business premises rental business. All these facilities should be privatized. The level of rent for business premises should be determined based on supply, demand, and location. Hard-to-reach localities should have lower rents.

No.	Issues	Explanation	Citizens/Taxpayers Response and Views
6	Administrative Allocation of Tax Benefits	Arbitrary administrative allocation of **tax benefits** such as tax holidays, investment incentives, and income tax exemptions to some businesses and not others is unfair and inequitable.	Many discussants suggested that tax exemptions and incentives must be standardized. The criteria for qualification must be published and made available to the public.
			In the discussants' views, including individuals from the Chambers of Commerce, these tax incentives are used for tax evasion and avoidance. A discussant suggested that the tax authority conduct a thorough audit, review the benefit to the country and society of handing out such incentives and communicate their findings to the public. The businesses that benefit from tax and investment incentives are directly and indirectly linked to the ruling political party.

No.	Issues	Explanation	Citizens/Taxpayers Response and Views
7	Assessment of Dutiable Values of Imports	Even when an importer presents a legitimate invoice showing the price paid on an imported item, the customs officers rely more on the Ethiopian Customs Commission (ECC)'s tariff book. If the tariff book is not up to date, it may show a different price than what the importer paid. The ECC also uses the World Trade Organization database to determine how much the imported item costs in the seller's country. Consequently, the assessed dutiable value of the imported item may differ from the importer's actual price. Suppose the importer buys a vehicle with a deep discount because of low demand in the seller's country; however, the ECC tariff book shows the vehicle's full price. While the computation of customs taxes and duties is straightforward, there are some issues regarding the value of the imported item. To verify the value of imported goods, Customs Proclamation No. 859/2014 provides six alternative	Many discussants indicated that the import duty on many items is exceptionally high. Duties and taxes paid on the total cost of an imported good are calculated as the sum of the price of the good at the place of origin (e.g., at the factory or dealership in Country A) plus insurance paid for the item while in transit, plus the transportation or freight cost and other charges, for example, loading, unloading, and storage charges. One of the discussants suggested that the assessment methods used by the ECC introduce bias and unfairness, and the government must change its assessment methodology. One option is reducing the customs duty and tax rates. For example, a flat 20% tax rate on all imported items would reduce corruption and eliminate the incentive to falsify invoices and bills of lading.

No.	Issues	Explanation	Citizens/Taxpayers Response and Views
		methods of determining the value of the imported article. Five of these methods seem arbitrary and introduce an element of corruption and unfairness, including: (1) valuation of identical goods (Article 91), (2) valuation of similar goods (Article 92), (3) deductive value method (Article 93), (4) computed value method (Article 94), and (5) fallback method (Article 95).	

No.	Issues	Explanation	Citizens/Taxpayers Response and Views
8	Use of Heavy Penalties	Some participants believe that the tax administrators have made the tax system complicated. The requirement that taxpayers make monthly filings has resulted in late payments and penalties. The tax declaration forms are complex. The complicated nature and slowness of the tax authority have raised the cost of tax compliance. Small and medium businesses must hire tax accountants at a great expense to prepare their tax declarations. Also, taxpayers spend several hours or days sitting in the tax office to file their tax declarations.	In the view of the discussants, simplifying the tax code, tax declaration forms, and tax filing process would facilitate the timely payment of tax liabilities. For example, the tax declaration can be through commercial banks or the post office. Establishing strategically located tax filing support centers would help medium and small taxpayers meet their tax obligations on time and avoid penalties.
9	Perception of Government Legitimacy	Political-party–unaffiliated businesses believe that the federal government is not inclusive and legitimate. For that reason, many have opted to operate in the shadow economy.	A sustained political discourse with the different political parties, improving the governance system, and increasing transparency would enhance tax compliance. We must change the ethnopolitical and kleptocratic governance system. We must implant politics of an inclusive, open, and collaborative society and begin to build law-abiding citizenship.

No.	Issues	Explanation	Citizens/Taxpayers Response and Views
10	Federal Government Grants to the Regional States	According to Article 62, sub-article 7 of the Constitution of the Federal Democratic Republic of Ethiopia Proclamation1/1995, the House of Federation determines the division of federal and state tax resources and the federal government's regional subsidies. First, although federal government subsidies are allocated to regional states based on population density, some regions' populations have been purposely undercounted. Thus, the subsidies and division of tax resources are unfair and skewed to benefit favored regional states. Some localities within regional states do not benefit from government expenditures on infrastructure and essential services. Citizens and taxpayers in these localities feel left out and robbed of their tax money.	The federal, regional, and local governments must ensure that all regions and districts are served equally. Where there are no schools, schools should be built and staffed. Where there are no health clinics, they should be constructed and staffed to serve the surrounding communities. Where there are no access roads, they should be built. The allocation and distribution of government expenditure must be inclusive and accommodate the needs of all ethnic groups. Using an internationally recognized method, a proper population census should be undertaken concerning federal grants or subsidies to states. The House of Federation must review and revise its grant allocation formula and use the new census data.

8.1 CONCLUSIONS

In the views of many citizens, the current Ethiopian tax system is unfair. Several businesses owned by the ruling political party and shell companies of high-level politicians and businesspersons associated with the ruling party are not paying their fair share of taxes. These businesspeople are afforded investment, tax incentives, and low rent for business premises.

Perceptions of tax equity and fairness have a direct impact on tax compliance. The Merkato traders and merchants affected by the presence of street vendors are unwilling to comply with the tax law until the city administration removes the street vendors from their storefronts.

Worldwide, the problems of tax equity and fairness revolve around tax relief and tax justice. On the one hand, high-income earners and the wealthy want to reduce the tax rate applied to their incomes. They use different tactics and strategies to hide their income. They claim the burden of taxation falls on them disproportionately. They want a reduction in the tax rate.

On the other hand, middle- and low-income taxpayers argue that the tax system benefits the high-income earners and the wealthy more. High-income earners and the rich benefit disproportionately from tax deductions, and they can also exploit tax loopholes and tax havens. The quality and equitable distribution of government services across the country also matters. Many peri-urban and rural communities that are poorly served continue to resist the government's taxation efforts.

Moreover, the tax audit and appeals processes are corrupt and unfair. Once an auditor makes a decision, it is not easy to reverse the decision through appeals. This has driven many taxpayers to close shop and transition into the shadow market.

ANNEXES

ANNEX 2.1 WHAT MATTERS
FOR QUALITY OF LIFE?

Quality of life is about well-being and happiness. In the 1950s and the 1960s, citizens' quality of life in the United States and Ethiopia was remarkably high, particularly for those exposed to formal education and skills training. In general, citizens had trust in their government and their community members. I grew up in a very cohesive community to the extent that if my parents were not at home, I could go to any household in the community and ask to be fed. These community members were like my family members. Of course, my family reciprocated.

Likewise, when the head of a household was temporarily laid off from work, the community collected money equivalent to the person's monthly salary and donated it to the family until the individual found a job. Ethiopia did not have a government-funded social safety net or unemployment compensation. However, there was a strong social bond and social capital whereby community members cared for each other.

As a child, I could walk around the neighborhood and surrounding communities without fear. Children were protected from crime or from committing a crime by neighbors, friends, and even strangers. In those days, children were not allowed, for example, to go to tea houses or movies. The reasoning was that once kids started going to these establishments, they would become addicted. Then they would begin stealing or demanding money from their cash-strapped parents, which was wrong. Any adult from the community could punish or prevent any kid from engaging in these activities.

Also, our village changed rapidly as the number of people employed in government and private enterprises increased. Houses were rebuilt, remodeled, and looked much more beautiful. The community also built better access roads. Garbage dumpsters were set up away from the river and the children's playground. People looked healthier and happier.

Better educational achievements garnered an increase in respect. Students who performed very well in school were respected. Students worked hard to be recognized and were proud of their accomplishments.

People in the community were happy and confident and respected each other. Most community members' gateway out of poverty was education and sound skills training, which began in elementary school.

There were opportunities to study abroad as we progressed through elementary and high school. Qualified students went to the United States and European countries to earn a bachelor's or higher education degree. However, those students who got the opportunity to study in the United States, Europe, and other countries did not seek asylum or stay a day longer after graduation. They flew back to Ethiopia immediately after graduation. They all said the quality of life in Ethiopia was much better. Today, however, everyone wants to live outside Ethiopia to pursue a better life for themselves and their children.

I arrived in the United States in the late 1960s. I lived and worked in New Jersey, New York, Pennsylvania, Virginia, and North Carolina. After graduating from the University of Pennsylvania, I worked in New York City and New Jersey. In New Jersey, I lived in a very welcoming community. The day we moved into our new house, which we bought at a reasonable price, the neighbors came to meet and welcome us. They brought cookies, pies, and wine. They showed us where to shop for groceries and where to find the best dental and medical care. The milkman introduced himself to us and asked if we needed milk. He would place a bottle of milk on our front porch before 6:00 a.m. each day, and on Saturday, he would collect all the bottles and the payment, which I put in an envelope and left with the bottles. We were also introduced to the butcher, and once he understood the cut of meat we liked, we could call him and get the meat delivered. I paid the butcher at my convenience. Being trusted gave me much pride.

In the winter, neighbors borrowed each other's shovels to clear the snow from our driveways. In the summer, we borrowed each other's lawn-mowers and had block parties, which was joyful. Everybody in the neighborhood was working and well-to-do. Many were also well-educated. Everybody seemed happy and satisfied with life. But in the late 1980s, people began complaining about life. Many neighbors saw the factories they and their fathers had worked closing down. AT&T, where I worked, was forced to sell off some of its assets and was broken into twelve telephone companies. It had to lay off close to 80% of its workforce. For many laid-off workers, life was a struggle. And with the arrival of these huge grocery stores, the small mom-and-pop stores had to close too. The milkman stopped coming, and the butcher and the corner grocery store closed shop. Kids who used to work at the family store after school began roaming the streets, sometimes getting into trouble. Our good neighbors moved out, and new people came in. It was not a welcoming community anymore because of the stress of life and creeping poverty. The quality of life began to decline.

From my experience and others, what matters for quality of life are:

- *Having economic well-being:* Having enough income to afford the necessities of life through employment or one's enterprise is key to one's quality of life. One of the indicators evaluated by the pan-European quality-of-life survey is employment.[1] Similarly, the European Foundation for the Improvement of Living and Working Conditions (2004) identified employment as key to people's quality of life.[2]
- *Being equipped with education, knowledge, and necessary skills:* A quality education system that prepares people with life and

1   Branislov Mikilic (2007). Quality of Life in Europe: Concept, Measurement, and Findings from the First Pan-European survey on the Quality of Life (EQLS), Foundation for the Improvement of Living and Working Conditions, Brussels, November 19, 2007.
2   European Foundation for the Improvement of Living and Working Conditions (2004). First European Quality of Life Survey 2003, Dublin, Ireland, p. 1.

workplace skills is crucial for the quality of life. Eurofound (2017) noted that "a central element in improving quality of life is enabling people to achieve their desired goals, whatever they may be."[3]

- *Having access to quality preventive and curative healthcare:* Individuals' ability to move about and be productive at work is critically dependent on their health status. Quality public health-care services that improve human health are critical for setting the conditions for quality of life. People with good health are productive and happy citizens. On the other hand, a healthcare system that results in drug dependency, such as the opioid crisis in the United States, is undesirable and prevents people from en-joying a fulfilling life. Many jobs go unfilled because employers cannot afford to hire drug addicts. Families have also increasingly become broken and dysfunctional because of the opioid crisis.

- *Having access to a quality living environment:* People's living envi-ronment affects their quality of life. Improperly placed garbage dumps make people sick and result in congenital disabilities and mental problems. Also, petty crime, gang harassments, rape, and kidnappings significantly affect people's quality of life.

- *Having access to political freedom:* A nation's governance system critically impacts citizens' quality of life. Access to an equitable and fair security and justice system, including human rights pro-tection, freedom to choose, political space to voice one's opinion and desires, and freedom of movement and assembly, are vital ingredients that enhance citizens' quality of life.

- *Openness and quality of communities:* Open communities are in-clusive and have substantial social capital, just like my childhood neighborhood. It is a human need to be accepted and respected by others in the community. Also, communities concerned about the quality of their living environment seek to volunteer

---

3 Eurofound (2017). European Quality of Life Survey 2016: Quality of Life, Quality of Public Services, and Quality of Society, Publication Office of the European Union, Luxemburg, p. 8.

and collaboratively solve community problems, respond to emergencies like fires or floods or collectively implement projects that enhance their living environment and experience a better quality of life.

While working in Iraq for the USAID/RTI International Local Governance Project between April 2003 and June 2005, my monitoring and evaluation team (MET) conducted a series of quality-of-life surveys.[4] One of the issues we looked at related to Iraqis' perception regarding the benefits of decentralized local governance and the state of their communities. The Quality of Life surveys collected data on Iraqis' reported sense of belonging and connectedness to communities and their perspectives on their well-being and safety. Most survey respondents said their communities are "friendly, safe, tolerant, and receptive to new ideas." Respondents reported that people care about their communities and trust community members. That community cohesiveness helped them survive the coalition forces' war and occupation. In addition to the above drivers of quality of life, some scholars include *balancing work and life* as additional drivers.[5] Lately, income inequality that prevents equal access to quality education, healthcare, and employment has hurt citizens' quality of life.

Over the past four decades, income inequality has steadily grown in many parts of the world, including the United States. Many middle-income households in the United States cannot send their children to the country's best schools. These families are also burdened with massive student debt with low returns. Even Community Colleges have become expensive. Many graduates are unqualified for high-paying jobs requiring science, technology, engineering, and mathematics proficiencies.

---

4 Catherine Elkins, Mansour Fahimi, and Samuel Taddesse (2006). The Quality-of-Life Surveys: Monitoring and Evaluation of Iraq Local Governance Project. Working Paper, RTI International, Research Triangle Park, 3049 Cornwallis Road, NC.

5 Martha Nussbaum and Amartya Sen, ed. (1993). The Quality of Life (Introduction). Clarendon Press: Oxford.

What Matters for Standard of Living?

Many economists measure the standard of living by the average per capita gross domestic product (GDP) growth rate. Per capita GDP is, however, not a good measure of the standard of living. It does not tell how much a person earns per year. Also, economists use the average per capita GDP annual growth rate to indicate a nation's economic progress and expansion. That does not mean the average citizen's earnings are growing at the same rate. For this reason, the United Nations Human Development Index (HDI) uses the median personal earning to measure a country's standard of living.[6]

However, GDP growth and economic goods and services diversification indicate a country's material well-being. Industrial development and technological advances create products and services that enable citizens to live better lives. For example, according to the Federal Reserve Bank of Boston, *"technology and increased productivity have freed us from the back-breaking labor and never-ending drudgery that was so much a part of everyday life in the 1800s or even 1900s. Life is also less limiting—and far more varied—than it used to be. We have more choices at the supermarket and the shopping mall and access to a much wider range of ideas, information, and amusements."*[7]

Moreover, in today's globalized world, material goods are plenty. These changes and advances positively affect citizens' standard of living. Access to material things that reduce daily life's hardship and provide more comfort enhances our standard of living. The question then becomes how many people can afford to buy and use these goods and tools to

---

6   Human Development Report (2020). The net frontier: Human development and the Anthropocene, United Nations Development Programme, NY, for calculation of the standard of living se *technical note 1* at http://hdr.undp.org/sites/default/files/hdr2020_technical_notes.pdf

7   Federal Reserve Bank of Boston (2003). "The Ledger: Spotlight on Standard of Living." *Economic Education Newsletter*, Winter 2003.

make their lives easy. Does the average person earn sufficient income to afford them?

Citizens with high earnings enjoy a higher standard of living than those with low incomes because they can afford to buy the goods and services that make daily life better. Also, people with a quality education that enables them to land a better-paying job or create and manage a high-earning enterprise enjoy a higher standard of living.

At this point, we need to ask what conditions generate a higher standard of living for citizens. Among the requirements for a higher standard of living that matter most are the following:

- *Availability and access to quality education:* Today, most Americans cannot afford higher education, and those who received higher education at a high cost are not qualified to fill jobs that require technical skills or a deeper understanding and use of science, technology, engineering, and mathematics (STEM). In 2017, fewer university graduates qualified to fill the available technology jobs in the United States. India, China, South Korea, and some Nordic countries are better preparing their youth for the future artificial intelligence and technology-driven world of work. Developing countries are way behind.

- *Availability and access to high-paying jobs:* Today, the earnings of most Americans are tied to the minimum wage, which in most cases is less than $12.00 per hour. And most people are temporary employees without any employment benefits such as health insurance. Well-paying factory jobs have disappeared with globalization. Low wages limit Americans in most regions of the country from enjoying a better standard of living. Wages have been declining since 1974 due to the flight of capital and the limit on the average number of hours worked in the service-oriented economy.

- *Availability of enabling investment environment:* In America, most manufacturing establishments have closed shops and moved overseas, searching for cheap labor and tax havens. While multinationals are doing very well and enriching their shareholders, small and medium-sized businesses are not doing so. We must reform the regulatory and tax regime to be more business-friendly. In addition, efforts are required to make capital affordable and available to small and medium-sized businesses. A competitive business environment is needed to enable small and medium-sized enterprises to expand and compete. Furthermore, America must invest more in research and development.

- *Availability and accessibility of quality healthcare:* Good health enhances an individual's productivity, which is key to higher incomes. Many Americans cannot access and use quality preventive and curative healthcare today. The cost of health insurance is exceedingly high. The Affordable Care Act, designed to lower health insurance costs, continues to be gutted by Republicans. Out-of-pocket expenses charged by healthcare providers keep increasing at an alarming rate.

  Moreover, the quality of disease diagnosis and treatment seems to have declined despite advances in medical technology. Many urban and rural Americans are drug dependent, as evidenced by the opioid epidemic. The opioid effect goes beyond the individual patient. It has destroyed families and communities.

- *Narrowing income inequality:* The income gap between the haves and the have-nots has expanded since 1974. This income inequality limits what the average American can buy and enjoy. In most cases, their meager income prevents them from enjoying the same material things the rich can enjoy. Current U.S. policy helps to widen the gap. The 2017 Tax Cut and Jobs Act is a case in point. The tax cut was a vast transfer of wealth from the poor to the rich. Children of the well-to-do have a more significant advantage over middle-income family children regarding admission to the best colleges and universities. They also have a family-and-friends network to land the best jobs available.

What Matters for Happiness

Happiness is about citizens' expressed feelings of well-being and life satisfaction. Happiness also includes a person's feeling of physical and mental well-being.

In 1967, the U.S. Peace Corps in Addis Ababa, Ethiopia, commissioned me to study and gauge the happiness and life satisfaction of the rural population primarily engaged in farming. The life of a typical farmer is challenging and very demanding. A farmer typically wakes up at 4:00 a.m. First, he carries his plow and drives his cattle to graze. After dispatching his livestock to the grazing area, he hooks up the plow to his oxen, plows his field until about 10:00 a.m., and returns home with his cows for breakfast. After breakfast, he returns to plowing his field, and the women in his household milk the cows, fetch water, and prepare lunch. At around 4:00 p.m., the farmer stops plowing and tilling the land. He unhooks the plow from the oxen, carries the plow on his shoulder, and drives his oxen and cattle back home. He then changes his clothes and begins relaxing with a gourd of homemade beer, "tella." The women are busy making dinner, milking the cows, and feeding the cattle and sheep. In the evening, everybody gathers around the fireplace, eats dinner, tells stories, and goes to bed. The next day, they get up and start all over.

During sowing and harvesting, the community works as a unit—sowing one family's land after another and then doing the same during harvest time. Wherever we went, we observed that the farm community was organized into a cohesive unit. They helped each other during good and bad times. We asked the men and women how they saw their lives and whether they were happy and satisfied. Ninety-two percent of the men and the women we talked to said they were very happy and satisfied. They lived an independent life. They had little interaction with the government.

Their interaction with government workers was only on market day when they carried their surplus produce to sell in the market. They paid nominal marketing tax.

These farmers did not possess modern furniture, household goods, or implements. Everything they owned was homemade. They did not even wear shoes, even though they were available in the market. At the end of our conversation, an elderly man said, "Boys, you are unhappy and unsatisfied because you want a foreigner's way of life and material things. We have lived this way for the last thousand years and always have been happy." The lesson of the study was that material possessions had nothing to do with happiness. It had to do with the following:

- *Good physical and mental health:* Healthy people are happy and friendly. Good health is, in many cases, a reflection of the quality of the healthcare system and the quality and ambiance of the natural environment. Industrial pollution, vehicular pollution, congestion, and the degradation of the natural environment have harmful health effects.

- *Cohesive and supportive community:* People who live in a supportive and cohesive society, in general, are happy, self-confident, and cooperative. People who live in closed and dysfunctional communities are unhappy and have low self-esteem because of exclusion from most community events. Sometimes these people revert to violence to assert themselves.

- *Freedom to associate freely with neighbors and friends:* People who live in a political environment where they are free to associate and meet others to discuss issues are happy. In 2010, during the pilot Ethiopian Social Accountability Program (ESAP-1) evaluation, we met several men and women who felt empowered. In addition to collaboratively solving community problems, many felt secure enough to discuss family and personal issues with their neighbors, which they had previously kept secret. That exchange of information enabled them to find solutions to the problems they had struggled with for a long time.

- *Access to markets:* People who have ready access to markets to sell their surplus production or buy what they need are happy people. The act of buying and selling, in many countries, is a social event. When I was a child, I used to go with my mother to Merkato, one of the largest markets in Addis Ababa. My mother had formed a special bond with many of the merchants. They would invite her to sit down and have coffee or lunch with them while the items she bought were already on their way to our house. They chatted about many issues—private and public. It felt like we were visiting relatives. She was happy and waited eagerly for the market day. I, too, was delighted because of the candies and other gifts I received.

- *A healthy living environment:* People who live in a clean natural environment are happy. Clean air, water, and large green areas benefit a person's health and well-being. Public policies that balance nature and human exploitation of natural resources and enhance the livability of the village, town, city, and region are essential.

- *Absence of vandalism and crime:* People who live in communities with no crime or vandalism are happy. On the other hand, people who live in crime-ridden neighborhoods are continuously traumatized and unhappy. Children are scared to go out of their homes to play with other kids. For example, some communities in Chicago, Los Angles, Boston, the District of Colombia, and New York are like war zones, with gun violence between competing gangs being used to control the neighborhood. Drug crime is another burden on communities.

- *Access to education:* People with a good education that enables them to learn about new information, ways of thinking, and doing things are happy. When I was a child, reading and writing were exciting experiences. I would pick up a book and read it aloud to my mother. Her supportive smile and encouragement were so empowering and made me happy. I would go to the library, bring home several books, and read them from cover to cover. The stories I read took me all around the real and imaginary world. Reader 4 took me to Tibet, Brazil, Iceland, and Siberia, countries I had never known. I met many characters, including the scientist Humba who had a herd of dinosaurs on an island off the coast of Brazil.

ANNEX 2.2: EMPLOYABILITY SKILLS FOR THE TWENTY-FIRST CENTURY

In 1989 when I started as an independent consultant, part of my assignment was to advise on organization capacity building and workforce development. Workforce development was a multi-faceted effort. It included reviewing the academic curriculum taught in high schools, colleges, and technical and vocational training institutions. The review focused on assessing if academic and training institutions equipped their students with skills and competencies suited to the current and future labor market. In other words, does the education provided lead to productive employment? To determine the academic and technical skills sought by employers now and in the near future, we constituted advisory councils representing academia, skills training institutions, and private- and public-sector employers. We also conducted a series of focus group discussions (FGDs) with private- and public-sector employers from a cross-section of industries and government agencies and with graduates from academic and training institutions.

The advisory council identified the primary academic knowledge and technical skills prospective job applicants should have. The educational and training institutions' curricula were revised, enhanced, and updated based on this input. The continued interactions between prospective employers and academic and training institutions ensured that the curricula remained current and relevant to employers' needs.

The curricula were upgraded based on annual longitudinal surveys on how easily graduates of the schools and training institutions got jobs in their chosen fields of employment. The surveys also assessed how satisfied employers were with the new graduates. While most (76%) of graduates could get a job within a year of graduation, many (46%) were not retained as permanent employees. They were fired after the six-month prohibition or trial period.

Our investigations suggested that employers wanted more than academic and technical competencies. These additional requirements are related to the recruits' attitudes and character. Graduates' low employability skills are the leading causes of why so many take a long time to find employment and why so many cannot be retained as permanent employees.

Employability skills are soft skills that make job applicants and employees successful in obtaining and keeping good-paying jobs. They reflect what most employers expect from job applicants and their employees. These soft skills are in addition to academic and technical competencies and include the following:

- **Decorum and etiquette:** Decorum and etiquette deal with how a potential job candidate should dress for an interview and their attitudes and manners during the interview. Most of our focus group discussants unanimously agreed that "The appearance and the attitude an interviewee showed during the interview was a major factor in the selection or rejection of the applicant for further consideration." Their concerns revolved around whether the job applicant was adequately attired and had the requisite attitude and manner. Focus group discussants indicated that "the way the applicant is attired in some ways is indicative of whether or not the applicant is serious about the job. And if the applicant will conform to the Organization's dress code once employed."

  While I was a high school student in Ethiopia in my senior year, our homeroom teacher advised us on how to prepare for a job interview. He said, "dress appropriately and wear clean clothes and polished shoes. But do not overdress." Also, he suggested that before going to the interview, "have an appropriate haircut and practice your smile." He also said to "stay calm and attentive and exhibit self-confidence and be polite, and respectful and thank everyone at the end of the interview."

- **Listening and communicating:** Listening attentively and answering questions when asked is a critical skill. Also, answering questions crisply, coherently, and persuasively determines whether the job applicant will be hired or rejected. Several focus group discussants noted that many job applicants looked nervous and began to respond to the questions before the recruiter had finished asking the question. As a result, these interviewees provided the wrong response and failed the interview. Listening indicates whether the applicant will follow orders from their supervisor or manager and execute the order as instructed orally.

During my senior year in high school, my homeroom teacher gave our class a vital piece of advice: "Before you go for a job interview, read and learn as much as you can about the job and the employer." He said, "This information is important for responding confidently to some of the questions the recruiters may ask. Also, be honest and avoid guessing the answer. It is better to say, 'I don't know the answer than give the wrong answer.'"

Good oral and written communication skills are essential in today's job market. Several focus group discussants indicated that many colleges and technical and vocational school graduates are weak communicators. Consequently, applicants who communicate effectively and efficiently are ranked higher than others.

Reading, understanding, and writing coherently and persuasively are essential skills. These skills apply to all industries, government agencies, and work environments. They demonstrate language, numeracy, and writing competencies. A job applicant may be asked to complete an application form and answer written questions. Some questions may be multiple choice, and others may require writing an essay about a particular subject. For example, "Why are you the best candidate for the job?"

Once hired, an employee may be required to

- produce reports such as inventory lists, maintenance and repair documentation, tenders and bid documents, or in-depth research reports on a specific topic.
- read and understand technical information, guidelines, and policies, including the latest company policies and procedures, and communicate with others.
- Communicate orally with peers, subordinates, and supervisors to accomplish assigned tasks or to communicate with customers. Face-to-face, phone, or radio communications are equally important with colleagues, supervisors, and associates.

At the behest of my homeroom teacher, we practiced listening, responding, and communicating through role-playing. Students sitting next to each other were paired. One of them was given the role of a recruiter and, using a prepared list of questions, "interviewed" the other student, who was playing the role of a job candidate. That student had to listen and respond to each question asked. The role-playing was then reversed until all students had a chance to practice both roles, i.e., recruiter versus job candidate.

- **Teamwork and collaboration:** The cutthroat competition in the workplace has caused employees to concentrate on individual success. However, as our focus group discussants suggested, individualism stands in the way of collaboration and teamwork. In the twenty-first-century business environment, success depends on teamwork, whereby each employee brings in a specialized skill.

Some employers intentionally organize employees into teams to accomplish specific results and outcomes. Teamwork is about the relationships, interactions, and collaborations among business colleagues when problem-solving or completing specific tasks to generate desired outputs, results, and outcomes. Teamwork requires that employees understand their roles and responsibilities and complete their assigned tasks on schedule.

A team member must have a positive attitude towards other team members and establish a smooth working relationship. Often teams consist of people who vary in age, gender, race, religion or political persuasion, and lifestyle; they have diverse backgrounds and skill sets. Successful employees fit in any team and are willing and able to work in unison with their colleagues. However, teamwork is not about individual success but a team's performance and success. When your team wins, you win. After the task's completion, some team members may be recognized for their outstanding individual effort and contributions. Still, each team member's individual effort ultimately led to the team's success.

Some team projects require constant interaction, and the work is highly interdependent on other team members' efforts. It requires close coordination of activities with others. In these cases, good and positive people skills are critical. Other team projects require independent work and input on a set timeline. In either case, one needs to learn how to coordinate and collaborate with other team members and produce outputs on a timely basis for the team's overall success.

- **Learning and problem-solving:** Our focus group discussants also value employees who recognize problems in the workplace and solve them. For this reason, recruiters may ask a job applicant to identify and solve some common workplace problems. Job applicants who easily recognize a workplace problem and attempt to resolve the issue are ranked higher than other applicants.

Learning and critical thinking skills also relate to recognizing and fixing what is wrong. Learning relates to observing and studying the work environment to identify process- or procedure-related problems. It is also about using past work experience to solve or suggest fixes to those observed problems.

A related learning element recognizes if one needs additional skills training to improve job performance and takes the initiative and responsibility to learn those skills. It is also related to actively seeking constructive feedback from team members, managers, associates, and peers and acting on that feedback to improve performance.

Problem-solving can include developing processes for identifying problems and devising ways to resolve those problems quickly without impacting production or customer service delivery. For example, an employee who can identify issues arising from the company's procedures concerning effective and efficient production and service delivery to customers and then offer suggestions to fix those issues is a valuable employee. The primary objective is saving money for the company and providing flexibility and convenience to customers.

Employees' suggested changes and fixes often save their organizations millions of dollars. For example, when I was working for AT&T in the 1980s, the company saved between $150 to $500 million annually using employee suggestions and fixes in different divisions of the company.[8] In return, it only spent about $15 to $25 million on bonuses and prizes for these fixes and suggestions. It had a dedicated office and hotline that collected employee suggestions and fixes. The office staff analyzed and sent the recommendations for implementation to the affected departments. At the end of the fiscal year, the office recognized all those employees who contributed their ideas with recognition certificates and cash prizes.

---

8   At that time, AT&T was one of the largest companies, with revenues of $45 billion.

- **Initiative and enterprise:** The soft skills of initiative and enterprise are related to the requirement of minimum supervision to achieve a given result. Many focus group discussants complained that they have to supervise their employees excessively, noting that they prefer employees who can work independently with minimal supervision.

  In general, initiative and enterprise are about an employee determining how to achieve work-related outputs, results, and outcomes without close or detailed supervision. Close supervision of each employee is time-consuming, stressful, and costly.

  Initiative and enterprise also relate to change management, identification of opportunities, and performance evaluation and improvement. It is also about proactively researching and promoting innovation with colleagues in a shared workspace.

  Employees who demonstrate initiative are more likely to be considered for promotion and offered career advancement opportunities. Employees can show initiative and enterprise at all levels. They can suggest ways to work more effectively, reduce costs, reduce customer complaints, improve customer service, and increase revenues. Initiative and enterprise are closely related to learning and problem-solving.

- **Honesty & Trustworthiness:** Honesty and trustworthiness were among the top employability skills identified by focus group discussants. They gave examples of businesses that folded because of untrustworthy employees. Trustworthiness is related to an employee being loyal, honest, and dependable.

  Trustworthy employees protect their company's resources and assets from waste, theft, or misappropriation. They act and behave as owners of the company and work for its success. The owners of these companies delegate responsibilities and rely on these employees to do the right thing for the company's benefit.

Many small and large businesses and government agencies lose millions of dollars every year due to dishonest and corrupt managers and employees. Many high-level and low-level employees engage in illegal behavior and corrupt acts detrimental to their employers' profitability and success. Businesses are spending millions of dollars to catch untrustworthy employees. They have hired security personnel to install security cameras and other devices to protect their assets and catch employees engaged in theft and corrupt practices.

- **Planning and organizing:** Employers seek individuals who can plan and organize work activities. Planning and organizing reflect an individual's ability to manage assigned tasks and deliver outputs and results within the stipulated timeline and due dates.

  Planning and organizing include time management, project management, scheduling, research, and strategic resource allocation to achieve the desired objectives effectively and efficiently within the expected timeframe. Individuals who plan and organize their daily work activities achieve more and perform better than those who don't plan or organize their work.

- **Self-management:** Self-management is about employees managing themselves to achieve given outputs, results, and outcomes of assigned tasks with minimum supervision. It is related to initiative and enterprise and learning and problem-solving.

  Many employers expect their employees to take responsibility for their workplace performance. Employees must know the Organization's mission, purpose, and values to take responsibility. What products and services does the Organization produce? Who are the Organization's stakeholders and customers? How is the Organization structured and managed? What are the Organization's regulations and procedures? Also, employees must understand their specific job responsibilities.

Self-management requires that the employee actively seek feedback from peers, subordinates, supervisors, and customers and act on it to improve workplace performance. It also requires the employee to adopt safe working habits and to refrain from any activity that could cause a dangerous situation for themselves or others.

- **Adaptability to technology:** It is hard to imagine jobs that do not rely on technology in today's work environment. Technology has changed the workplace significantly and abolished specific tasks. Desktop computers, laptops, digital printers, and emails entered the workplace in the 1980s and 1990s. These technological advances displaced administrative secretaries whose sole role was to take dictations and type letters, memos, and reports on typewriters. Technology decimated the typing pool and girl Friday businesses that supplied temporary administrative secretaries and typists to different organizations. Automation of assembly plants also displaced millions of factory workers.

Consequently, employers prefer job applicants who have information technology skills. Job applicants with the necessary skills in word processing, Excel and accounting software, or other applications have a better chance of being hired. Related skills include those needed to work with computer-controlled equipment and machinery. Computer coding skills may also come in handy.

To be successful, employees and potential labor market entrants need to learn, upgrade, and develop proficiencies in new and emerging technologies. In the United States, millions of people continue to be displaced by technology-driven changes in industry and government. These displaced employees must relearn and adapt to the new technological environment to return to their jobs or move to an equivalent position elsewhere.

ANNEX 2.3: BUILDING MAN-MADE AND NATURAL DISASTER RESILIENCE

Man-made and natural disasters can occur without warning. At times, they indicate that something disastrous is about to happen. Suppose a natural or man-made disaster, such as disease outbreaks, earthquakes, flooding, drought, forest fires, or conflict and war, occurs. How do we withstand their effects and recover quickly? In this sense, *resiliency* is about the ability of individuals, households, communities, and countries to prevent, cope with, endure, and recover from the effects of a disaster in a timely, effective and efficient manner. The recovery process includes preserving and quickly restoring essential physical and institutional infrastructure, basic services such as healthcare, water, and sanitation services and education, reestablishing peoples' livelihoods, and delivering direct emergency assistance to the affected population in an effective, efficient, equitable, transparent, and accountable manner.

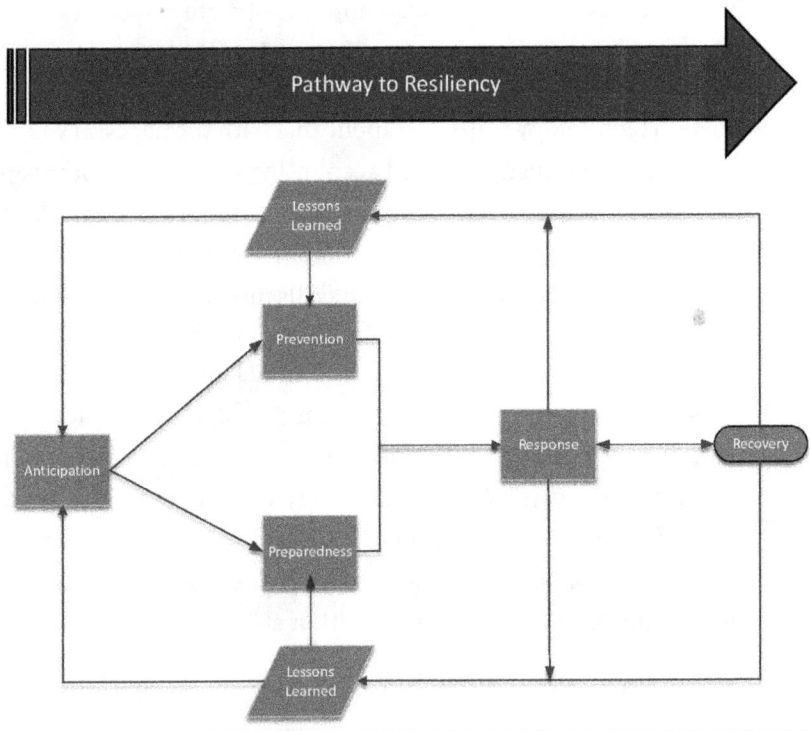

The disaster recovery and resiliency pathway includes anticipation, prevention, preparation, and pre-positioning of personnel and commodities. Anticipation requires sustained surveillance, intelligence, data mining, and research investment. Critical leading indicators are developed and monitored. The data is regularly analyzed to inform prevention and preparation plans, decisions, and policies.

Since natural disasters and hazards are recurring, a dedicated research unit can generate regular intelligence reports that inform emergency prevention and preparedness decisions and policies. The research unit must be adequately staffed with capable researchers. It must link with domestic and international research centers that work on natural and man-made disasters and coordinate information and analytics exchange.

Prevention means taking actions that avert, for example, conflict before it happens. Local and national discontent and disagreements can be addressed through dialogue and negotiations. Open discussion, consensus-building, and decision-making with all stakeholders engaged in problem resolution often result in averting devastating conflicts.

Climate-related and geophysical hazards cannot be prevented. Still, we can prepare for them and reduce their devastating effects on the affected communities. Anticipation, lessons-learning, and taking preventive measures might mean implementing policies that ensure, for example, human settlements are built away from known flood zones and earthquake-prone areas. It also means that appropriate building codes and risk avoidance policies are developed, implemented, and enforced. This may also include reinforcing the physical infrastructure to withstand the shock and minimize damage or building redundancy in essential services delivery to the affected population.

Also, water-saving and conservation methods are promoted, adapted, and used widely to deal with drought. Farmers are given drought-resistant seed varieties as well as a drought-adaptive production technology. Planning and utilizing early warning systems are necessary to temporarily resettle the affected populations and their livestock to less-affected regions until conditions improve. However, the relocation of the affected people must be carefully planned with the host communities to avoid conflict. Regarding flooding and mudslides, preventing or reducing the effects of flooding requires building adequate drainage systems that divert the water away from human settlements and essential infrastructure. It also involves building terraces, retaining walls on hillsides, and reforestation to slow down soil erosion and mudslides.

While putting preventive measures in place, we must simultaneously be prepared to respond to the hazard quickly to mitigate human suffering and restore peoples' livelihoods as soon as possible. One way to reduce the effects of disasters is by pre-positioning emergency assistance personnel and supplies. It also means having shovel-ready programs that can be immediately implemented to mitigate human suffering. The first 72 hours are very critical. Disasters that displace people from their homes and communities have a wide-ranging effect, including homelessness, hunger, malnutrition, and disease outbreaks. Emergency preparedness to provide temporary shelter, food, water, and medical treatment can reduce the effects of displacement. Small businesses are provided loans to restore their activities quickly. Pastoralists and farmers are assisted in restocking their livestock and grains. Families and communities are supported to rebuild their houses and restore essential services such as schools, water points, health facilities, and access roads. Emergency food items, bottled water, drugs, and other consumables are restocked regularly to avoid spoilage and maintain freshness and usability.

Natural disasters and man-made hazards are costly. Quick recovery requires a substantial financial investment, as we have learned from the natural disaster experiences of the United States and other countries. Our preparedness must include establishing a "disaster resiliency fund" partly funded through tax revenues and partly through the sale of interest-bearing bonds backed by the national government.

Each disaster recovery process provides valuable lessons that inform anticipation, prevention, preparedness, and response for future disasters and hazards. Lessons learned must be used effectively to improve responses and recovery and resiliency programs. That new knowledge must be captured through appropriately designed monitoring and evaluation systems.

ANNEX 5.1: ASSESSING AND BUILDING ORGANIZATIONAL CAPACITY: THE DELPHI METHODOLOGY

I. Introduction and Objective

Organizational capacity relates to the clarity of an organization's mandate, vision, and mission. It is also about the quality of its leadership, the financial, human, and technological resources available to it, and it's capacity to learn and improve. In this regard, we recommend using the Participatory Delphi Approach (PDA) for identifying (a) the organizational capacity gaps and (b) approaches for closing the gaps and improving organizational performance. PDA uses mixed qualitative and quantitative methods to determine the capacity gaps and the actions needed to eliminate the gaps and enhance the Organization's performance. Because of its participatory nature, the changes are driven and owned by the Organization's management, staff, and external stakeholders.

A participatory capacity assessment approach is vital for understanding and building fit-for-purpose capacity for better service delivery to customers for now and in the future. A participatory approach is a valuable method for assessing and scoring an organization's existing capabilities and how to improve and enhance the Organization's performance.

The Delphi technique was developed in the 1950s at the Rand Corporation by Helmer and Dalkey as a qualitative research methodology for forecasting and solving complex problems (Benarie, 1988; Woudenberg, 1991). It is a type of survey methodology that can capture the understanding and experiences of key stakeholders. It is based on three or more rounds of structured surveys and roundtable discussions. It uses the intuitive information of the participants, whose opinions and feedback are anonymous to each other. Giving written feedback and maintaining the anonymity of the feedback source are essential characteristics of the Delphi technique.

PDA is an interactive group communication process. Participants inter-act, rethink, and compare their thoughts in a "non-threatening forum" without being influenced by each other's opinions or fear of repercussions from supervisors and senior management. The following iterative steps are suggested whereby all the key stakeholders participate. The process requires two to three independent, unbiased, and knowledgeable facili-tators. Two facilitators take notes during the dialogue sessions, while the third moderates the discussion.

Regarding tax administration, the PDA participants are categorized as follows. First, the Organization of Revenue personnel is segmented into rank-and-file employees, middle management, and top management. Second, a random sample of taxpayers segmented into large, medium, and small taxpayers are surveyed separately. Third, participants from other federal government ministries and agencies such as the Organization of Trade and Industry (MTI), the Ethiopian Investment Commission (EIC), the Organization of Mines, and other business licensing and investment incentive granting agencies are identified and surveyed. The survey instru-ments and checklists are designed to solicit information on the current organizational capacity and performance and capture the capability gaps within the tax administration in three or more surveys and discussions.

II. But What Is Organizational Capacity?

Organizational capacity relates to performing and fulfilling an organiza-tion's duties and responsibilities. The question is how well and efficiently they execute their duties and responsibilities and achieve results.

An organization's capacity is its potential to perform—its ability to successfully apply its resources to accomplish its goals and satisfy its stakeholders' and customers' expectations (Horton et al., 2003). An or-ganization's personnel, facilities, funding, knowledge, and technology constitute its resource base. The Organization's leadership, business pro-cesses, procedures for service delivery, and external relationships make up its management capacity. Together, these resources and management capacities determine the Organization's potential to perform and achieve specific results.

Baser and Morgan (2008) define capacity as the overall ability of an organization to create public value. To do so, the Organization must have competent people committed to generating development results. Capacity is further defined from an operational point of view as the emergent combination of individual competencies and collective capabilities that enable a human system to create value. Orbach (2006) defines organizational capacity as the quantity and quality of goods and services produced to given specifications with available resources. According to this definition, the capacity assessment focuses on analyzing and understanding the utilized capacity, the unutilized capacity, and the added capacity needed to produce the desired goods and services. Thus, a capacity assessment determines the desired capacities against existing capacities (NDP, 2008).

The critical elements of organizational capacity include the legitimacy of the Organization's mandate, vision, and mission; its leadership; organizational structure and allocation of functions, job descriptions, and workflow; access to financial resources and effective financial management systems; access to sufficient physical and human resources commensurate with the duties and responsibilities of the Organization. It also includes effective and efficient human capital management (i.e., the skill mix, optimal staffing of organizations and departments, and personnel incentives and motivations). Thus, the organizational capacity-building exercise should focus on the following organizational capacity elements:

- **Legitimacy and clarity of the Organization's mandate, vision, and mission** related to the duties and responsibilities of the Organization as provided by law. It also relates to the questions of where the Organization is today and where it ought to be in the future, concerning

    - the impact on society of its goods and services,
    - the quantities and qualities of its goods and services,
    - the way it arranges and manages resources to produce the goods and services efficiently and effectively, and

- the available resources it can mobilize to deliver the desired level of goods and services.

An organization's vision is what an organization, or a unit within it, wishes to achieve in the medium and long term. An organization's mission is what it has to do in the short term within given cost/resource constraints based on its vision (or its legal mandate or explicit terms of reference).

Mission = Targets + Time (within given cost + resource constraints)

- **Leadership** provides clear direction to an organization and determines its future regarding the needs of key constituents, stakeholders, and clients. Quality leadership ensures that the Organization's future is planned for and acted on. Also, effective leadership keeps employees on track, pursuing the direction given (through a mix of motivation, performance monitoring, and guidance).

The discussion on organizational leadership will involve assessing leaders' tools to think of and provide directions. It may include discussing the conceptual framework leaders use to give direction and guidance to the Organization. The conceptual framework relates to how leaders think of a system, a function, or a phenomenon they are managing—it is their "working theory." Managerial activities include planning, goal setting, determining and assigning responsibilities, leading, empowering, allocating resources, incentivizing and motivating, supervising staff members, and maintaining stakeholder relations. Leadership is critical for the performance and success of an organization (Horton et al., 2003). We define leadership in terms of

- the capacity to assess and interpret needs,
- identification of the challenges and opportunities outside the Organization,
- establishing strategic direction,

- influencing and aligning others toward a common goal,
- motivating others, committing them to action, and giving them responsibility, authority, and space to take action, and
- holding them accountable for their performance and recognizing them for their accomplishments.

Project management is a critical capacity that directly determines the quality of services delivered to customers and impacts an organization's performance (Biafore, 2006). Project management skills and procedures, such as planning, project formulation, implementation and management of project activities, project cycle management, and technical reviews, affect an organization's performance. If an initiative is started but is not followed through to completion, it fizzles out without producing any tangible result.

Likewise, process management, which is concerned with managing resources and processes that support the production and delivery of services to customers, is a critical capacity that affects an organization's performance. Process management encompasses staffing of the organization and staff development, financial management, facilities management, and more. This also recognizes that an organization is robust to the extent that it taps the capacities of its staff members, shares them with others, and assimilates and institutionalizes them. Such organizations can effectively utilize staff members' skills and professional training.

- **An organization's strategy for achieving its vision and mission** includes a clear plan and strategy for executing the mission statement and specific actions that must be taken within a given time frame.

- **The management structure and the division of labor within the Organization** also affect the Organization's performance. An optimal division of labor within an organization exists when

  - every essential function has an agreed organizational home that makes sense within the mandate of the Organization;

– there is complete clarity on the nature and scope of all functions;

– functions and processes are not split unnecessarily among too many departments, and there are no parallel structures;

– when split horizontally or vertically into sub-functions or tasks, there is total clarity as to who is doing what, and the split makes sense;

– when a function is split, accountability for the overall function remains unitary; and

– there are no functional gaps, overlaps, or duplications.

When a process has an organizational home, there is a better chance that somebody will

– formulate a conceptual framework, a vision, and a strategy for it;

– develop plans for the implementation of its strategy;

– apply quality standards and best practices to it;

– guide, monitor, and control its execution; and

– enforce accountability for it.

However, when a function is split among several organizations, organizational units, or governance levels,

– it is not easy to get an overall picture due to its fragmentation;

– it is difficult to coordinate it due to many fragments;

– there is often a lack of clarity on the division of responsibility and labor, resulting in functional overlaps, role conflict, and waste of time and resources;

– there are often operational and output gaps due to misinterpretation of the responsibilities of others or a conscious decision to let others take action; and

– it is much more challenging to retain overall accountability for the function or operation.

- **An organization has financial resources and financial management capacity** if it can

    - mobilize funds sufficient to match its mandate,
    - allocate funds in line with operational needs, and
    - manage funds efficiently and control expenditures effectively.

The capacity of an organization to mobilize and allocate resources effectively depends on

    - its ability to present a better case to the providers of its budget and external funding agencies, which hangs on the availability of evidentiary information and staff with financial analysis, strategic planning, proposal writing, and presentation skills;
    - its ability to link resource allocation to operational requirements through well-defined norms and standards; and
    - the ability of customers to pay for the services they get and the Organization's ability to collect the fees.

The capacity of an organization to control expenditure effectively, in turn, depends on

    - the existence of rules and procedures for cash management and the release and use of funds;
    - the existence of rules and procedures to monitor operations, collect information, conduct internal audits, and produce reports regularly;
    - the design and structure of the budget, particularly the system of classification used, the coding, and even computerization; and
    - incentives for following and sanctions for not following the required rules and procedures, mechanisms for enforcing the rules, and political-administrative desire to use these mechanisms.

- **An organization's existing physical resources and capacity to manage them effectively influence its performance further.** An organization's capacity is constrained when infrastructure, information technology, and physical resources do not meet operational requirements. To perform better, the Organization would need these resources in the right quantities, at the proper specifications, and at the right location and time.

- **Human capital is an essential ingredient to organizational capacity and performance.** A higher-quality human capital would result in a higher level of organizational performance. The capability of an organization is robust if it has an optimal number of people with the right mix of skills, competencies, and motivations. Management practices and work habits directly affect effective human capital utilization. Practices are ways of doing things: what we do when performing given tasks and how we do it. Application of best practices, in general, enhances performance. Examples of management best practices include the following:

    - Formulation of conceptual frameworks, vision, mission, strategies, and policies
    - Budget planning and operational planning
    - Division and Organization of work into coherent components
    - Creation of teams, allocation of work components to them, and enhancement of team spirit
    - The setting of individual and group objectives and performance appraisal and reward systems
    - Enhancement of staff participation in thinking and acting
    - The motivation of individuals and teams
    - Development of staff to achieve professional proficiency
    - Recognition of staff for good performance
    - Monitoring and regularly evaluating operations, outputs and outcomes, and client and customer satisfaction
    - Timely and rational decision-making and problem-solving

III. Participatory Organization Capacity Assessment

For capacity-building efforts to be sustainable, interventions need to adopt participatory approaches and develop into empowering partnerships. Those involved feel a high degree of ownership (Blagesus and Young, 2006). The participatory organizational capacity assessment process can be capacity enhancing. For example, consider those often-involved experience *changes in thought and behavior due to the learning during the assessment process.*

Information about the Organization's mandate, vision, mission, and performance is widely shared when managers and staff are engaged in the organizational capacity assessment processes. For example, discussions about the Organization's mandate, vision, and mission can enhance the staff's understanding and awareness of their responsibilities. As a result,

a. the capacity assessment can yield specific insights and findings that can change business practices and be used to build capacity, and

b. those who participate in the assessment process learn to think more systematically about their roles and responsibilities, relationships with the Organization's customers, and needed capabilities.

Involving the Organization's managers, staff, and other key external stakeholders in the evaluation process from the outset can facilitate the identification of critical capacity gaps hampering the Organization's performance. It can also ensure that the capacity built will be used effectively, efficiently, and sustainably.

The capacity assessment process filters out what needs to be measured to enhance organizational performance. What we choose to measure impacts how people react and behave. If staff, for example, get rewarded (or punished) for measured things, then those things take on added importance. Waste and undesired outcomes occur when the wrong things are measured and used. Often using what is measured inappropriately increases the likelihood that the wrong things will get done.

Capacity development is "the process through which individuals, organizations, and societies obtain, strengthen and maintain the capabilities to set and achieve their development objectives over time" (UNDP, 2008). It includes strengthening the processes, systems, and rules that influence collective and individual actions and performance. And it requires enhancing people's technical ability and willingness to play new roles, take on new responsibilities, and adapt to new demands and situations. Thus, the capacity gaps identified in the Delphi sessions should form the basis for delivering capacity-building assistance to that Organization.

Capacity building requires a learning-by-doing approach (Schacter, 2000). Development partners have supported the legislation, administration, diagnosis, planning, and monitoring capacity (Lafontaine, 2000). However, the capabilities of many assisted organizations failed to develop within a reasonable timeframe, partly due to technical advisors doing the work themselves instead of showing and guiding their counterparts on how to do the job. Many technical advisors say, "I am too busy to teach my counterpart the job." This is partly due to senior managers' high day-to-day demand for their time.

Capacity development initiatives are often successful when they recognize and build on existing strengths, knowledge, and experience within the Organization. Also, a clear definition of roles and responsibilities, accountability of all parties, and transparency in decision-making can contribute to the success of capacity development activities. An organization's capacity can be developed successfully through an iterative process involving local experts and stakeholders and robust monitoring and evaluation processes.

Capacity development aims to improve the potential performance of an organization embodied in its physical, human, and information technology resources and management. Performance is the ability of an organization to meet its goals and achieve its overall mission. As noted above, an organization's performance is influenced by its existing resources, internal environment, and prevailing external environment in which it operates. Technical assistance in building an organization's capacity must address these performance dimensions. Four key indicators, listed below, can gauge an organization's performance:

- *Effectiveness:* the degree to which the Organization is achieving its goals and delivering the services expected by stakeholders
- *Efficiency:* the degree to which the Organization utilizes its available resources cost-effectively in producing and providing services expected by stakeholders
- *Relevance:* the degree to which the timing, scale, and quality of services delivered by the Organization reflect the needs and priorities of stakeholders
- *Sustainability:* the degree to which the scale and quality of goods and services produced and delivered are within the limits of the Organization's financial, operational, and technological infrastructure and human resources at its disposal. The service levels are maintained at the desired levels.

The external factors that can affect the performance of an organization may include

- the administrative and legal framework in which it operates,
- the national policies and the political environment under which it operates,
- the social and cultural setting in which it operates,
- the technology available to it, and
- the socioeconomic trends that affect its revenue-generation abilities.

The performance of an organization is also affected by internal factors that influence its direction and the energy displayed in its activities. The internal dynamics influence how the Organization uses its capacities to achieve its goals and perform at its potential. The internal environment relates to the Organization's character, which makes up what might be called the Organization's personality and influences its cohesiveness and energy in pursuing its goals. The following are examples of an organization's internal environment:

- Managers' leadership and management style
- Employee incentives and rewards systems
- Employees' feelings of acceptance, inclusion, and being valued
- Legitimacy, clarity, and acceptance of the Organization's mission
- Organizational structure and delineation of roles and responsibilities
- The extent of shared norms and values promoting teamwork and the pursuit of professional excellence in the quest for the Organization's goals and objectives

IV. Applying the PDA

The PDA is a mixed qualitative and quantitative approach with several steps in its implementation. However, there are three guiding principles for any successful organizational capacity building. First, the people working in the Organization better understand its functions, strengths, and weaknesses as they experience them in their daily work activities. Thus, all employees must be engaged, including frontline service providers, backroom support staff, and middle and top management. Second, the Organization's customers understand its services' quality, effectiveness, and efficiency, and their opinions matter. Since they are directly affected, the organizational transformation processes must involve a statistically significant number of randomly selected large, medium, small, and individual customers. Third, governmental organizations that interact with the Organization or its customers must be engaged, as what they do affects its effectiveness and performance.

Under Step 1, the Technical Assistance Team (TAT) must do its homework. It must understand the Organization's mandate and how it manages and operates. It must also map out the services delivered to customers and who does what based on the Organization's structure and business processes. The TAT must understand the flow of information from bottom management to top management and vice versa and use available data. It must also assess the current and past performance of the Organization using selected performance indicators to identify areas of weak performance.

The TAT must also identify the primary customers and stakeholders of the Organization. These include the management and employees of the Organization, customers, and other stakeholders. Experiences and perceptions of each group are critical for determining the current organizational capacity and performance and what needs to change for improved future performance.

Under Step 2, the TAT designs separate survey questionnaires for the three groups of stakeholders. The survey questions asked may differ by stakeholder group. The first survey questions are intended to solicit the opinion and experiences of internal stakeholders—top and middle management and rank-and-file employees. The second survey questions address customers. The third survey questions are structured to get feedback from other stakeholders. Exhibit 1 provides an example of questions to ask stakeholders. The survey questionnaires must be designed to gather relevant information regarding improving the Organization's capacity for better service delivery and performance. The expected outputs of the exercise, however, are as follows:

1. A clear and straightforward statement of the mandate, mission, vision, and value of the Organization
2. Revised and streamlined organizational structure and business processes aligned to the Organization's mandate and vision
3. The actual and authorized level of staffing and the required optimal staffing levels for each department and division
4. Prioritized capacity gaps
5. Action plans for addressing the identified capacity gaps

6. Estimated budget for implementing each action plan
7. Timelines (i.e., start and end dates) for implementing and completing each action plan

Under Step 3, the TAT executes the survey questionnaires and analyzes the results. **Ensure that the survey instruments do not ask for the respondents' names.** The anonymity of survey respondents is critical for getting honest opinions from respondents. The survey instrument may have preassigned numeric codes to identify respondents by category, for example, different numeric codes for senior management, middle management, and rank-and-file employees. Customers should have unique numeric codes, and there should be a separate numeric code for other stakeholders. At this stage, the TAT summarizes the results of the surveys for discussion with the stakeholders.

Under Step 4, the TAT organizes and executes an offsite workshop to review the survey findings with each stakeholder group. Box 1 provides a sample Workshop Agenda. Before the workshop, the TAT must prepare all the required material and send invitations and announcements with sufficient lead time to ensure all stakeholders

Box 1: Workshop Agenda

- Introduction (includes a welcome statement by the MOR)
- Explanation of the objective of the workshop and the rules of engagement
- In-depth discussion of organizational capacity
- Presentation and an in-depth roundtable discussion of the results of the first round opinion survey
- Summarization and discussion of the first roundtable discussion
- Execution of the second round opinion survey
- Presentation and an in-depth roundtable discussion of the results of the second round opinion survey
- Summarization and discussion of the second roundtable discussion
- Execution of the third round opinion survey (if needed)
- Presentation and an in-depth roundtable discussion of the results of the third round opinion survey
- Summarization and discussion of the third roundtable discussion
- Participatory identification and prioritization of capacity gaps within the MOR
- Collaborative Action Plan Development

are available. Ensure that the workshop is conducted in a **stress-free environment**. Also, suggest that all participants must voice their opinions and suggestions unreservedly. Have enough markers, easels, and flipcharts to note participants' comments, suggestions, and questions. Assign two people to take notes while two people facilitate the discussions.

If needed, have someone available to tell stories or jokes during breaks to relax the audience. Begin the sessions immediately after registration with introductions and opening remarks. Let the participants circulate and socialize during workshop breaks.

At the start of the workshop, the TAT should describe the purpose and objectives of the exercise and then state and explain the rules of engagement. The aim is to establish a forum for the open and free exchange of information and experiences among managers, staff, and other stakeholders. The organization staff should speak out and share their negative and positive experiences without fear of repercussions from senior management. Make sure one or two individuals do not dominate the roundtable discussions. All present at the roundtable must have an equal chance to express their views.

The TAT should define and discuss organizational capacity. After a sufficient and detailed explanation, the TAT should invite participants to speak out, comment, and ask questions. Give everyone a chance to speak and note the questions and remarks of the participants.

Next, the TAT should score and tabulate the initial survey findings and solicit comments from the participants. The scoring criteria and definition are provided in Exhibit 2. Exhibit 2 defines the maturity stage of the actions implemented to enhance the target organizational capacity.

For the roundtable discussion, discussion participants should be divided into four to six groups. Allow for a detailed discussion of the findings and their implications. Let each roundtable present its comments and questions through its elected spokespersons. Summarize the main remarks and issues. At this point, end the first session, and indicate to the participants that the workshop will commence the following day.

Under Step 5, the TAT should summarize the workshop participants' feedback. A revised survey questionnaire must be prepared, incorporating feedback received during the first session. The TAT should begin the workshop session by reviewing the previous day's main findings and welcoming additional comments. After that, the TAT should administer the second round of the survey. Once all the participants have submitted their completed survey, there should be a lunch break. During the lunch break, the TAT should analyze and summarize the survey results to review with the participants in the afternoon session. The team's findings should be presented during the afternoon session, followed by a thorough roundtable discussion. Again, note participants' agreements, disagreements, comments, and suggestions, and adjourn the session until the next day.

Under Step 6, the TAT should summarize the previous day's findings, clarify the objective of the exercise, and begin to identify and consensually agree on the Organization's capacity gaps. Let the participants prioritize the capacity gaps through a roundtable discussion. Each group then presents its prioritized list. After all the roundtable groups have finished explaining their prioritization, a detailed group discussion should occur in which the four to six prioritized lists are reconciled. A final prioritized list is produced, which reflects the group's consensus.

Under Step 7, the TAT should ask participants to develop an action plan for the prioritized capacity gaps using the roundtable discussion format. Each roundtable should discuss the action plans created. Devote sufficient time for exploring and adjusting the action plans.

Under Step 8, the TAT should present the final draft of the consolidated action plans and ask the participants to develop an implementation timeline for each action plan. That then serves as a basis for delivering capacity-enhancing technical assessments such as business process redesigning and staffing. Under Step 9, the TAT should establish baselines and targets and develop a tracking matrix, as shown in Exhibit 3.

EXHIBIT 1: SAMPLE ORGANIZATIONAL CAPACITY SELF-ASSESSMENT SCORING SHEET

CODE: Alphanumeric Code for identifying the level of management

Please indicate your level of agreement or disagreement with the following statements:

Organizational Feature	Issues	Scores				
		Strongly Agree 4	Agree 3	Disagree 2	Strongly Disagree 1	Don't Know 0
Mandates and Core Functions	1. The Organization's mandates, functions, and responsibilities are identified and reported by a proclamation and implementing laws and regulations.					
	2. The Organization has a clearly articulated organizational structure that delineates the functions and responsibilities of each department within the Organization and the supervisory and reporting hierarchies.					
	3. The function, responsibilities, and resources allocated to the Organization are implemented and enforced through a clearly defined legal framework and regulatory mechanisms.					

Organizational Feature	Issues	Scores				
		Strongly Agree 4	Agree 3	Disagree 2	Strongly Disagree 1	Don't Know 0
	4. Each department has developed its scope of work and plan and uses them according to its assigned responsibility and mandate.					
	5. Each department and function is adequately financed and staffed with qualified personnel to perform its essential functions.					
Decision-Making	1. Decision-making authority is exercised by the Minister only.					
	2. Decision-making authority is vested with the Minister and his Undersecretary only.					
	3. Decision-making authority is delegated to directors. Directors can make decisions without approval or sign-off from the Minister or the Undersecretary.					
	4. Decision-making authority concerning the procurement of goods and services is delegated to the proper level. Limits are set at each level. For example, a division head can authorize the procurement of goods and services up to 5,000 ETB.					

Organizational Feature	Issues	Scores				
		Strongly Agree 4	**Agree** 3	**Disagree** 2	**Strongly Disagree** 1	**Don't Know** 0
Management Systems	1. The Organization's organizational chart identifies the different departments and their functions.					
	2. The nature and scope of the functions of each department are clearly defined, and there are no functional gaps, overlaps, or duplications of functions.					
	3. The Organization has established and published written procedures and processes for each business function.					
	4. All employees are trained in the Organization's processes and procedures. They consistently follow these processes and procedures in their daily business transactions.					
Human Resources— Staff	1. The Organization has personnel with the appropriate skill mix.					
	2. The Organization personnel has the skill and competency to perform their assigned tasks adequately.					

Organizational Feature	Issues	Scores				
		Strongly Agree 4	Agree 3	Disagree 2	Strongly Disagree 1	Don't Know 0
	3. The Organization has a training and career advancement program to enhance its employees' competencies.					
	4. The staff possesses adequate technical skills to perform the tasks they are assigned.					
Human Resources— Systems	1. The Organization has identified all the necessary skills, technology, and jobs to carry out its mandate.					
	2. There are written recruitment procedures and job descriptions for all jobs and positions.					
	3. Merit-based hiring, promotion, and reward systems are institutionalized and consistently used.					
	4. Personnel performance appraisal and career development plans are formalized and practiced system-wide					
Diversity— Women	1. The Organization has adopted and put into practice gender equality and equal employment opportunities policies.					

Organizational Feature	Issues	Scores				
		Strongly Agree 4	Agree 3	Disagree 2	Strongly Disagree 1	Don't Know 0
	2. The number and percentage of women employees in the Organization are proportional to the composition of women in the general population.					
	3. Women are adequately represented in all key decision-making positions.					
	4. Women participate effectively in all decision-making forums.					
Diversity— Regions	1. The Organization's recruitment, training, and hiring policies favor equitable regional representation.					
	2. Regional representation of staff is proportional to the general population.					
	3. The Organization has designed and implemented programs, such as scholarships and accelerated training to increase equitable regional representation.					
	4. Personnel in key decision-making positions are regionally balanced.					

Organizational Feature	Issues	Scores				
		Strongly Agree 4	Agree 3	Disagree 2	Strongly Disagree 1	Don't Know 0
Public Information	1. There are formal and regular staff meetings for information sharing.					
	2. Formal and regular procedures for disseminating information to the public are established and used.					
	3. Civil society and the public are regularly consulted in budget formulation and expenditure planning.					
	4. Annual performance and audit reports are published and disseminated widely to the public.					
Public Participation in Government	1. Formal systems and procedures are established and used for obtaining citizens' feedback and input into the Organization's decision-making processes.					
	2. Key Organization policy decisions are discussed and vigorously debated with civic groups and citizens and adjusted before they are implemented.					

Organizational Feature	Issues	Scores				
		Strongly Agree 4	Agree 3	Disagree 2	Strongly Disagree 1	Don't Know 0
	3. Town hall meetings and workshops are regularly conducted to obtain input from civic groups and citizens to inform the Organization's planning, budgeting, and programming decisions.					
Financial Management – Budgets (*Does the Organization have the staff and other resources to manage and control the Organization's financial transactions?*)	1. The Organization has a planning and budgeting department staffed with qualified personnel.					
	2. The Organization has established and is using a coherent financial management system.					
	3. The Organization can develop, present, and defend the Organization's annual budget.					
	4. The Organization's financial management system is integrated with the government-wide Organization of Finance's financial management information system.					

Organizational Feature	Issues	Scores				
		Strongly Agree **4**	**Agree** **3**	**Disagree** **2**	**Strongly Disagree** **1**	**Don't Know** **0**
Anti-Corruption	1. The Code of conduct for Organization employees is published and disseminated, and all the staff are provided mandatory training.					
	2. Fraud and anti-corruption mandatory training are provided to all employees of the Organization.					
	3. The Organization has established and uses best-practice procurement procedures and processes (e.g., competitive bidding, etc.).					
	4. Internal audit policies and procedures are established and used.					
	5. Internal and external audits are conducted regularly, and results are published and disseminated to the staff and the public.					

EXHIBIT 2: ORGANIZATIONAL CAPACITY ASSESSMENT SCORING CRITERIA*

Organization Features	Start-Up (0 Points)	Development (1 Point)	Expansion (2 Points)	Consolidation (3 Points)	Sustainability (4 Points)
		Criteria for Each Progressive Stage			
Mandates and Core Functions	The ministerial structure is under deliberation.	Organization and departmental mandates/structures and core functions are defined (by decree or law); initial hiring started.	Core functions put into practice; initial hiring completed.	Core functions are fully operational; other functions are at minimum capacity.	All processes operational with a critical mass of staff hired; agreed divisional/sectional mandates established and used.
Decision-Making	The Minister makes all decisions with no delegation.	Executive decision-making structures are defined (written procedures in place), but most management decisions are taken by Undersecretary, not the Minister or Deputy Ministers.	Formal decision-making is system operational: management decisions are increasingly delegated to department managers.	Management decisions are increasingly delegated to department managers.	Management decisions are consistently delegated to the appropriate level of the Organization.
Management Systems	No administrative procedures are formalized.	Few administrative procedures are formalized.	The administrative manual is in place, although they are not been thoroughly tested and revised.	Procedures are increasingly formalized.	The administrative manual is tested and revised and considered the procedure's arbiter.
Human Resources—Staff	Existing staff is not fully capable of providing the skills required for their positions.	The majority of the staff is participating in training for technical skills.	Staff members possess the minimum technical skills required for their positions but lack broader communication skills.	Staff members possess complete technical skills required for their positions, and the majority are participating in training for broader skills.	The staff possesses all skills, including communication, leadership, team building, management, and a gender-balanced view of the role of women in government and society.

Organization Features	Start-Up (0 Points)	Development (1 Point)	Expansion (2 Points)	Consolidation (3 Points)	Sustainability (4 Points)
			Criteria for Each Progressive Stage		
Human Resources— SYSTEMS	No formal personnel systems exist (i.e., job descriptions, recruitment and hiring procedures, etc.).	Some but not all necessary human resources management systems exist.	All necessary personnel management systems are virtually implemented (written procedures, recruitment practices in place and operational, etc.). However, there is little to no recognition of employee performance.	Performance (merit) is beginning to be recognized formally.	A formal personnel system and a standard performance appraisal system with merit-based rewards and promotion provisions are in place.
Diversity— Women	Staff is severely under-represented by women.	Some women are on staff but not in decision-making positions (or rarely contribute to decisions).	There is an increased number of women on staff, with some participating in decision-making positions.	Significant representation of women among staff, and women regularly participate in decision-making.	The composition of the staff represents women, and they participate effectively in decision-making.
Diversity— Regions	Regions are disproportionately represented.	A policy has been established to increase hiring from regions.	The policy was implemented for hiring from regions, and hiring has begun.	Regional representation has noticeably improved.	Regional representation is proportional.
Public Information	There is little to no dissemination of information.	Dissemination of information occurs but is not formalized or institutionalized.	Formal and regular procedures are established for the dissemination of public information.	Formal and regular procedures for the dissemination of public information are in use. Civil society and the public are beginning to use public information from the Organization.	All public information is disseminated regularly and effectively. Civil society and the public actively use public information from the Organization.

Organization Features	Start-Up (0 Points)	Development (1 Point)	Expansion (2 Points)	Consolidation (3 Points)	Sustainability (4 Points)
			Criteria for Each Progressive Stage		
Public participation in government	There is little to no interaction with civil society or citizens.	Some interaction with civil society and citizens is marked by procedures or events that allow public input and discourse with the Organization, although informed or irregular.	Formal systems/procedures exist for obtaining public input.	The Organization engages in a public debate with civil society; the interaction is regular.	Citizens and civil society input are incorporated into Organization activities. Systems and procedures for feedback and discourse are institutionalized.
Financial Management— Budgets	There is no budget for Organization administration or programs.	The Basic Organization budget and financial management system exist.	The Organization staff can develop the annual budget. A sufficient number of employees are skilled in financial management.	The financial management system is integrated with government-wide FMIS.	Actual Organization expenditures are within 10% of the budget.
Anti-Corruption	No anti-corruption systems are in place.	Anti-corruption systems are defined and accepted by the Organization and government officials.	Anti-corruption systems are established. Employees are informed, and training is taking place.	There are some standard outputs from the systems, such as reports or visible enforcement.	Anti-corruption systems are fully institutionalized. The public begins to perceive the Organization as noncorrupt.

*Adapted from USAID TIPS Number 15, "Measuring Institutional Capacity."

EXHIBIT 3: CAPACITY ASSESSMENT AND BUILDING TRACKING MATRIX

OBJECTIVE:

PROGRAM AREA:

PROGRAM ELEMENT:

ACTIVITY:

Organizational Feature	Aspects of Capacity Strengthened (What capacity gaps are targeted?)	Activities and Actions Carried Out (What actions are taken to address the targeted capacity gaps?)	Capacity Changes (What capacity improvement was achieved?)				Performance and Results (What difference did your activity make?)
			Capacity Building Indicators (How is capacity improvement measured?)	Existing Capacity Baseline	Additional Capacity Needed Targets	Change in Capacity Achieved Actual	
Mandate and Core Functions							
Decision-Making							

Organizational Feature	Aspects of Capacity Strengthened (What capacity gaps are targeted?)	Activities and Actions Carried Out (What actions are taken to address the targeted capacity gaps?)	Capacity Changes (What capacity improvement was achieved?)				Performance and Results (What difference did your activity make?)
			Capacity Building Indicators (How is capacity improvement measured?)	Existing Capacity Baseline	Additional Capacity Needed Targets	Change in Capacity Achieved Actual	
Management Systems							
Resources— Staff							
Human Resources Systems							
Diversity— Women							
Diversity— Regions							
Public Information							

Organizational Feature	Aspects of Capacity Strengthened (What capacity gaps are targeted?)	Activities and Actions Carried Out (What actions are taken to address the targeted capacity gaps?)	Capacity Changes (What capacity improvement was achieved?)				Performance and Results (What difference did your activity make?)
			Capacity Building Indicators (How is capacity improvement measured?)	Existing Capacity Baseline	Additional Capacity Needed Targets	Change in Capacity Achieved Actual	
Public Participation in Government							
Financial Management— Budgets							
Anti-Corruption							

REFERENCES

Baser, Heather, and Peter Morgan. "Capacity, Change, and Performance. A Study Report." Discussion Paper No. 59B, European Center for Development Policy Management, April 2008.

Benarie, M. "Delphi and Delphi Like Approaches with Special Regard to Environmental Standard-Setting," *Technological Forecasting and Social Change* 33(2) (1988): 149–158.

Blagescu, Monica, and John Young. "Capacity Development for Policy Advocacy: Current Thinking and Approaches among Agencies Supporting Civil Society Organizations." Working Paper 260, Overseas Development Institute (ODI), London, UK, January 2006.

Bolger, Joe. "Capacity Development: Why, What, and How." *CIDA Occasional Series* Vol. 1, no. 1 (May 2000).

Brinkerhoff, Derick W. "Organizational Legitimacy, Capacity, and Capacity Development." RTI International, Paper presented at Public Management Research Association 8th Research Conference, University of Southern California, School of Policy, Planning and Development. Los Angeles, California, September 29–October 1, 2005.

CIDA. "Capacity Development—Occasional Series." *CIDA Occasional Series* Vol. 1, no 1 (2000).

Cohen, J. M. "Building Sustainable Public Sector Managerial, Professional and Technical Capacity: A Framework for Analysis and Intervention." *HIID* (October 1993).

DANIDA. "Capacity Assessment and Reviews of NGOs with Framework Agreements: Synthesis Report," Organization of Foreign Affairs, Ref. No. 104. N.1–14, June 2000.

Hilderbrand, M., and M. Grindle. "Building Sustainable Capacity: Challenges for the Public Sector," UNDP Report on Project INT/92/676, 1994.

Horton, D., A. Alexaki, S. Bennett-Lartey, K. N. Brice, D. Campilan, F. Carden, J. de Souza Silva, L. T. Duong, I. Khadar, A. Maestrey Boza, I. Kayes Muniruzzaman, J. Perez, M. Somarriba Chang, R. Vernooy, and J. Watts. "Evaluating Capacity Development: Experiences from Research and Development Organizations around the World," The Netherlands: International Service for National Agricultural Research (ISNAR); Canada: International Development Research Centre (IDRC); the Netherlands: ACP-EU Technical Centre for Agricultural and Rural Cooperation (CTA), 2003.

Jacobs, Bruce. "Echoes from the Field: Proven Capacity-Building Principles for Nonprofits." The Environmental Support Center and Innovation Network, Inc., October 2001.

Lafontaine, Alain. "Capacity Development Initiative: Assessment of Capacity Development Efforts of Other Development Cooperation Agencies," GEF-UNDP Strategic Partnership, July 2000.

Lusthaus, Charles, Marie-Helene Adrien, Gary Anderson, and Fred Carden. "Enhancing Organizational Performance: A Toolbox for Self-Assessment," International Development Research Centre (IDRC), Ottawa, Canada, 1999.

Lusthaus, Charles, Marie-Helene Adrein, Gary Anderson, Fred Carden, and George Plinio Montalvan. "Organizational Assessment: A Framework for Improving Performance," IDRC, 2002.

Lusthaus, Charles, and Stephanie Neilson. "Capacity Building at IDRC: Some Preliminary Thoughts." Prepared for IDRC's Evaluation Unit, Universalia, April 2005.

Mckinsey & Company. "Effective Capacity Building in Nonprofit Organizations," Prepared for Venture Philanthropy Partners, 2001.

Missika-Wierzba, Bathylee, and Mark Nelson. "A Revolution in Capacity Development? Africans Ask Tough Questions," Capacity Development Briefs No. 16. The World Bank, May 2006.

Morgan, P. "Capacity and Capacity Development: Some Strategies," CIDA Policy Branch, 1998.

OECD. The Paris Declaration on Aid Effectiveness. Paris, 2005. Available at: http://www.oecd.org/daqtaoecd/11/41/34428351.pdf

OECD/DAC. "The Challenge of Capacity Development—Working Towards Good Practice," 2006.

Orbach, Eliezer. "The Capacity of the Nigerian Government to Deliver Basic Education Services," Africa Region, Human Development Sector, The World Bank, April 2004.

Orbach, Eliezer. "Organizational Capacity, Capacity Building, and Management in the Public Sector: A Framework for Analysis," Presentation to RTI, Education and Policy Systems Group, August 21, 2006.

Robinson, M., and S. Friedman. "Civil Society, Democratization and Foreign Aid in Africa," IDS Discussion Paper No. 383, Brighton: Institute of Development Studies, 2005.

Schacter, Mark. "Capacity Building: A New Way of Doing Business for Development Assistance Organizations." Policy Brief No. 6. Institute on Governance, Ontario, Canada, 2000.

UNDP. "Capacity Assessment Practice Note," Capacity Development Group (CDG), New York, New York, September 2008.

UNEP. "Capacity Building for Sustainable Development: An Overview of UNEO Environmental Capacity Development Initiatives," December 2002.

UNDP. "Capacity Development," UNDP Management Development and Governance Division, Technical Advisory Paper No. 2, 1997.

USAID-CDIE. "Measuring Institutional Capacity. Recent Practices in Monitoring and Evaluation." *TIPS* Number 15, 2000.

World Bank. "Partnership for Capacity Building in Africa. Strategy and Program of Action," Washington: The World Bank, 1996.

Woudenberg, F. "An evaluation of Delphi." *Technological Forecasting and Social Change, 40*(2): 131–150 (1991).

ANNEX 5.2: KEY PERFORMANCE INDICATORS

Level	Content	Indicator	Baseline[9]	Target[10]	Source[11]	Frequency of analysis and reporting
Impact	GOE self-finances its development program through sustainable tax revenue collection	• Tax revenue as % of total annual government expenditure[12] disaggregated by: – Tax type – Customs and other import duties			MOFEC/MOR	Annual
Strategic Outcome	Increased domestic revenue collection	• Tax revenue collected disaggregated by – Individuals – Businesses by segment – Customs			MOR Planning Directorate	
		• Tax revenue as a % of GDP			MOFEC	

9   **Baseline data** will be established during the period August to October 2019.

10   **Target data** will also be established during the period August to October 2019.

11   **Data sources** will be refined as we collect the baseline data during the period August to October 2019.

12   What we want to demonstrate is that tax revenues are able to collect are increasingly covering most of the government's budget for service delivery and social and economic development

Level	Content	Indicator	Baseline[9]	Target[10]	Source[11]	Frequency of analysis and reporting
Strategic Outcome	Increased voluntary compliance	• % of tax declarations filed by the due date disaggregated by – Businesses (LTO, MTO, STO) – Individuals (disaggregated by sex)			MOR/LTO MIS Directorate	
		• % of taxpayers paying the correct amount of tax by the due date disaggregated by – Businesses (LTO, MTO, STO) – Individuals (disaggregated by sex)			MOR/LTO MIS Directorate	
Strategic Outcome	A tax environment that encourages business and investment and facilitates trade	• Number of new businesses registered annually			Organization of Trade	Annual
		• World Bank Doing Business Indicators – Paying tax – Aggregate score and ranking – Scores and ranking for individual indices			World Bank Doing Business Indicators	
		• World Bank Doing Business Indicators – Trading across borders – Aggregate score and ranking – Scores and ranking for individual indices			World Bank Doing Business Indicators	

Level	Content	Indicator	Baseline[9]	Target[10]	Source[11]	Frequency of analysis and reporting
Outcome	A tax and customs system that is more integrated, effective, and efficient	**Audit:** • % of audits completed from a national plan • Average revenue yield per audit			MOR—Audit Directorate	Annual
		Debt: • Total debt stock as a % of total revenue			MOR—Debt Directorate	
		Registration and Filing: • % of registered taxpayers using new filing/submission platforms – Businesses (LTO) – Individuals disaggregated by sex			MOR/LTO MIS	
		VAT: • The average number of days for receipt of VAT refund – Businesses (LTO) – Individuals disaggregated by sex			Taxpayer Survey	

Level	Content	Indicator	Baseline[9]	Target[10]	Source[11]	Frequency of analysis and reporting

		Customs:
		• The average time from the arrival of goods to their release
		  – Time required to submit a goods declaration
		  – Time required from submission of goods declaration to the assessment of duty and taxes
		  – Average time for examination of goods
		  – Time required to pay duty and taxes
		  – Time from payment to release of goods
		  – Time taken for interventions from other agencies and stakeholders
					Customs Commission
					
					WCO Time Release Study	

Level	Content	Indicator	Baseline[9]	Target[10]	Source[11]	Frequency of analysis and reporting

Outcome	A tax and customs system that is more transparent and accountable	**Tax Policy/Communications:**
		• % of taxpayers who report that they understand their tax obligations
		  – Businesses (Large, Medium, Small)
		  – Individuals (disaggregated by sex)
		  – Importers
		  – Exporters
					Taxpayer Survey	

		Cross-cutting:
		• % of taxpayers who rate the professionalism of tax and customs administration as high
		  – Businesses (Large, Medium, Small)
		  – Individuals (disaggregated by sex)
		  – Importers
		  – Exporters
					Taxpayer Survey	

		• % of taxpayers who rate the tax assessment and customs process as fair
		  – Businesses (Large, Medium, Small)
		  – Individuals (disaggregated by sex)
		  – Importers
		  – Exporters
					Taxpayer Survey	

Level	Content	Indicator	Baseline[9]	Target[10]	Source[11]	Frequency of analysis and reporting
Outcome	An increasingly customer-centric revenue administration	**Customs:** • % of surveyed importers/exporters who indicate that they are satisfied with the process of submitting a goods declaration and paying the taxes and duties - By category/segment			Taxpayer Survey	

		Communications:
		• % of survey respondents who noted that it is easy to access information about their tax obligations
		  – Individuals (disaggregated by sex)
		  – Businesses (by category/sector)
		  – Importers
		  – Exporters
					Taxpayer Survey
					MOR—Communications Directorate	

		Registration and Filing:
		• The average number of days to submit a tax declaration
		  – Individual taxpayers (disaggregated by sex)
		  – Business Taxpayers (by category/sector)
					Taxpayer Survey
					MOR/LTO
					MIS Directorate	

Level	Content	Indicator	Baseline[9]	Target[10]	Source[11]	Frequency of analysis and reporting
Output	Standardized and streamlined functions across domestic tax and customs	**Audit:** • Number of audits per auditor			MOR—Audit Directorate LTO	Annual
		Key functions: • Development of new SOPs in functional areas (linked to the BPT) • Indicative number of days to complete the process (new process versus old approach)			TTO	
		Organizational Health: • % of positions within core functions with an updated job description			MOR—HR Directorate LTO	
Output	Optimized services and engagement for taxpayers and customs clients	**Communications:** • The proportion of taxpayers surveyed who indicate that they are satisfied with the process of filing and paying taxes – Businesses (large, medium, small) – Individuals (disaggregated by sex)			Taxpayer Survey	Annual
		Registration/Payment: • % of registered taxpayers filing and paying taxes using an online platform (i.e., e-filing or e-payment) – Businesses (large, medium, small) – Individuals (disaggregated by sex)			MOR/LTO Registration Directorate	

Level	Content	Indicator	Baseline[9]	Target[10]	Source[11]	Frequency of analysis and reporting
		Customs: • The total value of goods declared and processed electronically			Customs Commission	
Output	Enhanced capacity[13] and accountability of staff	**Organizational Health:** • Employee attritions as % of total staff disaggregated by sex – MOR (HQ, LTO, MTO, STO) – Customs			MOR/HR	Annual
		• % of new hires who complete the staff induction program disaggregated by sex (HQ, LTO, MTO, STO)			MOR—HR Directorate	
		• Number of management-level staff completing leadership self-assessment (HQ, LTO, MTO, STO) • Number of staff with a follow-up leadership coaching plan (HQ, LTO, MTO, STO)			MOR Employee Survey	

13 TTP assistance will be provided for stakeholder engagement through strengthening the communication and taxpayer education functions of MOR.

Level	Content	Indicator	Baseline[9]	Target[10]	Source[11]	Frequency of analysis and reporting
Output	Improved IT capability and data quality	**IT:** • Delivery of case management systems (audit, VAT refund, withholding, customs)[14]			MOR / LTO, MIS Directorate	Annual
		• Delivery of a data quality framework and risk management/data security strategy			TTO	
		• Average hours of system downtime at branches each month (LTO, MTO, STO)			MOR—MIS Directorate	
		Registration and Filing: • % of taxpayer records updated annually (LTO, MTO, STO)			MOR—Registration Directorate	

		Registration and Filing:
		• The number of taxpayers deregistered annually
		  – Businesses (LTO, MTO, STO)
		  – Individuals (disaggregated by sex)
					MOR—Registration Directorate	

14 Milestone will be established for development and implementation of the specific case management systems in the period August to October 2019.

Level	Content	Indicator	Baseline[9]	Target[10]	Source[11]	Frequency of analysis and reporting
Output	Revenue policy that is data-driven, efficient, and equitable	**Tax Policy:** • Number of person-hours of training delivered by type of course • Number of trainees by subject disaggregated by sex			MOFEC—Tax Policy Directorate	Annual
		• Improved revenue forecasting models completed and delivered • Revenue forecasting and tax expenditure estimation required datasets identified • Estimated tax expenditure reported • Annual revenue forecast outturn variance				
		• Number of stakeholder consultations conducted for tax policy revisions • Number of stakeholders' consultation recommendations endorsed • % of endorsed recommendations adopted for tax policy revisions/new tax policy development				

Level	Content	Indicator	Baseline[9]	Target[10]	Source[11]	Frequency of analysis and reporting
Output	Compliance with risk-driven tax and customs functions	**Audit:** • Number of person-hours of training delivered by type of course (HQ, LTO, MTO, STO) • Number of trainees by course disaggregated by sex (HQ, LTO, MTO, STO)			MOR—Audit Directorate	
		• % of audits based on risk-based selection criteria (LTO, MTO, STO)				
		Customs: • Undervaluation as a % of the total value of declared goods			Customs Commission	
		• Additional tax and duties collected as a result of customs examinations disaggregated by risk level (red, yellow, green, blue) • Total tax and duty recovered from non-compliant customs declarations by risk level (red, yellow, green, blue)				

www.ingramcontent.com/pod-product-compliance
Lightning Source LLC
Chambersburg PA
CBHW071319210326
41597CB00015B/1281